THE GOLD OF TROY

OTHER BOOKS BY ROBERT PAYNE

Mao Tse-tung
The Revolt of Asia
Red Storm over Asia
Fathers of the Western Church
Forever China
Zero
The Holy Fire
The Three Worlds of Albert Schweitzer
The Terrorists

THE GOLD OF TROY

The story of Heinrich Schliemann
and the
buried cities of ancient Greece

ROBERT PAYNE

FUNK & WAGNALLS COMPANY • NEW YORK

PRINTED IN THE UNITED STATES OF AMERICA

Tu, genitor, cape sacra manu patriosque penates:
me, bello e tanto digressum et caede recenti,
attrectare nefas, donec me flumine vivo abluero.

The gold which the Griffins dig up consists of rock encrusted with golden drops like fiery sparks; they quarry the gold with the power of their hard beaks.

These creatures are found in India and are sacred to the Sun, having the size and strength of lions whom they excel by reason of their wings; and they can vanquish elephants and great serpents. The tiger, however, they cannot vanquish, for he excels them by his fleetness. . . .

—FLAVIUS PHILOSTRATUS
in his *Life of Apollonius of Tyana.*

CONTENTS

THE GOLD OF TROY

An Enchanted Childhood

During the seventies and eighties of the last century an old gray-haired scholar, wearing a high collar and a sun helmet, was to be seen wandering over the ruins of an obscure mound in Asia Minor. He was short and wiry, with dark brown eyes, high cheekbones, a heavy nose, and a sensual mouth; there was something of the peasant about him, something too of the Lübeck merchants who were his ancestors. He spoke in a high-pitched nervous voice, dressed shabbily, walked with a curious gliding motion, and always carried in his coat pocket a dog-eared paper-bound edition of the *Iliad* or the *Odyssey*. To the friendly inquirer he would explain that he had uncovered the ancient city of Troy and found in its walls a secret treasure hoard of gold, which he kept securely locked in his house in Athens. He believed that the ashes of Odysseus, the crown jewels of the Trojan Empire, and the golden death masks of Agamemnon and many other Greek heroes were in his possession, and it is just possible that his claims were justified. Until he was long past middle age he never touched a spade, but during the last seventeen years of his life he excavated continually. The most unscientific of archeologists, he founded the modern science of archeology.

Luck helped him—luck, and a fierce hunger for gold. At various times in his life he made four immense fortunes; one fortune came from profiteering during the Crimean War, but the greatest came from the Californian gold-fields. And this fortune he merely stumbled upon when he went out to California to collect the estate of his brother who had died of fever. Just as some people seem to have the power of divining water, so he seemed to have some sixth sense which told him where gold was buried. He discovered the treasure of Troy when he least expected it, and he stumbled upon the treasure of Mycenae where no one else had suspected it. One day in Indianapolis, shortly after his divorce from his frigid Russian wife, he wrote to a bishop of the Greek Orthodox Church in Athens, asking the bishop to find him a wife. Once more his luck held. In all the world there was hardly another woman so understanding of his needs as the beautiful wife selected for him. Luck pursued him like a fury.

When he was born on January 6, 1822, in the parsonage of the obscure village of Neu Buckow in Mecklenburg, not far from the Polish frontier, there was no hint of the millionaire banker he was to become or the great treasures he was to unearth. Two years later his father became pastor in the village of Ankershagen, so small a place that it is rarely shown on any maps. Slavs and Teutons had once fought across the plains of Mecklenburg with their lakes and brooding mists, but at the beginning of the nineteenth century all Mecklenburg had become a backwater. "Stupid as a Mecklenburger," said Berliners, but it was not true. Mecklenburgers produced few artists and few poets, but they produced food. They drank heavily, laughed hugely, cultivated their potato fields, raised beef, and amused themselves on long winter evenings by telling stories around the hearth-fires. In all of Germany there were no people so deeply attached to the earth.

In later years, whenever Heinrich Schliemann remembered his childhood, he remembered the little parsonage with the cherry blossoms in the garden, the treasures reputed to be buried in the neighborhood, and the ghosts who haunted the place. One ghost lived in the little garden house under a linden tree: it was the ghost of Pastor von Rustdorf, his father's predecessor at the parsonage. On the other side of the wall, in a pond, there was a maiden who was believed to rise each midnight with a silver bowl in her hands, while less than a mile away stood the burial mound of a child buried in a golden cradle. At the center of Ankershagen stood a medieval castle with secret underground passageways. Once the castle was owned by the famous robber baron Henning von Holstein, who made war against the Duke of Mecklenburg. He offered to parlay with the Duke, who marched up to Ankershagen and would have been murdered if a cowherd had not warned him in time. Henning von Holstein captured the cowherd, roasted him alive, and kicked him for good measure after broiling him. The Duke brought a larger army up against the castle, and when Henning von Holstein saw there was no escape, he hid his treasure near the crumbling round tower and killed himself. The long flat stones in the churchyard marked his grave, and every year his left leg—the one that had kicked the unfortunate cowherd—grew out of the grave like a strange flower. The sexton said he had seen the leg clothed in a black silk stocking, but none of the village boys ever saw it.

The young Heinrich grew up among these legends. He visited the castle and saw the terra-cotta relief on the north wall which showed Henning von Holstein riding to war. He saw the fireplace where the cowherd had been roasted, and knew the hill where the cowherd had hidden to warn the Duke of Mecklenburg. He penetrated the underground galleries of the castle and thought he knew the entrances to the secret passageways which meandered across the whole countryside. He was fed on legends and stories of hidden treasure. In a sense, he never stirred from his native village, never so much as stepped out of his father's parsonage. To the end of his life he resembled the child with his face glued to the parsonage window, shuddering with joy as he gazed through the mists at the flame-lit, mysterious, and legendary world outside.

For him the ghosts were everywhere—he had only to put out his hands and touch them. It was the world of the Brothers Grimm and E. T. A. Hoffmann, with their strange fairy tales drenched in blood. The horror came unawares, at every turning in the road. There were good fairies, but there were also crab-apple women with silver cords in their hands ready to hang you on the nearest crab-apple tree. There were worse things than crab-apple women: there were strange whispers at night, lights moving about in the garden, and at any time the legless Henning von Holstein might descend from his castle. Heinrich had his own way of dealing with ghosts—he would cut his initials on trees and benches and windowpanes, and somehow these boldly carved letters kept the ghosts at bay. On the great linden tree in the garden he once carved his initials in letters two feet high, and they were still there, very clear, when he examined the tree again nearly fifty years later.

Perhaps, too, he carved his name everywhere out of a need to assert himself in the crowded parsonage. There were four daughters and two sons—one other son had died the year he was born and he was baptized with the name of his dead brother. He was closest to his two sisters, Dorothea and Wilhelmine, and perhaps closest of all to his mother, a quiet woman, the daughter of a burgomaster, who seems to have found little joy in her marriage with a gruff and domineering pastor. She was thirteen years younger than her husband, having married him when she was sixteen. She wore lace cuffs and played the piano, and the villagers disliked her because they thought she gave herself airs. The children adored her; her husband despised her, and had affairs with the kitchen maids. To the end of his long life—he lived to be over ninety—the pastor was a center of scandal.

Before entering theological school, the pastor had been a schoolmaster. He had a gift for teaching. He taught his children their letters and liked to show them the fine plates in his books. One day when the pastor raged against poverty, Heinrich asked why he did not dig up the silver bowl or the gold cradle. The pastor smiled. He seemed to know that he was dedicated to poverty, and no riches would ever enter the drab parsonage.

He was a man of moods, generous and close-fisted by turns, with a strange sternness which would sometimes give way to light-hearted garrulity. He told stories well. He liked playing practical jokes. He especially liked to take his children on long walks through the countryside, telling them the history of every field and hamlet, inventing everything at the spur of the moment, spinning out his stories until they became completely ludicrous and still credible; and then he would throw back his head and roar with laughter at the spectacle of his children open-mouthed in wonder. And sometimes, to keep them quiet on winter evenings, he would tell stories out of Homer until the little parsonage reeled with the thunder of the Trojan wars.

The parson knew no Greek and had never read Homer in the original, but there was nothing in the least surprising in his deep interest in the *Iliad* and *Odyssey*. All Germany was aware of Homer. Goethe and Schiller and a host of other German poets paid Homer the tribute of imitation and celebrated him to the skies. Excellent translations were available, the best and most famous being by J. H. Voss, who had spent some months of his unhappy youth as a tutor in the very castle where Henning von Holstein had roasted a cowherd. Accordingly the children in the parsonage felt a proprietary interest in the Homeric heroes and listened breathless to the stories of the war between the Achaeans and the Trojans, and it was not difficult for them to imagine the war taking place among the ruined towers and battlements of Ankershagen. In their childish imaginations Troy and Ankershagen overlapped, became part of one another; and the lives of the heroes entered their own childish lives.

At Christmas, 1829, when Heinrich was seven years old, he received as a gift from his father Ludwig Jerrer's *Illustrated History of the World*. He turned immediately to the page showing Troy in flames. In the foreground was Æneas, plumed and helmeted, wearing a corselet, striding through the smoke and flames of the doomed city, while carrying his father Anchises on his back and holding his son Ascanius by the hand. The picture fired the boy's imagination. Everything in it helped him to identify Troy with Ankershagen. The round towers, the huge castle walls, the great gateway—all these could be found at Ankershagen.

But the most extraordinary thing of all was the resemblance between Æneas as depicted in the engraving and the old pastor, as we recognize him in surviving photographs. There was the same high forehead, the same enormous eyes, heavy nose, and bearded jowls. Æneas looks like a prosperous grocer, and so does the father. He is not fleeing from Troy in mortal terror. Quietly, calmly, with no backward glance, the hero emerges through the smoke, his son beside him.

When he grew older, Heinrich liked to say that this engraving was the turning point of his life, and that from the moment he set eyes on the picture he decided to excavate the buried city. He remembered turning to his father and pointing out that in spite of the fire the walls were still standing. He told the pastor that he thought Jerrer had actually seen the city.

"No, all of Troy was burned to the ground," the pastor replied. "It's just a fanciful picture."

"But Troy had walls like that—"

"Yes."

"And these walls are much too large to be destroyed by fire, so there must be something left?"

The pastor was fairly sure nothing remained, but the boy held fast to his opinion. He told himself that one day he would make the journey to Troy and discover the walls and towers depicted so realistically in the *Illustrated History of the World*.

Fifty years later, when he told this story in an autobiographical fragment, scholars raised their eyebrows. It seemed inconceivable to them that the discoverer of Troy should be able to remember a conversation so deeply buried in the past. Schliemann answered that hardly a day passed in his mature life when he was not dreaming and planning to uncover Troy, and all his energies were directed toward the day when he would stand in triumph on the Trojan walls; and once again the scholars raised their eyebrows. It is unlikely that Schliemann was exaggerating, for the dreams of a seven-year-old child are so vast that they can encompass the whole future and dictate his journey through life.

The boy dreamed his way through school. He was seven when he fell in love with Minna Meincke, the daughter of a local farmer. Minna was his own age. She had yellow hair, blue eyes, and was pretty in a doll-like way. They met at dancing class, and thereafter they were inseparable. She enjoyed listening to Heinrich telling her stories. One day, when the whole Meincke family came on a visit to the parsonage, Heinrich vanished from sight. He had disappeared upstairs, and was sprucing himself up. Usually untidy, he appeared in the drawing-room wearing his best suit, his face shining from soap and water, his hair neatly combed. The Schliemann family was thunderstruck, until they realized that Heinrich was determined to produce a good impression on Minna.

Even at the age of seven he loved Minna to distraction. He sat by her side at school, attended her at dancing class, and accompanied her on long rambles through the countryside. They haunted the castle and the cemetery, and gazed at the spot where Henning von Holstein's black-stockinged leg had once grown through the stones. Together they examined the fireplace and the secret passageways, and interrogated everyone who could throw light on the fierce robber baron's existence in the castle. From the sexton and the sacristan they learned that at the turn of the century the leg had appeared regularly each year, but more recently someone had taken it into his head to pluck the leg from its roots and use the bones for knocking pears off trees. They believed everything they were told. There was Peter Huppert, "Hopping Peter," the village tailor, who had only one

eye and one leg, but he too liked to tell stories. He told
them well, and had a prodigious memory. Like many illiter-
ate people he could remember everything he ever heard—he
could repeat the whole of Pastor Schliemann's last Sunday
sermon, and his recital was word perfect. One day he told
them how, during the time of Pastor von Rustdorf, he had
been wondering where the storks built their nests in winter,
and so with the help of the sexton he caught one of the
storks which nested on the parsonage barn. He fastened a
strip of parchment round its leg with a message saying the
stork had spent the summer in the village of Ankershagen in
Schwerin-Mecklenburg, and would the finder kindly report
where it had spent the winter. The following spring the
stork flew back, and Hopping Peter said he found a strange
runic message written on parchment around the stork's
foot:

Schwerin-Mecklenburg ist uns nicht bekannt;
Das Land wo sich der Storch befand
Nennt sich Sankt Johannes-Land.

Unknown to us is Schwerin-Mecklenburg;
The country where the stork was found
Is known as St. John's Land.

"We believed him," the boy wrote later, "and would have
given years of our life to know where that mysterious St.
John's Land was to be found." Perhaps, after all, St. John's
Land was only another name for Troy, that ruined and improbable land where the heroes walk unharmed through the
flames and every stork carries a mysterious message and
black-stockinged feet grow out of churchyards.

From listening to Hopping Peter the children would go to
the church, to amuse themselves by turning over the pages
of the ancient church registers, in which the names of long-

dead villagers were inscribed in heavy Gothic script in the hands of Johann Christian von Schröder and his son Gottfriedrich. For ninety years, between 1709 and 1799, father and son had occupied the parsonage, and Heinrich felt a protective right over those heavy books, whose covers could only be lifted with difficulty. And when the children wearied of examining these parchment pages with their endless records of births, marriages, and deaths, there was always the possibility of visiting Gottfriedrich's daughter, an old woman eighty-four years of age, who knew all the village lore and showed them the portraits of her ancestors. The portrait of her mother, Olgartha Christine von Schröder, especially pleased Heinrich because it resembled Minna.

So for nearly two years the children wandered hand in hand through a legendary landscape, confiding their secrets to one another, always inseparable. They swore to marry each other and live the rest of their lives together. They would remain in Ankershagen, because it was the only world they knew—the high church steeple, the cherry blossoms in the garden, the graveyard, and the great castle on the hill. They promised faithfully they would never allow anything to interfere with their dream.

Quite suddenly their dream came to an end, and they saw all around them a world in ruins.

For a long time Heinrich's mother had been ailing. She had known for many years that her husband had been sleeping with the kitchen maid. She had watched in silence when the parson gave the girl expensive presents, jewels, clothes and money. She had borne her husband's children and suffered his fierce temper, and she knew the maid was only waiting for her to die to become the mistress of the parsonage. The kitchen maid wore about the house the heaviest satin dresses and velvet shawls, and was not above taunting her. Two months before her last confinement, the parson's wife wrote a strange letter to her eldest daughter, thanking her for the affection she had always shown to her "forsaken mother." She went on:

In the coming days always remember that I am waging the battle of life and death. If you hear that death has prevailed, do not grieve too much, but rather rejoice that my sufferings are at an end in this, to me, so thankless world, in which patience, prayers, entreaties to God in the silence of the night, beseeching Him to change my hard lot, have not prevailed. . . . If God helps me happily to survive my time of suffering, and my life afterward becomes such that I once again find joy and happiness among men, I promise you to wear my pretty cap very often. I must now conclude, as I am in the middle of killing the pigs, and it goes so against the grain.

This letter, which seems to have been written in blood, was almost the last she wrote. A few weeks after giving birth to a son, she was dead.

The villagers knew why she died. They had long known about the affair with the kitchen maid. Now they turned against the parson in silent anger, watched him from behind their curtained windows, and hoped to make life intolerable for him. But they only succeeded in making life intolerable for his children, who were sent away to stay with relatives until the storm blew over. The kitchen maid was glad: now at last she had the parson to herself.

Heinrich was sent off to stay with an uncle who was a parson at Kalkhorst in Mecklenburg. He did not leave immediately. For some weeks, while arrangements were being made for the journey to Kalkhorst, he remained in the parsonage, and sometimes he would steal away to the house of Gottfriedrich's daughter and contemplate in stunned silence, with tears streaming down his cheeks, the portrait of Olgartha Christine von Schröder, which was so like the

Minna he was no longer allowed to see. His mother's death made little impression on him. "To be separated altogether from Minna—never to behold her again—this was a thousand times more painful to me than my mother's death," he wrote later, "for I forgot my mother in my overwhelming grief for the loss of Minna. I have since undergone many great troubles in different parts of the world, but none of them caused me a thousandth part of the grief I felt at the tender age of nine years for my separation from my bride."

So he spoke in the authentic voice of grief, which he was never able to hide from others or from himself. For the rest of his life he dreamed despairingly about her. He told himself he would serve her all the days of his life, and in some mysterious way, after great hardships and many perilous journeys, he would find her again. Minna, Troy, St. John's Land—these were the names of the unavailing landscape of his dreams.

But no one can live with his grief every moment of the day, and at Kalkhorst the boy settled down to school, worked hard, and was regarded as a promising Latinist. His uncle, Friederich Schliemann, was a kindly and unobtrusive mentor. There was a bust of Homer in the school, and his professor of Latin was a certain Carl Andres from Neu Strelitz, who recognized the boy's brilliance, corrected his grammar, and saw to it that the boy wrote his Latin themes on subjects that interested him. In spite of everything that had happened, Heinrich still worshiped his father. Accordingly, as a present to his father at Christmas in 1832, he wrote a Latin essay on the Trojan wars. It was a long essay describing the principal events of the war and the adventures of Ulysses and Agamemnon, and though "not entirely faultless," it seems to have pleased his father. The next year, when Heinrich was eleven, it was decided to send him to the Gymnasium at Neu Strelitz, where he was placed in the

third class, which meant that he was considerably above
other boys of his age in intelligence. A pale, brilliant, unhappy youth, possessed of driving ambition, he could look
forward to years of quiet study and eventually to some
post in a university, perhaps at the University of Rostock,
one of the most ancient and distinguished in all of Germany.

Within three months these dreams, too, were shattered
by his father's uncompromising determination to do as he
pleased. The village was up in arms against him. Determined to ruin him, the villagers whispered that he had embezzled church funds and for other reasons as well was incapable of leading his flock. He was censured by the bishop,
suspended from the ministry, and threatened with expul-
sion from the church. Since he could no longer afford to
pay the school fees at the Gymnasium, Heinrich was forced
to enter the Realschüle, the ordinary common school,
where he spent the next three years in a state of quiet and
relentless misery. He drowned himself in work. He was a
good pupil and advanced rapidly—in the spring of 1835 he
had already advanced to the first class. The blow fell the
following spring, when he learned that his father could no
longer afford to pay the relatively small sums necessary to
keep him at the common school. He must go out and earn a
living, by himself, without friends, with no hope of ever
pursuing a career of letters or entering a university.

His whole world shattered, he went blindly about the
business of obtaining a menial job—anywhere, as long as it
would give him food to eat and a bed to sleep on. In the end
he decided to become an assistant in a grocer's shop in the
neighboring village of Fürstenberg, remembering perhaps
that in a grocer's shop he would at least have enough to eat.
He had left school just before the Easter holidays. He had
decided to go to work immediately after Easter, and he was
still staying at Neu Strelitz when an unhoped-for accident

occurred. Visiting the house of Herr Laue, a musician of the court, he came face to face with his beloved Minna, and for a few moments he was alone with her.

Five years had passed since he had last seen her, but he recognized her instantly. She was dressed very simply in black, and the very simplicity of her dress only enhanced her beauty. She was fourteen years old, and carried herself like a grown woman. They gazed helplessly at each other, burst into tears and fell speechless into each other's arms. Several times they tried to speak, but no words came. They were still gazing at each other in the anguish of their grief and separation when Minna's parents entered the room. They were forced to separate, and it was more than five years before he saw her again, and then only for a brief moment. She came to him when he was most lonely, and most in need of her, and then vanished. To the end of his life he remembered her as she stood in the court musician's house, wearing a black dress, the tears streaming down her cheeks.

Long afterward he wrote: "I was sure that Minna still loved me, and this thought fired my ambitions. From that moment I felt within me a boundless energy, and filled with an unshakable confidence in my ability to progress in the world by untiring effort and to prove myself worthy of her. And so I implored God to grant that she would not marry before I had obtained an independent position for myself."

A few days later the boy rode off to Fürstenberg, to become a servant in Herr Holtz's grocer's shop, at the beck and call of everyone who wanted herrings or a bottle of potato whiskey.

The Storm

╔══════════════════════════╗

He hated the shop and everything about it. He hated old Herr Holtz, who was as wooden as his name, and he hated his servitude and the niggardly sums of money he received. He hated waking up at five in the morning to open the shop, sweep the floors, dust the counters, oil Herr Holtz's boots, and arrange the counter. Above all he hated losing Minna and being so weary at the end of the day that it was impossible to study, impossible even to remember the lines of Virgil he had memorized at school or anything else he had ever been taught. Outside in the sunlight boys went to school and played leapfrog and sauntered home in the afternoon with their satchels on their backs. In the grocer's shop it was always dark and cold and miserable, and there were no legends to feed his imagination, and no pictures of the ancient world to remind him of burning Troy.

For the next five years of his life he seems to have lived in a state of mindless abandon. Ambition gnawed at him, but there were no prospects of wealth in sight. The village was poor, and sometimes Herr Holtz had difficulty in making ends meet: if they sold 12 talers worth of groceries a day, about $8, they thought they were lucky, and their total sales in a year hardly amounted to 3,000 talers, or $1,800. Profits were small, hours were long, and there was no end to the eternal drudgery.

The best hours were in the early morning when the boy was left to himself. At eight o'clock in the morning Herr Holtz came down and sent him off to the local distillery with a sack of potatoes—in Mecklenburg everyone drank potato whiskey, and Herr Holtz was the chief purveyor of it in the obscure village of Fürstenberg. Then he would hurry back to stand behind the counter until eleven in the evening, retailing herrings, butter, milk, salt, coffee, sugar, oil, candles, and the inevitable potato whiskey. The shop reeked of herrings and whiskey. He was always trundling heavy casks around the shop, counting the cases of herrings, and running errands. There was no opportunity for study, though he would sometimes read for a little while at night before going to bed under the counter, his brain weary with figures, his hands damp with herring-oil, and his clothes sprinkled with wood shavings. He never had enough money to buy clothes, and therefore he wore the same patched suit summer and winter. So it went on, year in, year out, until it seemed that all ambition was crushed in him.

Yet all this time he was dreaming of wealth, vast wealth. The more miserable he became, the more earnestly he thought of Minna and the day when he would be able to marry her and provide for her. The wretched people who came to the stop nauseated him. He would become a scholar. He would grow rich. He would show himself to advantage in an unbelieving world. Inevitably ambition became a monstrous growth, like Henning von Holstein's leg, clothed in black silk, growing in the churchyard.

There were occasional interludes of contentment. One night a drunken miller lurched into the shop, and Heinrich watched him as he declaimed a hundred lines of Homer in the light of the oil-lamps. Heinrich was fascinated. He could not read or understand Greek, but the rhythm of the words struck a chord in his soul, and when the drunken miller had recited a hundred lines, he was asked to repeat them, and then, still not satisfied, Heinrich asked him to repeat them a third time. He was so pleased that he gave the miller three glasses of potato whiskey for his trouble, even though it cost him all the money he had.

In time Heinrich came to know the drunken miller well, and always looked forward to his coming. His name was Hermann Niederhoffer, and he was the son of the Protestant pastor at Roebel. A twenty-four-year-old ne'er-do-well, he had been expelled from school for some misconduct or other, but not before he had learned those famous hundred lines, which he always repeated in exactly the same way, with the same flourishes and the same sweetness of tone. Heinrich wrote long afterwards that hot tears flowed down his cheeks as he listened to the words. "From that moment," he said, "I did not cease to pray to God that by His grace it might one day be permitted to me to learn Greek."

He did not imagine the incident, but he may have imagined his prayer. He was always dreaming of escape—to America, where the streets were paved with gold and a man might buy books to his heart's content. He was eighteen when he signed a contract with the land-steward of a neighboring estate, which would have permitted him to make the journey to New York, if he could get together enough money to pay some of the expenses. It was 1840, with the immigrants flocking in thousands to the Western prairies. Heinrich applied to his father for a loan, but that strange secretive father was engaged in one of his innumerable love affairs and no money was forthcoming. With a heavy heart and no hope at all of ever escaping from bondage, he returned to the little grocer's shop, and he might have served behind the counter for the rest of his life if an accident had not happened.

Sometimes, when he was older, he would find himself trembling in a cold sweat when he remembered how a cask of chicory had altered the whole course of his life. It was not a very large cask, but it was heavy. He strained himself, and suddenly spat blood, and while the blood poured over the sawdust on the floor, he knew he could not go on carrying sacks of potatoes and lifting milk churns for ever. He was pale and weak-chested, and in danger of dying surrounded by packages of herrings and whale-oil candles. He decided to go to Hamburg, which was on the sea, and therefore close to America. He had saved 30 Prussian dollars, amounting to about $18. With this money and the clothes he stood in, he walked to Hamburg by way of Rostock, where he paused long enough to learn bookkeeping "on the Schwanbeck system," completing in a few days a course which normally kept a student busy for a year or a year and a half.

Even if he had wanted to return to the pitiable little village of Ankershagen, there was nothing there to attract him. His father had married a woman of the people, given her two children, separated from her and brought her back again. There were ghosts in Ankershagen, but there was something far worse than ghosts—scandal. There was no peace between his father and the new wife. They screamed at each other and fought like wildcats, with alternating bouts of hate and lust, and matters grew so grave that the new wife hid herself in the woodshed for fear of being murdered and the old clergyman was summoned before the court and ordered to treat her kindly or make her an allowance of 300 Reichstalers a year. All this was known at Fürstenberg and Rostock, and so Schliemann hurried off to Hamburg, a vast anonymous city where he could lose himself and forget his misery and his yearning for Minna, who still dominated his thoughts, although sometimes he found himself dreaming of his cousin, Sophie Schliemann, the daughter of the rector of Kalkhorst, who was slim and graceful and blushed easily. It was Sophie who saw him off on the coach which brought him from Rostock to Hamburg, and he was dreaming of her all the way until the five great towers of Hamburg came in sight.

The towers fascinated him—he was to be fascinated by towers for the rest of his life—and he stood outside the city spellbound by its silhouette against the September sky, saying "Hamburg! Hamburg!" over and over again. All his life he had known only small towns and villages, but here was a city with great avenues bordered by the palaces of merchant princes, with huge painted signs hanging from the second stories of the mercantile houses, and markets everywhere. Wagons rattled along the paved streets; clocks chimed; there were carillons from the high belfries of the churches. Excited beyond measure by the magnificence of the roaring city, deafened by the noise, he forgot his own misery. He was like a sleepwalker, or a dreamer. And thinking of how he would soon make his fortune, he wrote to his sister: "Hamburg has raised me to the seventh heaven and turned me into a dreamer."

But who in Hamburg wanted to employ a youth with a

weak chest who was continually spitting blood? He knew something about serving behind a counter in a grocer's shop and he possessed a precocious knowledge of double entry bookkeeping. With his sickness and his pallor he was not a very attractive youth. He was a little astonished to discover that no one wanted him. At Lindemann's grocery shop overlooking the fish market, he got a job which paid him about $36 a month, but he was dismissed eight days later. It was the last time he was ever to tend groceries, for his next job was as a bookkeeper, and this lasted only a week. He was in desperate straits, and wrote to an uncle for a loan to tide him over until Christmas. The money came by return mail with a letter so insulting that he would have sent the money back if he had not had so much need. The loan amounted to no more than ten Reichstalers. It barely kept him alive. And when Christmas came, he had abandoned Hamburg for ever.

Luck had worked for him in strange ways. The heavy cask of chicory brought salvation and suffering, and now a chance encounter with a shipbroker, who had known his mother, led him to hope he might escape from Germany altogether. The kindly shipbroker introduced him to the captain of the brig "Dorothea," bound for La Guayra in Venezuela. There had been a time in Schliemann's youth when he had dreamed of the pampas of South America, and now he jumped at the opportunity of making the journey. His health was broken and he was penniless, with no money to buy even a blanket. Then he remembered his silver wristwatch; he sold it for three dollars and went out on a spending spree. He had spent all his money when he came on board the sailing vessel, but he had bought in a secondhand market two shirts, a coat, a pair of trousers, a mattress, and a blanket of sorts. He was to lose most of them a few days later.

He had never sailed before, and he knew nothing about ships. The "Dorothea" sailed out of Hamburg on November 28, 1841 with a fair wind. There was a crew of eighteen and three passengers: Schliemann, a joiner from Hamburg, and the joiner's son. Schliemann was seasick even in calm weather, and he was ill when the ship put in at Cuxhaven three days later. They berthed for only a short while at Cuxhaven, sailed out into the North Sea, and two days later found themselves in the path of a hurricane. The ship took on water, the pumps were manned continually, and Schliemann found himself suffering from an unappeasable hunger, which he allayed as best he could by chewing on ship's biscuits. He roped himself to a bench, set himself to learning Spanish from a Spanish grammar, and sometimes fell with a crash onto the deck. The other passengers suffered in silence in their bunks.

It was the worst weather Schliemann had ever known —the storm pouring out of the skies, the waves breaking over the sides, the ship in danger of foundering. On December 10 the gale was still raging, but the captain succeeded in maintaining his course with the help of the main topgallant sail, the only sail he dared to use. In spite of all the efforts of the crew the ship was being blown south by evening, and hardly anyone believed the ship could survive the incessant pounding of the waves. The wild snow was falling, and sea gulls kept circling around them in great flocks—this was thought to be a bad sign. It was intensely cold with six degrees of frost, and on the afternoon of the next day the storm grew worse, with the waves piling up like mountains and then hurtling down on the ship, which seemed to be no more than a shuttlecock at the mercy of the waves. Toward evening the main top-gallant sail broke away. The storm sail was hoisted, but this too broke away. And then a strange thing happened—for a brief while the clouds parted and they all saw the blaze of the setting sun. When the clouds closed over them again, most of them thought they had seen the sun for the last time.

Schliemann was by this time too sick to worry, and he listened with an odd sense of abstraction to the joiner who was trembling with horror at the fate which awaited them. The joiner believed in dreams: he had known some terrible dreams the previous night. Then, too, the ship's cat had been whining throughout the whole day, and the captain's dog had howled. At about seven o'clock the cabin boy came down to the cabin with tea and biscuits. The boy was weeping and saying he would never bring them anything any more. A little later the captain and the second mate came to the cabin and spoke gravely to the passengers, and they were graver still when the first mate came to report he had seen two lights in the distance. The captain gave orders for the anchors to be dropped, but the anchor chains snapped like broken twine a few moments later. By this time Schliemann had undressed and gone to bed, so completely exhausted that he was beyond fear.

Around midnight the cabin door blew open and the captain was shouting at them: "All passengers on deck! The ship's going down!" A moment later an enormous wave smashed all the portholes, flooding the cabin, and the ship lurched violently to port. Schliemann sprang out of his bunk, tried to dress, could not find his clothes, and rushed up on deck stark naked. Badly bruised, he somehow caught hold of the rigging and managed to crawl to the starboard gunwale, clutching at loose ends of rope and silently commending himself to God. He was afraid of sharks. He had seen them coming to the surface when the storm broke on them. He said his prayers and thought of his sisters, and all the time he could hear the joiner scream-

ing to the Virgin Mary for help. The strangest thing of all
was that the ship's bell was tolling continually. It was like a
death knell.

Naked, on the coldest night of the year, the snow falling
round him, the sky like a black cloud, he awaited his fate.
When the ship was sinking, the captain ordered the crew to
man the lifeboats. One lifeboat fell perpendicularly into the
water and vanished. The second was smashed to a pulp
against the side of the ship. There remained the small stern
boat, slung between the masts, but by this time the crew
was too frightened to do anything except climb the rigging.
The ship was waterlogged and slowly sinking. Two hours
passed. At last with a violent lurch the ship keeled over to
port, and sank. Schliemann went down with it, but soon
rose to the surface. When an empty cask floated by, he
clutched at it, his fingers curling convulsively around the
rim.

So he remained for half the night, hanging between the
sky and the sea, until the first mate pulled him out of the
water and somehow got him into the stern boat, which
had been thrown free. There were fourteen people in the
boat, and no oars. They drifted until the dawn, only to be
thrown up on one of the sandbanks off the island of Texel,
off the Dutch coast. The storm was dying down, and the
people of Texel were hurrying to the shore to gather all
the cargo which was drifting onto the banks. Schliemann
was in great pain. Three of his front teeth were broken,
there were deep cuts on his face and body, and his feet
were swollen. All the survivors lay gasping in the sand
until a friendly farmer came along with a cart and carried
them off to his farmhouse, where a fire was kindled and
they were given coffee and black bread. For three days
the survivors remained at the farmhouse, recuperating
from their ordeal.

Schliemann was given some wooden shoes, a pair of torn trousers, a blanket, and a wool cap. He liked the farmer, but what pleased him more than anything was that his sea box with his shirts and stockings, together with his pocketbook, which contained his "letters of recommendation for La Guayra procured for me by Herr Wendt," was found on the sand bank. None of the sea boxes of the other survivors floated to shore, and inevitably Schliemann was christened "Jonah." A heavy cask had nearly killed him when he was a grocer's clerk at Fürstenberg; an empty cask had saved him. His luck was holding. When he took the ferryboat to the mainland, still haggard and coatless, wearing heavy wooden *sabots*, with his sea box under his arm, he was amused to find himself greeted by a crowd of impudent bootblacks who, seeing him as ragged as themselves, pretended he had come to join their ranks.

But there were few things that amused him in those days. Desperate and miserable, without money, in a strange country, he realized he had survived by a miracle. He told himself he had survived the ordeal only because he had hardened himself with cold baths at Hamburg and because he had worn two pairs of under-drawers and two woolen waistcoats during the winter. He had no coat, no leather shoes, and no prospects. He refused to return to Hamburg with the other survivors, announcing that he had been inexpressibly miserable there and felt that his destiny lay in Holland.

Needing money badly, he went to the consul for Mecklenburg in Amsterdam, a certain Herr Quack, but the consul's servant, thinking he was a beggar, shut the door in his face. Schliemann rang the bell again, and when the door opened he had time to throw inside the house a short note saying he was a citizen of Mecklenburg in need of assistance. Herr Quack read the letter and sent his servant out into the bitterly cold street with two gulden, about fifty cents, for his compatriot. The servant informed Schliemann that he must count himself lucky to receive the gift, and the consul hoped it was the last he would hear from him.

Schliemann was angry. When he grew older, he would become capable of vast and volcanic rages, but now he was angry with the cool bitterness of a poor man desperately in need of assistance. He found a sailors' lodging house, kept by the Widow Graalman on the Ramskoy in Amsterdam, and when his funds were low and he could no longer pay his rent, which amounted to one gulden a day, he resorted to a ruse. He wrote to Herr Quack, saying he was ill and demanding to be taken to hospital—it was the least the wretched consul could do for him. There was no difficulty in getting the message into the consul's house, for the widow was only too anxious to help, afraid she would have to keep and feed him until he died or recovered. The ruse was successful. He spent eight days in the hospital.

He wrote to Herr Wendt, who had befriended him in Hamburg, a detailed account of the shipwreck and his present fortunes, and by a lucky accident the letter was delivered while the shipbroker was entertaining guests at dinner. Herr Wendt read the letter aloud. Everyone sympathized with the unlucky youth, and they made a collection, which amounted to the sum of 240 gulden, a very small fortune. Herr Wendt also enclosed a letter of introduction to the consul-general for Prussia, requesting his assistance. Within a few days Schliemann was at work in the counting-house of F. C. Quien and Co., as a supernumerary messenger boy. His job consisted of stamping bills of exchange and getting them cashed in the town. From that moment there was no turning back. He had found what he wanted to do, abandoned grocers' shops for

ever, and set his foot on the path which would lead
him to a fortune.

From the beginning he saw that the only way to make a
fortune was to dedicate his whole life to it. He would
sharpen his wits and strip himself to the bone, surrendering
himself to the task with an act of dedication so complete that
he would in time find himself incapable of leading any other
life. First, he reduced his expenses to a minimum. He was
paid thirty-six gulden a month, and out of this eight gulden
were reserved for his cheerless room in a lodging house.
Second, he would waste no money on entertainment—his
sole entertainment consisted of evening walks in the town
to admire the shops brightly lit with gas, or wandering
down to the railway station to see the trains coming in.
Third, he would have nothing to do with women. This was
not particularly difficult, for he found a substitute in
gazing at the exquisite wax models in hairdressers' windows.
There was one hairdresser who had six models made of
brightly colored wax, with elegant coiffures, revolving on
turntables. With the passion of a poor man dedicated to
making a fortune, he gazed at them with the hopeless
abandonment of a suitor who knows that the fairy princess
will never pay him a moment's attention, and sometimes
he thought of Minna and hoped he was worthy of her.
Fourth, he would acquire an education, even if it meant
starting from the bottom by learning the elements of
German calligraphy. In twenty lessons he learned how to
write a passable German hand, and then he went on to
learn Dutch and English by reading aloud, taking lessons
every day, writing essays and having them corrected by a
tutor. Fifth, he would train his memory, so that nothing
that ever happened to him, no book he read, no figures he
encountered in the ledgers, would ever pass completely

from his mind. Sixth, he would spend his money only on books or on the means to advance his education.

That lonely, spartan life left ineradicable marks on him, and he never recovered from it. He had the pride and single-mindedness of the self-taught; and if he grew bitter in his personal relationships that was the price he paid for his stern devotion to the duty of improving himself. He had no adolescence, or rather he experienced all the emotions of adolescence between the ages of nine and eleven, when he was seeing Minna every day. Now the steel was entering his soul, and with the steel went quirks of behavior, terrible rages, and titanic resolutions. Ruthlessly, dispassionately, with appalling lucidity, he mounted the steps leading to the temple of Success, and for long years the vision of Troy and even the thought of marrying Minna were to succumb to an all-consuming passion for gold.

Now every moment he could spare from the office was devoted to study—not the study of the Greek and Roman empires which were the passion of his youth, but the study of all the languages used in business. He learned English in six months by attending the English Church in Amsterdam twice every Sunday, and repeating under his breath every word spoken by the parson; and it seems never to have occurred to him that he was modeling himself on Hopping Peter, the old tailor in Ankershagen who was able to recite his father's sermons without in the least understanding what was being said. At night he read and reread *The Vicar of Wakefield* and *Ivanhoe* until he knew them by heart. His brain worked best at night, and therefore he allowed himself little sleep. He grew ill and pale, and had no time for his friends; he became a kind of memory-machine, learning nouns and verbs and conjugations by rote, divorced from the ordinary world of Amsterdam all around him.

After learning English in six months, he spent the next six months learning French. At the end of the year his powers of concentration had improved so vastly that he was able to learn Dutch, Spanish, Italian, and Portuguese with astonishing rapidity, claiming that it took him no more than six weeks of concentrated study to speak and write these languages fluently. Before he came to Amsterdam he knew only German, and that only in the *Plattdeutsch* of Mecklenburg, and a good smattering of Latin. Now he knew seven languages well: he could read and write them, could draw up business reports in them, and read foreign newspapers. To accomplish this, he had stolen time from his employers and maintained a ruthless schedule, learning long lists of words even when he was running errands in the rain, or memorizing whole passages while waiting for stamps at a post office. Never for a moment did he relent. He knew that in time, if he survived the rigors of his self-composed discipline, he would come into his reward.

The reward came shortly after his twenty-second birthday, on March 1, 1844, when he stepped into the office of Herr Schröder, who headed the vast import and export business in Amsterdam. Schliemann appealed for a job, explained his qualifications—seven languages, a head for figures, and two years' experience as an errand boy—and was immediately put to the test. At first glance Herr Schröder recognized a man who might be useful to him, and within a matter of minutes Heinrich was appointed a bookkeeper at 600 gulden, and within a few weeks the salary was increased to 1,000 gulden. The kindly Herr Schröder seems to have been amused and amazed by his new bookkeeper, who bore his own Christian name and who was so very apt in his understanding of the complexities of trade. Schliemann abandoned his study of languages for a few

months, and instead put his studies to use. He advanced
rapidly. He soon became one of the chief correspondents
in the office and was attached to the small circle surrounding Herr Schröder. When letters from Russia came to the
office, Heinrich announced that he would learn Russian in
a few weeks, so that he would be able to answer them.

He learned Russian in the same way he had learned
English—by pitching himself head foremost at the language, without troubling about grammar, though he would
sometimes permit himself a cursory examination of gram-
matical rules. He obtained a poor translation into Russian
of Fénélon's *Les Aventures de Télemaque*, which tells
in an extremely long-winded fashion the story of the son
of Ulysses. He bought a dictionary and an old grammar.
The first time he read the story he simply looked up all
the words in the dictionary, and by dint of hammering at
the text in front of him succeeded in extracting some sense
from it. He had a prodigious memory, and never needed
to look up the same word twice. He wanted a tutor, but
none was forthcoming. He took the trouble to go to the
Russian Consulate at Amsterdam and begged the vice consul
to give him lessons, but the vice consul had other matters
on his mind, and refused.

So he returned to his lodgings, wrote short stories and
essays in uncorrected Russian, and, because he felt lonely
and needed an audience for his recitations, he hired a poor
Jew at four francs an hour to listen to him reciting whole
chapters of *Les Aventures de Télemaque*, which he had
learned by heart. He liked to have an audience, and liked
shouting the heavy and sonorous syllables of the Russian
language, but the walls and floorboards were thin and the
lodgers complained at these nightly exercises, and he was
twice forced to change his lodgings. The method was singularly successful. At the end of six weeks he sent off

his first letter in Russian, addressing it with all the proper salutations to a certain Vassily Plotnikov, the London agent of a large firm of indigo merchants in Moscow. That letter was to shape the next twenty years of his life. In time he was to acquire a huge fortune, and perhaps the largest part of it was derived from selling indigo in Russia.

In those days Amsterdam was still one of the great centers of trade in indigo, which was imported from India and the Far East. Periodically indigo auctions were held there, and Schliemann would be sent to attend the auctions. With his consuming interest in all things Russian, he sought out the Russian merchants, who were surprised to find a German in Holland talking to them in their own language. He asked about conditions in Russia, made himself agreeable to them, inquired about prospects, and spoke about leaving Amsterdam for Moscow and setting up as an importer in partnership with an established Russian firm. He even drew up a contract with a Russian importer named Zhivago, who promised to open a business agency to be called "Zhivago and Schliemann" with a capital of 60,000 silver rubles to be supplied by the Russian partner, the profits to be shared equally. Evidently he was being regarded as a man of substance, and Heinrich Schröder, while paying him well, had to contemplate the possibility that he would leave for finer pastures.

For a year and ten months Schliemann continued to live in a series of dingy lodging houses, always saving his money, spending as little as possible on himself, his only apparent vice being innumerable cups of sweetened tea—it was a pleasant vice which he permitted himself to the end of his life. Sugar gave him sudden spurts of energy, and kept him awake during the long nights of study and contemplation. And now more and more he began to write letters to his father couched in the tones of an elder brother, anxious to save the family from disaster. He was continually cajoling his father to lead a more profitable life. He showered his father with gifts—from his first savings he sent two casks of Bordeaux and a box of cigars to the old reprobate, and he continued to send gifts in an endless torrent, always accompanying them with moral maxims and admonitions to follow his son's example—and all the time he was dreaming about marrying Minna. He told himself that the years of apprenticeship were nearly over. Soon he would marry and settle down with a healthy bank account. He would become a merchant prince, modeling himself on the Brothers Schröder, his knowledge of eight languages enabling him to carry on a vast trade across the length and breadth of the earth.

Toward the end of December, 1845, he was summoned to the inner office and asked whether he would like to represent the Schröder business interests in St. Petersburg. It is possible that news of his negotiations with Zhivago had already leaked out, and the firm was anxious to retain his services at any cost, even the cost of sending him as their chief representative to the capital of Russia. Told that he would be allowed to represent all the wide-flung Schröder interests with their branch offices in Bremen, Trieste, Smyrna, Le Havre, and Rio de Janeiro, he accepted at once; and he spent his last weeks in Amsterdam interviewing the heads of other businesses and suggesting that he could act as their representative as well. He was so sure of himself and the profits he would make that he requested that no fees be paid to him until he had actually shown a profit. "I will incur no expense for you," he wrote to the head of one business, "until you are satisfied that my activities on your behalf are productive of remunerative results, and accordingly I ask you to address your letters to me in unfranked envelopes."

Just before setting out for St. Petersburg he thought of writing to his friend Herr Laue, the court musician at Neu Strelitz, to inquire about Minna and to suggest that the time had come to marry her. Then it occurred to him that it would be better to postpone the matter until he had established himself in St. Petersburg. He wrote to his father, explaining his good fortune, the result of his own relentless single-mindedness. "Such gifts," he said, "do not fall from Heaven on those who are unworthy of them." He had made few friends in Amsterdam, and he felt no greater wrench in parting from Amsterdam than he felt in parting from Hamburg. For the rest of his life he was to be a wanderer over the face of the earth.

So in a mood of profound self-satisfaction, at the age of twenty-five, only four years after being shipwrecked off the coast of Holland, he set out from Amsterdam as the chief representative of one of the greatest trading firms on earth, and sixteen days later, February 1, 1846, after an arduous journey by coach and sleigh, he arrived in St. Petersburg.

The Search for Gold

ᄅᄅᄅᄅᄅᄅᄅᄅᄅᄅᄅᄅ

In the 1840's of the last century St. Petersburg was a city still coming to birth. Nicholas I was on the throne, a stern square-chinned man, six feet tall, who despised his ministers and preferred to think of himself as a cavalry officer who had inherited the Czardom by the grace of God and was therefore entitled to enjoy himself to the utmost. Among his major amusements was the construction of glittering white Italianate palaces on this bleak northern shore of the Baltic. He held himself well, his waist tightly compressed, as befitted a cavalry officer, and he pursued indiscriminately all the women at his court. Nearly everyone who came into his presence trembled, for his left eye was so much brighter than his right that he seemed to be somehow inhuman,

removed from the common preoccupations of humanity—
a trait which he shared with Alexander the Great, whose
terrible eyes also made solid soldiers tremble in their shoes.

St. Petersburg in the time of Nicholas I was a city of
extremes: wide streets, a few factory buildings, innumerable
palaces, the hovels of the poor. Visitors remarked on the
absence of traffic on the streets, the emptiness of the place,
the sense of abandonment which had come over this new
city built on marshlands by Peter the Great and now rebuilt
by Nicholas I, who saw himself as the destined successor
of Peter. In winter the whole city was white, the only color
coming from the bright scarlet liveries of the royal coach-
men. At night ghosts wandered through the icy streets.
While the courtiers endured the endless frivolities of the
Court, and the serfs endured their slavery, students were
already planning to overthrow the monarchy. It was the
year when Dostoevsky's first novel, *Poor Folk*, appeared,
and already that group of conspirators known as the
Petrashevsky circle was plotting against the Czar, with the
young Dostoevsky among them. Throughout Russia there
was a gradual awakening of a feverish social conscious-
ness: the bitterness and despair of a people enslaved.

In all the years he spent in St. Petersburg, Schliemann
never showed any sign of being aware of the deadly poison
in the air. He told himself continually he was living in the
best of all possible worlds. For him St. Petersburg was a
good substantial city, eminently suitable for business, and
far safer than most cities. He spoke of "the beautiful and
clean houses, the fine streets and delightful climate." In
his letters the Czar becomes "the wise and most glorious
emperor Nicholas." He had no illusions about the Russian
businessmen—they were as grasping and difficult to handle
as all the other businessmen everywhere, but at least he
possessed advantages over them. He knew his trade better

than most, and as the chief representative for Schröder he was in a position to make himself heard. Restless, energetic, ambitious, he was constantly on the move. After seven days in St. Petersburg he drove off by sleigh to Moscow, to establish connections with firms he had been corresponding with. He was at ease in the company of merchant princes, and was soon on intimate terms with them.

From the moment he arrived in St. Petersburg he acted out the part of international merchant with resounding success. He represented the Schröder interests, and six or seven other interests as well. Even with a commission of ½ percent, which was all he allowed himself in those early years, he earned 7,500 gulden during his first year, and this represented a turnover of 1,500,000 gulden—a sum beyond his dreams two or three years before. He achieved his success by a meticulous attention to detail, by standing at his desk from early morning to late in the evening, by following every clue which would lead him to a profit, however small.

He made four separate journeys to Moscow that year, and by October things were going so well that he permitted himself a combined business and pleasure trip through Germany, France, and England, stepping off for a few hours in Amsterdam to renew acquaintance with Heinrich Schröder, for whom he felt an intense gratitude. What interested him most of all was the vast progress in industry —locomotives, bridges, factories, the telegraph, the whole of Europe surging forward into the new age of industrialism, and Russia so backward that it seemed as though he were specially selected to bring the advantages of industrialism to his adopted country. Gradually he came to regard himself as a Russian. He spoke of the Czar as "our Czar" and Russia as "my country." And while enjoying his riches, he also enjoyed his old habits of thrift. So it happened on all his travels that he would put up at the best hotels, while choosing the least expensive rooms, usually on the top floor. He had a passion for being under the roof, and perhaps it went back to those days in Amsterdam when he learned seven languages in two years in the garrets of cheap lodging houses.

He liked London, though he knew the cold chill of a typical Victorian Sunday. He wandered into the British Musuem and made careful lists of the Pharaohs in their sarcophagi, and of Greek and Roman vases. He was delighted with the train which took him to Manchester, traveling so much more quickly than any other trains in Europe. At that time Manchester was the greatest industrial center in the world, a vast humming factory lit with the fires of coke furnaces and the blaze of innumerable chimneys. There he saw the giant locomotives being built for export to Germany and watched iron being cut "as easily as paper," and everything pleased him. Steamships, dockyards, iron foundries, the telegraph which could send a message from the south of England to the northernmost tip of Scotland—it was all wonderful beyond belief, and at the same time magnificently arranged by the Creator for the furtherance of trade. No one ever looked upon the industrial revolution with a less jaundiced eye.

He returned to St. Petersburg by way of Le Havre, Paris, Brussels, Cologne, Düsseldorf, Hamburg, Berlin, without pausing in Mecklenburg. There were excellent reasons for avoiding the places where he had spent his childhood. Some time during that year he had written to Herr Laue in Neu Strelitz and asked for the hand of Minna Meincke, only to learn that she had married a local farmer. The marriage took place a few weeks before he wrote his letter. The shock nearly killed him. Sixteen years had passed since he first set eyes on her. He told himself that through all those sixteen years he had lived for her, and for her alone. What did it matter to him that he was slowly acquiring a fortune, influence, and prestige, when he had no one to share them with? So he grew sullen and embittered, nursing his grief, telling himself that there was a kind of curse on him, but the time would come when, with a great fortune at his command, he would marry any Russian beauty he desired. To a man of wealth all things were possible, even a happy marriage.

At the beginning of 1847, shortly after his return to St. Petersburg, he was inscribed as a merchant of the First Guild. This meant that he was now properly established, could obtain bankers' credit, and was on an equal footing with long-established merchants. He attended the monthly meetings of the Guild, made speeches in impeccable Russian, and was welcomed in the Guild club. He sat at the tables of the wealthiest people in the land. Peter Alexieff, "who is worth 100 million rubles and has a private fortune of 12 million rubles besides," greeted him affably at the club and invited him into his home. The prominent sugar and timber merchant Ponomareff took a fancy to him and spoke of advancing 100,000 silver rubles if he would enter a business arrangement with him. Then there was "my friend Zhivago, who is worth several millions"—the man he had met by accident at the Amsterdam auction sale, and who was therefore largely responsible for his journey to Russia —who lived in a palatial house in Moscow and entertained him whenever he visited the city. Zhivago was childless, but his niece Ekaterina, "an angel of virtue and beauty," was staying with him. She was sixteen, and completely captivating, and Zhivago himself seemed to desire the match, for he invited Schliemann to stay in the Moscow house for four or five months, evidently with the intention of acquiring a partner and a relative by marriage. Schliemann was a little nervous about these Moscow prospects.

He liked Ekaterina, but was unsure of himself. He wrote to his sister in Mecklenburg, begging her to make the journey to Russia—she would stay for a few weeks in St. Petersburg and then accompany him to Moscow, where she would observe the behavior of the beautiful Ekaterina. In effect, Schliemann wanted a business report on Ekaterina, just such a report as he was in the habit of receiving from his agencies abroad. What was she really like? How did she behave in the seclusion of her own apartment? Was she a person of fire and temperament? Could she cook? He wrote to his sister: "I am sure there is no lack of brides: the difficulty is to choose among a hundred would-be brides. You will help me in my choice. I myself am blind, and passion clouds my vision. I see only the virtues and never the failings of the fair sex. I have a large bath, so you can take your baths at home."

This astonishing letter proved only that Schliemann was incapable of relying on his own judgment in matters of the heart. Nothing came of the invitation to his sister, and in time he realized that no one could help him and only a miracle would provide him with a wife as adorable as Minna. So he temporized, made excursions among the daughters of the gentry and wealthier businessmen, and usually retired from the battle, hurt and confused. He was full-blooded, violently jealous, and self-opinionated. Accustomed to having his orders obeyed immediately, he found quite early in his career that the laws governing business are inappropriate in the boudoir; and in the presence of women he became more and more baffled. It was not that he lacked the social graces; it was simply that he could not trust himself, did not know exactly what he wanted, always hoped to marry a rich heiress, but could never find one who possessed the beauty, simplicity, and grace of Minna.

And while Minna still dominated his dreams, the search for a fortune dominated his life. He had opened his own business agency, while continuing his connections with Schröder. He trafficked in every kind of merchandise and took appalling risks, but never gave credit "except to merchants of the very first standing." He explained to Schröder that he had worked exceedingly hard on their behalf, and felt that he was now in a position to demand more than the miserable ½ percent which they had granted him in the days when he was unknown. Now everyone knew him. Was he not regarded as a man of dazzling accomplishments, with a business which extended over the whole world? Accordingly Schröder permitted him to draw off 1 percent of the value of the merchandise passing through his hands, and from that moment Schliemann knew that only a few years would pass before he had acquired an immense fortune.

So matters progressed until the end of 1848, when for the fifth time he made the journey by sleigh to Moscow, to spend Christmas and the New Year with the Zhivagos. He enjoyed the visit, but on the return journey through the snow he suffered agonies of cold when a storm blew up, and fell ill with influenza. He thought he was dying. For four months he remained in bed, and as soon as he was recovered, he threw himself so violently into his work that by June he was in a state of collapse. The doctors put him in a dark room and refused to let him continue with his business. He raged at the doctors, but admitted the justice of their accusations. He was discovering that to make a fortune a man has to live on his nerves, in a perpetual state of intellectual fever, in a landscape where the only comfort consisted in the sight of the gold which was always just out of his reach.

When fall came he had learned his lesson. He worked a little less avidly, and attended more social engagements. He gave dinner parties, served the finest wines, and surrounded himself with merchants and their eligible daughters. All thoughts of Ekaterina vanished when he fell hopelessly in love with a certain Sophia, who possessed no fortune, but was thrifty and spoke three European languages fluently. He was madly in love with her. He wrote off to his father that he had found the girl of his dreams, only to write in the next letter that he had taken her to a party, where she showed unpardonable interest in a young officer, and at the sight of "giddy, stupid Sophia" behaving in this lamentable fashion, he had broken off the engagement. On the whole he was glad he had escaped from her. He would have the opportunity of cultivating a romance with the adorable Ekaterina—the Zhivagos were always asking him to visit him in Moscow. So in February 1850 he journeyed by sleigh again to Moscow, and as usual stayed with the Zhivagos. No one knows exactly what happened. Within a month he was journeying at high speed across Europe, drowning himself in business, never staying in one place for more than a few days, his letters full of sound business advice, with not a word about Ekaterina in any of them.

Like a man hounded by the police, he slipped from one hotel to another. It is possible that he thought of settling in northern England, for he spent most of the time there, visiting Edinburgh, Glasgow, Liverpool, Bangor, Chester, and London. He took notes of everything he saw, and every night wrote up his diary; the industrial progress of England continued to amaze him. At the end of a few weeks he was back again in St. Petersburg, his pockets bursting with contracts. But it is unlikely that he made these sudden journeys only for the sake of business. Most of his long journeys in those early years seem to have taken place immediately after the collapse of a love affair. These hurried and precipitous excursions abroad were in fact surrogates for the sexual experience he lacked. There were moments when he detested St. Petersburg and thought of settling down on a farm in Mecklenburg with a poor peasant girl for a bride.

But St. Petersburg summoned him. There, at least, he had established the foundation of his fortune, and he told himself that for a few more months he would attempt to live in that cold northern city. He settled down to work, attended parties, and some time in the summer of 1850 he was introduced to a certain Ekaterina Lishin, a tall statuesque beauty, the niece of another business acquaintance. She had a pale oval face, dark eyes, and carried herself like a princess. Schliemann admired her, discussed the possibility of marrying her, but with his Mecklenburg caution decided to bide his time. Since she was extremely haughty in her manner and possessed no fortune of her own, he was a little wary of her. So the summer passed, and fall came, and business prospered, and he still did not know what to do with his life or the small fortune he had already built up, largely in indigo.

He was a man who rarely committed himself. He saw the world in harsh colors—riches, poverty; food in abundance, starvation; life in one of the glittering capitals, or on an obscure farm. As he stood at his desk in St. Petersburg, sending hurried messages to agents all over Europe, he was always close to nervous prostration. Sometimes it occurred to him that there must be easier ways to make a fortune.

Early in 1850 he received news that his younger brother Ludwig had reached the California gold fields. For some time Ludwig had acted as Heinrich's agent in Amsterdam. He lacked his brother's spark of genius, but possessed an equal amount of temperament. Headstrong, nervous, with a talent for languages—he corresponded with his brother in French, English, and Spanish—Ludwig also possessed a burning desire to make a fortune. Once he thought of opening a shop and asked Heinrich to lend him sufficient capital, and when Heinrich offered to lend him 500 talers he rejected the offer with indignation—he had supposed his brother to be a little less niggardly. On another occasion he wrote that he intended to kill himself unless Heinrich brought him into the business in St. Petersburg, and signed the letter with his own blood. Heinrich answered at length, pointing out that it was not a small matter to introduce a partner into the complicated affairs of St. Petersburg, and he had no intention of providing for Ludwig during the long years of apprenticeship. It would take him four years to learn Russian sufficiently well to be able to use the language properly, and there was absolutely no guarantee that he had the makings of a businessman, and in particular he was lacking in the necessary driving ambition. "I myself have had to fend for myself for thirteen years without asking a penny from anyone," Heinrich wrote, and it was quite clear that he intended Ludwig to do the same.

One day in Rotterdam, while walking along the banks of a canal in a mood of desperation and anger, Ludwig on an impulse decided to sail to America. Once in New York, he became a teacher of French, and then entered business. When he had saved enough money he struck out for the California gold fields, where he became a banker, and progressed so well that he soon made a small fortune. In the infuriating manner of a younger brother who has always lived in his older brother's shadow, he wrote a long taunting letter, explaining the advantages of California over any other place on earth, and suggested that Heinrich would be well-advised to sell everything he had and come to Sacramento.

The letter must have stung Heinrich to the quick. He could hardly have failed to observe the innuendoes, the challenge, the implied superiority of the younger brother who spoke so casually of making a vast fortune in a few months. Heinrich knew that such fortunes were being made by men who did not possess a tenth of his discipline or his dedication to wealth—in a few weeks Ludwig had apparently accomplished more than Heinrich in all his years as a businessman. Ludwig's final jibe was the most painful: he promised to take full financial care of his sisters and hoped to send Heinrich "a fat remittance" in the fall.

The remittance never came. Instead, there came a clipping from a Sacramento newspaper announcing that "on May 25, 1850, Mr. Louis Schliemann, of German nationality, lately of New York, died from typhus in Sacramento City, at the age of 25 years." The news reached Heinrich in the middle of August. Together with the clipping came a brief covering letter which said little more than that Ludwig had left a large estate.

For the rest of the year Heinrich continued to supervise his business, uncertain what was demanded of him. He had a profound horror of death, and his brother's death shook him. So that grief would not fall too heavily on his sisters, he wrote them a strange letter, saying that he had seen his brother lying dead in a dream. "I, who have not wept for twenty years, a man who is never shaken by things of this kind, found myself weeping continually for three days, and all because of a dream." A few days later he wrote that Ludwig had died in Sacramento and left a large fortune.

By the end of the year he had made his decision. Out of a sense of brotherly duty he would go to the gold fields and make a fortune, following in his brother's footsteps. He would start business with the money left by his brother, and grow rich far more rapidly than in St. Petersburg. He would build a proper gravestone for his brother's tomb, and remain in America for the rest of his life. Nothing held him: there were no attachments in St. Petersburg close enough to keep him there, though he still admired Ekaterina Lishin and sometimes it crossed his mind that he might return to Russia and marry her, but only if he possessed a fortune so large that it would dazzle her. In all his life he had never stayed very long in one place. He had thought he would be able to strike deep roots in St. Petersburg, but it was all a mistake. He decided to begin his life again, and once more he was a wanderer on the face of the earth.

On December 10, 1850, he gave his last dinner to his friends, the merchants Melin and Lishin, and said farewell to St. Petersburg. The Neva was frozen over, and an icy wind blew across St. Isaac's Square. His friends accompanied him to the post office, where the sleighs set out for the long journey to Germany; and as he passed the gleaming white Winter Palace, the Admiralty, and the equestrian statue of Peter the Great, he saluted them as though he never expected to see them again. At that moment he could not have guessed what misadventures would come to him before he stood by his brother's grave at the other end of the world.

As usual, he kept a diary. Very often during his travels the diary reads like an extended timetable. He notes the times of the trains, where he stayed, how much he paid for his room on the sixth floor, how much money he exchanged at the bank, and the names of the businessmen who met with his approval. One wonders what satisfaction he derived from those endless pages which announce the names of the railway stations he passed through. He wrote on December 15, 1850:

> By 7 o'clock in the morning we breakfasted at Elbing, at 11 o'clock we passed Marienburg and at 4 o'clock P.M. we went at Dierschau on a large floating bridge over the Vistula. On the 18th Decbr. at noon we arrived at Woldenberg, where we got a bad dinner and at 1 o'clock we started by the railroad over Stargard to Stettin, where we arrived at 5½ o'clock P.M. At 6½ o'clock we started again by rail and arrived at 9½ o'clock at night in Berlin.

Mercifully, he does not always write like this. The diary of his journey to America, which he wrote in English, contains some of his best writing. It was not intended for publication, or to be read by any eyes but his own, but it was written carefully, and sometimes there is a direct, tortured honesty in his story which enables us to share his experiences. When the diary opens, he is still the businessman with a consuming interest in acquiring the fortune he had promised himself. He goes about his affairs pompously, doing the right things at the right moment, very sure of himself. By the time the diary ends, the raw edges of human experience had shaken him to the depths: storm, tempest, and sickness have laid him low. He has looked into the face of horror, and become a man.

No one who turns to the opening pages of the diary is likely to believe that he is about to read a human document comparable with Conrad's *Heart of Darkness*. Schliemann arrived in Amsterdam, called on B. H. Schröder and Co., acquired letters of introduction to agencies and banks in America, and conducted himself as a proper businessman. On December 23, a Sunday, he arrived in London and took up lodgings "with Mr. Keizar, the Royal Hotel, Blackfriars Bridge." On Christmas Eve he discounted the bills on

London he had brought with him from St. Petersburg and sold his gold to the Bank of England, and in the afternoon visited the Crystal Palace, which delighted him—it was only one more illustration of England's undoubted advances in industrialization. He attended services at Westminster Abbey on Christmas Day. It seems to have been a lonely Christmas. He notes in his diary that on December 26 he saw "the celebrated tragedian 'Macredy,' who played for the last time before retiring from the stage." This is a puzzling entry, for Macready spent the entire Christmas holiday with his family at Sherborne and did not retire from the stage until two months later, the gala performance at the Prince's Theatre occurring in an atmosphere of wild excitement, with Dickens and Bulwer-Lytton in the audience, on February 26, 1851. On the day following the imaginary performance he took the train to Liverpool, staying as he always did in the huge square Adelphi Hotel, which must have reminded him of the heavy-set hotels of Germany. Then he arranged for his passage to New York, paid £35 for passage, sauntered around Liverpool, and went to bed. He did not know it, but very soon the mask of the imperturbable businessman—that mask which he liked most to show to the world—would be torn to shreds.

The S.S. "Atlantic," 3,000 tons, on which he sailed for New York the following day, was one of the fastest ocean-going steamers of the time. They were eight days out from Liverpool when they struck a storm. A huge wave smashed the port wheel with such force that the main shaft broke, and the ship was thrown to the mercy of the waves. Both engines were disabled. They were in mid-Atlantic, 1,800 miles from Liverpool and 1,400 miles from New York. With a strong westerly gale blowing, the captain decided to make for the American coast, and put up a mainsail and maintopsail, hoping to be blown across the ocean. Schliemann noted in his diary that "the sails looked like handkerchiefs" and none of the passengers approved of the captain's desire to make his way against the prevailing winds—it would be better to return to England. There were long debates. It was pointed out to the captain that the ship would almost certainly capsize if he continued to fight against the storm: it would be much safer if he turned round and sailed to the nearest port. In the excitement of the storm seasickness miraculously stopped, and Schliemann discovered to his surprise that he was in good heart, and even a little amused by the behavior of the famous ocean-going steamer which sailed home under her pathetic sails.

Sixteen days later the ship put in at Queenstown, and soon Schliemann was making his way back to Liverpool by way of Dublin, where he heard that there was some outstanding business in Amsterdam to be attended to. He hurried off, but he was back again in Liverpool on February 1, ready to sail to New York on the S.S. "Africa." This time the journey was uneventful.

He liked New York—"a very regularly built, nice, clean town with many many elegant and even colossal buildings" —though he felt it did not compare with the European capitals. He found little to admire in New York women, and noted in his diary that "at the age of 22 they look just as old and worn out as they are beautiful and symmetrical at 16 and 18." He complained of their tendency to be amusing and frivolous. Also, he disliked the railroads, and commented sternly after a trip to Philadelphia: "The American railroads are merely laid out with the design to make money, and not the least notice is taken as to convenience and accommodations for passengers." Later he invested huge sums in American railroads.

In Washington he called on President Fillmore. "I made my introduction by stating my great desire to see this beautiful country of the West," he wrote in his journal, "and to make the acquaintance of the great men who govern it." Soon after attending a *soirée* at the White House, he hurried off by ship to the Isthmus of Panama, at that time the most direct route to the Far West. There was no Panama Railroad. Prospectors journeyed by mule train across the Isthmus, where yellow fever was prevalent and there were bandits in the surrounding jungles. Schliemann went armed with a revolver and a long dagger. He saw alligators in the Chagres river and butterflies as large as pigeons. It was the first time he had ever set foot in the tropics, and he paid the tribute of his grudging admiration to the natives:

> The isthmus of Panama is an immense Eden in which the descendants of Adam and Eve seem to have retained the manners and customs of their primitive forefathers; for they go quite naked, and live upon the fruit which the splendid tropical vegetation puts around them in magnificent abundance. Their chief characteristic is a horrible laziness, which does not permit them to occupy themselves with anything; they cannot find themselves happier than lying in their hammocks and eating and drinking. They are very fantastic.

Fantastic or not, he feared them—and not only for their laziness. The bones of many prospectors, killed by these Indians, littered the mule trail. He was no happier when he reached Panama City and discovered that the Spanish inhabitants suffered from the same laziness, and in addition possessed the vices he attributed to the young women of New York. "The characteristic of the Spaniard in this country," he wrote sententiously, "is a great inclination for the frivolous and amusing, a great laziness, and a great lightness of character." It did not occur to him that in a tropical climate vast ambitions are sometimes at the mercy of the weather.

But though he detested everything in Panama, he was curiously content. The journey was nearly over, and the prospect of acquiring gold in California pleased him. Because he had to wait several days for a ship, he amused himself by visiting the old city of Panama, destroyed by Morgan and his pirates and now half overgrown with jungle. It was the first time he had paid any attention to ruins since leaving Ankershagen, and though he showed no particular excitement—what puzzled him most of all was how the roots of trees became embedded in the ancient walls—this visit to the old city must be accounted his first archeological exploration. He noted that the guide was stupid, and seemed to know nothing at all about the ruins, and the whole journey was a waste of time.

He sailed for California on March 15, 1851, on the S.S. "Oregon," and hated every moment of the journey. He complained bitterly about the food: no ice, no fresh meat, only salt pork and corned beef. He liked to take his baths in seawater, but the ship's servants were curiously uncooperative. A week after leaving Panama the ship put in at Acapulco, and his intense distrust of the Spaniards was exchanged for a still more intense distrust of the Mexicans—they were all false, ignorant and arrogant, and Acapulco itself was nothing but a huddle of huts "like an African village." Nor did he have anything good to say about the port of San Diego, which he dismissed as a small village with a few wooden houses around a bay thick with yellow seaweed. Hating the earth and his fellow-passengers, he took to reading about astronomy and spent long hours at night gazing at the stars. He might have exploded altogether with ill temper if they had not arrived quickly at the Golden Gate. San Francisco delighted him, but he had no time to waste. He was off immediately to Sacramento, in search of his brother's grave.

Sacramento was still in its infancy, and as he went about that strange clapboard town which owed its existence to the neighboring gold fields, he had the same feeling which came to him with surprising force when he visited St. Petersburg for the first time: here was undreamed-of wealth for the asking. But he noted, too, that the number of graves in the cemetery exceeded the total population of the town. He found his brother's grave. There was no marker, and so he gave $50 to a local undertaker for "a beautiful marble tombstone." He asked about the fortune his brother had left, and learned that Ludwig's partner had absconded with it. He made some inquiries about whether the police would be able to trace the partner, but came to the conclusion that nothing would be gained by an attempt to pursue him. The fortune had vanished into thin air.

When Ludwig arrived in Sacramento in July, 1849, the whole town consisted of exactly one frame building and a few huts. In two years it had mushroomed into a city of 16,000 inhabitants, and was likely to continue expanding at the same pace. Schliemann liked the town, and in his customary fashion set about exploring its potentialities by making trips into the surrounding areas. He visited Sutterville and the Yuba River gold fields and Nevada City, which he described as "a small and extremely nasty place in the midst of a pine forest." He was always searching for people who shared his interest in languages, and he was delighted on a journey through the Sonoma Valley to encounter a certain Professor Reeger, who spoke English, French, German, Italian, Portuguese, and Dutch; and it pleased him to sit up half the night with a stranger who could slip from one language to another with his own ease.

Though Sacramento pleased and intoxicated him, he was still undecided about his future. He lent a little money on short-term mortgages, but otherwise showed no particular desire to take root there. He had often thought of making a prolonged journey to the Far East, and it occurred to him during moments of weakness that he might return to Germany by way of the Pacific, taking a boat from San Francisco and visiting all the ports of China, India, and Egypt, and then taking a train through Italy. But these moments of weakness passed, and as the excitement of being in a strange country wore away, he began to think seriously once more of the fortune which was only waiting for him to gather in his hands. So April and May passed in a preliminary reconnaissance, and June found him once more in San Francisco in conferences with the agents of Messrs. Rothschild and other businessmen, while he prepared to set himself up as a buyer of gold dust, with headquarters at the corner of J and Front Streets in Sacramento.

He was attending these conferences on June 4, 1851, and had retired to his hotel room after an exhausting day, when the whole city burst into flame. That was the night of the famous San Francisco fire, and Schliemann in his downtown hotel was caught in the middle of it. Awakened by the clanging of fire bells, he dressed hurriedly and ran out into the street. A gale was blowing and fanning the flames. For a few moments he watched the houses all round him melting in the flames, and then he found himself hurrying up Telegraph Hill. "The roaring of the storm, the cracking of the gunpowder, the cracking of the falling stone-walls, the cries of the people and the wonderful spectacle of an immense city burning in a dark night all joined to make this catastrophe awful in the extreme." So he wrote the next day, the flames still dazzling his eyes. There was a rumor that foreign incendiaries were responsible for the conflagration, and Schliemann reports casually that many foreigners, especially Frenchmen, were murdered by the people of San Francisco on suspicion of setting the fire. He was amazed by the coolness of the Americans, who went about rebuilding their city while the ashes were still hot and the flames were still burning. He spent the whole night on Telegraph Hill, and in the morning set out for Sacramento.

Because he was afraid of fire, he leased an office in the only fireproof stone-and-iron building in Sacramento, and because he was afraid of theft he bought a huge iron safe and stood over it from six in the morning to ten at night, working himself and his two assistants, one Spanish, the other American, to the bone. Prospectors were flocking to California from all over the world, and so in a single day he would find himself speaking all the eight languages he knew. There were some languages he did not know, including the Kanaka spoken by the natives of the Sandwich Islands who had mysteriously appeared in Sacramento. During his rare moments of leisure he inspected the Californian Indians. They were a small copper-red people, extremely dirty, and suffered from syphilis. "They lived," he said, "like ants in their heaps of earth."

He had dreamed of a fortune, and now within a few months a fortune was within his grasp. There were days when 180 pounds weight of gold passed through his hands. His wealth increased from week to week, until he became almost afraid of it, and like his assistants he went about armed with a Colt revolver. He wrote later that he felt no particular fear of the rascals he met in the course of business: he could always outwit them. But he repeats himself too much, and boasts a little too often of his expertness: there were days when he seems to have lived in mortal terror of the gold which came so easily into his hands. And sometimes he remembered that he might die of typhus, like his brother, and there would be nothing to show for those long hours spent at his desk.

He had reason to be afraid, for in October he was lying

on his back, vomiting and raving like a madman, his body covered with yellow spots, while the doctor fed him with quinine and calomel, which were the usual medicines against yellow fever. In his absence his clerks carried on the business, thieving to their heart's content. When he returned to his desk the fear came back again. In a revealing letter to a friend in San Francisco he described the misery and loneliness which goes with acquiring a fortune:

> I had a *very hard time* here during the week, and never a negro slave worked harder than I did.
>
> But that is all nothing to the danger of sleeping the night alone with so immense accounts of gold in cash. I always spend the night in a feverish horror and loaded pistols in *both* hands. The noise of a mouse or a rat struck me with terror; —I could eat only once a day viz: at 6½ at night, and other wants of nature I was forced to forget entirely. In one word: it was a most awful time.

He had hardly recovered from one bout of fever when he caught the fever again. In January 1852 he went to recuperate in the Santa Clara Valley, a sick man, drained of energy, worried beyond measure because his doctor had told him he had the same constitution as his brother and was likely to die in the same way. Yet he knew his strength, and possessed a driving compulsion to acquire a fortune before he left Sacramento, and he was back again at his desk at the beginning of February. Once more he rose at five in the morning, took his place behind his desk, weighed gold dust, wrote out banker's drafts and talked to prospectors in eight languages—a stiff, unsmiling, punctilious man, with a curiously shrill voice and the air of a scholar resolved to solve the mystery of wealth and harness it to his own purposes, though he was still unsure what these purposes were. He called himself an American, spoke of "our gold-fields" and "our cemetery," and sometimes thought of settling in

America for the rest of his life. More often he found himself dreaming about a farm in Germany, though he must have known he possessed no skill as a farmer. He had put Russia behind him. Sitting over his horde of gold, he lived a life of quiet desperation, at odds with himself, certain of only one thing: he must make his fortune, or perish.

He very nearly perished at the end of March, when the fever came again and once more his body was covered with yellow spots. He had given his clerks instructions—as soon as he showed himself incompetent to carry on his business, they were to wrap him in a blanket and send him by steamer to San Francisco. Seven days later, on April 7, he had made his resolution. Miraculously recovered, he visited the Rothschild bank in San Francisco and arranged for the transfer of his assets and the liquidation of his business. He had made his fortune. Others had made larger fortunes from the Californian gold mines, but few had made them so quickly, or at so little risk. In the course of nine months he had amassed $400,000. He was not in the least staggered by his staggering good fortune. It seemed to him that this was no more than his due reward, earned by remorseless attention to detail and a consuming passion for hard work. He was to learn during the following weeks that the gods sometimes punish those to whom they have shown excessive favors.

He admired the Americans, but found them curiously uncouth, their manners reprehensible, and their women unattractive. Accordingly, he now decided to spend the rest of his life among the Russians, whose social graces he respected and whose women showed the proper seriousness he demanded. His fortune would enable him to lead a life of baronial magnificence in Moscow or St. Petersburg. He decided to return to Russia in style, paying $600 for a stateroom in the steamer taking him from San Francisco to

Panama. He would cross the Isthmus, take a ship to New York, and then make his way in a leisurely fashion to Russia.

The first warning from the gods came in the Gulf of Tehuantepec, seven days out from San Francisco. The ship was caught in a typhoon, and nearly foundered. The second warning came in Panama City, when an attempt was made to steal his luggage—he sat over it grimly with a Colt revolver in one hand and a dagger in the other. A few miles of the Panama Railroad had been laid, but thereafter the journey across the Isthmus was along the mule trail.

He had chosen the worst season of the year for his journey. It rained continually. They were abandoned by their guides. They had no food, and were forced to live on iguana lizards, which they ate raw. They were attacked by scorpions and rattlesnakes. It was a landscape of nightmare and terror. He suffered excruciating pain from a wound in his leg, which became gangrenous. There were no bandages, no medicines. For fourteen days they pushed forward along the forest trail, their clothes sticking to their skins, in danger of attack from the Indians, without maps, without any reason to believe that they would ever reach Colon. They shot monkeys, skinned them, and ate the flesh, and quarreled violently among themselves. Some died of dysentery, others of yellow fever, and their bodies were left beside the trail for the jungle animals to feed on. And still the rain came down, a bitter cold rain which sucked their energy and gave them the appearance of drowned men wandering at the bottom of the sea.

For Schliemann the most terrible thing of all was that he trusted no one and therefore could not afford to sleep. With his dagger and revolver he stood guard continually over his luggage: the gold bars, the drafts on Rothschild, the letters of introduction to merchant princes all over Europe. He was a man who rarely wrote vividly of his own emotions, but sometimes emotion comes through. So it was when he described the storm off Texel, and so it is again in a short paragraph he permitted himself when describing the agonies of the journey across the Isthmus:

> We became so familiarized with death that it lost for us all its terror, that we began to like it and to look upon it as a lingering of our sufferings. Thus came that we laughed and amused ourselves at the convulsions of the dying and that crimes were perpetrated among us; *crimes so terrible!* that now at a later date I cannot think of it without cold and trembling horror.

He never revealed what crimes were committed, or whether he himself committed them. Rape, murder, cannibalism—there are no clues. In later years, whenever he wrote about his life, he always passed quickly over the years he spent in America, and he never again referred to his journey across the Isthmus of Panama. He did everything he could to forget those terrible fourteen days, and became more merciless and demanding of himself and of others. His sisters had always complained of his coldness, the air of indifference which he showed to the world; now he was to become colder, harder, sterner, and more than ever in love with wealth. In a strange way he was becoming more and more like the Greek heroes who slumbered in the depths of his imagination, for they too had laughed and amused themselves at the convulsions of the dying, and like him had pursued wealth avidly, with barbaric abandonment.

So he made his way back to Europe, pausing only long enough in New York to have his wound bandaged, and in London to have the gangrene burned out with *lapis infernalis*, and then he was back in Mecklenburg for a few weeks, renewing old acquaintances and flaunting his wealth, giving expensive presents to his uncle, his father, and his sisters.

He had abandoned the idea of settling down on a farm. He would have a mansion of his own, or at least a large apartment, and marry a Russian girl of good family, and perhaps in time he would be elevated to the Russian nobility. He was thirty; he had made his fortune; and he feared no one. As he rode back in the sleigh to St. Petersburg, he counted himself the most fortunate man in the world. He had only to lift his finger, and everything he had ever dreamed of during his poverty-stricken days in Fürstenberg and Amsterdam —books, wine, women, servants, houses—would all be given to him in double measure. He did not know, and could not guess, that for seventeen long years his wealth was to taste like ashes in his mouth.

The Merchant Prince

‖‖‖‖‖‖‖‖‖‖‖‖

Outwardly he was a man of the world, the very type of the successful business executive, with his gold-rimmed spectacles and long coat with an astrakhan collar. He wore his mustache *à la Tartare*, carried an ebony cane, and possessed his own carriage. His vast apartment on one of the best streets of St. Petersburg consisted of two salons, seven bedrooms, five other rooms, a kitchen, stables, cellars, and a coach house. The best available wines were in the cellars and three of the most expensive horses were in the coach house. Princes and merchants clamored for invitations to the house of the adventurous businessman who was believed to have made a vast fortune in the California gold fields. He had an air of authority. He was cultivated and well-mannered. He spent money lavishly—had he not spent a thousand rubles to furnish a single guest room? In St. Petersburg he was regarded as the most fortunate of men, the most desirable of acquaintances, a man in line to become president of the Chamber of Commerce.

The inward man, however, bore very little resemblance to the image he showed to the world. Fires blazed in him, and sexual passion drove him almost insane. Above all he wanted a wife and children, and with all the women in Russia to choose from, he had to choose a cold virago who married him only for his money, refused to share his bed, taunted him continually, and lived out her life as though she were waiting for him to die so that she could inherit his fortune. Again and again in letters to his father and sisters he complains in a tone of bewilderment against the horror of being married to a woman who despised him.

Perhaps it was unavoidable. Perhaps he was so full of his wealth that no woman would have married him on his own merits. Ekaterina Lishin had refused him before, when he was already a wealthy merchant. Now that he was wealthy beyond the dreams of avarice, she accepted him. He called on her the day after he reached St. Petersburg and continued to call on her during the following weeks. He told himself he was in love with her, and would always love her. She possessed all the virtues: she was good, kind, simple, attentive. She held herself well, and was equally at home in her own salon and at the receptions given by wealthy merchants. He adored her, and promised to do everything to make her happy. On the day of his marriage, October 12, 1852, he wrote to his family:

> Today I became the happy husband of Catherine Lyschin, who is a Russian lady of great accomplishment of body and mind. My wife is a very good, simple, clever and sensible girl, and I love and respect her more with every passing day.

Because I am so happily married, I have decided to make St. Petersburg my home for the rest of my life.

No one ever entered upon a marriage with such high hopes, or regretted them so quickly. Within a few weeks he was writing to his sisters that his marriage was a mistake and he was being driven to the verge of madness. He had hoped for warmth from his wife, but received only implacable coldness. "There are some phlegmatic people," he wrote, "whose passions glow with a gentle, almost imperceptible flame, but in me passion becomes a consuming fire when obstacles prevent me from obtaining the objects of my desire. I know that intense desire and hopeless passion can drive a man to madness. . . ."

He was so shocked that he wrote a series of confidential letters to his friends, begging for advice and consolation. Little consolation was forthcoming. A friend in Amsterdam urged him to remember that even if Ekaterina had married him without love, at least by the very fact of marrying him she had sacrificed herself for him. She was perhaps not wholly bad. Probably she was only terrified by his parsimony, and if he was more generous to her, she might return his affections in time. His sisters wrote in the same strain, pointing out without malice that his own forbidding coldness might be the cause of the coldness in his wife. He must learn to be human, to be warm, to give himself to others. But there was no school where he could learn the art of being human, and so he plunged voraciously into the world of business. In this world he was master, and knew exactly how to behave and what was expected of him.

By instinct he was a gambler. Returning to Russia he put his entire fortune into indigo, and he controlled the market. His headquarters were in St. Petersburg, but a few weeks after his marriage he established a branch office in Moscow, placing his friend Alexei Matveiev in charge of it. He still worked twelve and sometimes fourteen hours a day. He saw little of his wife, preferring to stay in his office or to travel around Russia rather than face her temper. He showed no interest in the arts. Work was his opium: he drugged himself steadily, compulsively, and without any enjoyment except the enjoyment which came to him when he sent copies of the *Kronstadt Shipping Journal* to his father. The *Journal* gave the names of incoming and outgoing vessels, the owners and consignees, and likely as not there would be a long list of vessels filled with indigo and consigned to the firm of H. Schliemann and Co. There were thirty-three incoming vessels and three outgoing vessels shown against his name in the report for 1853, but this was only part of the story. Thousands of freight wagons were bringing consignments to him from Königsberg and Memel. He wrote to his father that his cash turnover amounted to a million silver rubles a month, and there was no end to it—fortune piled on fortune, gold on gold, and he was still no nearer the happiness he yearned for. And just as previously he had dreamed of ending his days on a farm in Mecklenburg, so now there would come to him the thought of returning to America and buying a farm there. "I believe I would enjoy country life," he wrote to a friend in America, "and I am sure I would find plenty to occupy me in the cultivation and development of my land."

He had none of the instincts of a farmer, who waits patiently for the seed to flower. He was always in a hurry, always working at a breath-taking pace, angry if there were any moments in the day when he was not actively concerned with business. About this time he wrote a revealing letter to his father, saying: "I cannot follow your well-meant advice to retire from business and devote myself to a quiet life. I was so accustomed to living a life of intense activity that inactivity, even under the most favorable circumstances, would drive me into an insane asylum." He was close to madness, and knew it, a strange sallow-featured high-strung genius of finance who sometimes broke into screams of rage and whose letters to his agents all over the world were often written in tones of demoniac fury, because his orders were not instantly obeyed. The dream of an escape to America pursued him during the early years of his marriage.

But for a man to dream of America while living in Russia in the middle years of the last century was to invite disaster. America was as legendary as Atlantis, a place of perfect freedom, where men never suffered from the infuriating attentions of the bureaucracy. In *Crime and Punishment* Dostoevsky tells the story of Svidrigailov, who had always dreamed of going to America. We see Svidrigailov wandering through the dirty yellow fog of St. Petersburg on a winter day, making his way along the wooden pavements covered with slippery mud. Suddenly through the fog there looms up a strange little man muffled in a gray soldier's cloak, with a brass Achilles helmet, evidently the guard outside one of the great official buildings. Svidrigailov and Achilles glare at each other.

"You've got no business to be here," says Achilles.

"Well, good morning to you—that's true," says Svidrigailov.

"Then explain yourself."

"I'm going away."

"Where to?"

"To America."

"To America, eh?"

Svidrigailov draws out his revolver and cocks it. Achilles raises his eyebrows.

"You mustn't do things like that here," Achilles says. "What sort of joke are you playing?"

"It's all right—"

"I assure you it is not all right!"

"Oh, there's no harm done," Svidrigailov says. "This is just as good a place as any other. If they ask you any questions, tell them I was going to America."

Svidrigailov puts the revolver to his right temple.

"You shouldn't do it," Achilles protests. "This isn't the right place at all."

Then Svidrigailov pulls the trigger.

Such was Dostoevsky's story written only a few years later, and though Schliemann showed no interest in Russian literature or the strange upheavals in the spiritual atmosphere of Russia, he was inescapably involved in the Russian temper, and perhaps all the more involved because he believed himself so detached. Like the Russians he felt the terrible yearning for the freedom of America, which he had known for a few months in California, and like them he possessed a revulsion from freedom and contempt for American ways. Those dreams of America, which enter so casually in his letters, had the stuff of tragedy in them.

Meanwhile business held him. Half-mad with anxiety, hating his wife, at odds with his agents, he found security in attending to his ledgers. The richer he became, the less use he had for his riches. Yet business was the air he breathed, and his Pole Star. Whatever he looked upon must be turned to profit—there was no other law. At rare intervals he permitted himself the solace of writing letters to his father and sisters, presenting them with moral maxims and encouraging them to live in the utmost sobriety. His letters must have set their teeth on edge, but they always thanked him for the small sums of money he sent. He wrote to his father:

By today's post I have forwarded instructions for 500 talers to be credited to your account. I have high hopes that you will use this sum in establishing yourself at your new address in Danzig in the manner befitting the father of Heinrich Schliemann.

In placing this sum at your disposal I must however insist that in future you keep a respectable manservant and a respectable maid, while preserving a decent standard of cleanliness in your house. I expect your plates, dishes, cups, knives and forks to be shining and clean, and the floorboards should be scrubbed three times a week, and you will have food on your table befitting a person of your station in life.

The 500 talers he sent his father were a pittance compared with the money he was making. Wherever he turned, luck pursued him. He heard that the Czar was about to issue a new legal code, and it occurred to him immediately that the code would be printed on paper of fine texture and distributed in thousands of copies. Accordingly, he made a corner in the best available paper, offered to sell it to the government, and his offer was accepted. He branched off in a hundred different directions, and always made money.

Occasionally there were moments of tension. In the fall of 1854 he was returning to Russia after attending the indigo auctions in Amsterdam. The Crimean War had broken out. The Russian ports were being blockaded, and all merchandise intended for St. Petersburg had to be shipped through Königsberg and Memel, then forwarded overland. Hundreds of chests of indigo and huge quantities of other goods had been shipped by his Amsterdam agent to Memel. He arrived at Königsberg on October 3, and as usual put up at a hotel near the Green Gate. The next morning he looked out of the window, and saw, as he had seen many times before, the words written in large gold letters on the gate-tower:

Vultus fortunae variatur imagine lunae:
Crescit, decrescit, constans persistere nescit.

The face of fortune varies as the image of the moon,
Waxes and wanes, and knows not how to remain constant.

For some reason the words with their ominous warning threw him into a panic. Years before he had mentioned this strange inscription to his father, and sometimes his father had quoted them back at him. This time, however, the words came to him with surprising force. He was sure something terrible had happened. He rode off to Tilsit, and then to Memel, and learned on the stagecoach that large areas of Memel had burned to the ground during the night. Smoke drifted over the city, and the ruined warehouses were still smoldering when he arrived. Almost insane at the thought of losing those hundreds of chests of indigo, convinced that he was ruined, he sought out his agent, who simply pointed at the smoking ruins and shrugged his shoulders.

Schliemann panicked easily. Whenever he suffered losses, he thought he was on the verge of bankruptcy. He told himself that he would have to start again from the beginning, and in his confused state of mind began to make plans: he would write to the Schröders and beg them for credit, sell his houses and estates, live at the bare minimum of subsistence. He had done all this before, and triumphed. He told himself he had lost everything, and would return immediately to St. Petersburg and attempt to put his affairs in order. All that day he trembled in an agony of hysterical misery, too sick at heart to think of anything else except his loss.

He was moaning about his loss to the people standing around the stagecoach that evening, as he was about to continue the journey to St. Petersburg, when someone tapped him on the shoulder. The stranger introduced himself as the chief clerk of Meyer & Co., Schliemann's agents in Memel, and said none of his chests of indigo had been lost. The warehouses were full when the ships put in at Memel, and some wooden storehouses had been hastily erected at a distance from them. The flames had not touched the storehouses. Schliemann was so overwhelmed by his good fortune that he remained speechless for some minutes. Once again, so it seemed to him, divine providence had saved him when he was in desperate straits. The only one saved from the general ruin, he saw the finger of God pointing at him and he exulted like a child.

There was no need to hurry on to St. Petersburg. Instead, he stayed at Memel and superintended the sale of his goods at a vast profit, turning his money over again and again, and closing deals on terms which sometimes astounded him. He had the Midas touch, and no objection to playing the part of a war profiteer—he sold indigo and other dyes, but he also embarked on trade in saltpeter, sulphur, and lead, to be used for gunpowder and bullets. He had made one fortune in the California gold fields, and he made another in the Crimean War. By the end of 1855 he was worth $1,000,000.

In other respects, too, fortune smiled on him. For the first time he was enjoying happy relations at home. His greatly increased wealth made Ekaterina more amenable and more loving, and that year she presented him with a child, who was called Sergey. For a few brief months he was overwhelmed with gratitude towards his wife. He bought an estate near the summer residence of the Czar at Peterhof, gave his wife jewelry, and promised to let her have a holiday in the south of France. At odd moments during 1854 he had learned Polish and Swedish. This *annus mirabilis*, which gave him a second fortune and a son, was to be crowned with one further gift—the gift of the Greek language, which he had always hesitated to learn because he was afraid he would fall completely under its spell.

Ever since he had heard the drunken miller reciting a hundred lines of Homer in the grocer's shop at Fürstenberg, he had told himself he would learn Greek. He had suffered agonies of misery when he was forced to leave the Gymnasium at Neu Strelitz just when he was about to enter the Greek class. Over the years he had acquired a library of books concerned with Homer and the Greek heroes in a multitude of languages, but he deliberately avoided books written in Greek for fear that he would set everything aside until he could recite whole books of Homer by heart. Now at last he could afford to permit himself this supreme luxury. But characteristically he did not allow Greek to interfere overmuch with his business.

For six days a week he worked at his office, but on Sundays he shut himself up in his study, sometimes alone, sometimes with a teacher, and after six Sundays of prodigious mental activity he was able to compose long, complex sentences in ancient Greek, and soon he was writing in modern Greek as well. The fountain burst forth. He was overwhelmed by the beauty and clarity of this language, which was even more glorious than he had anticipated. He was so delighted that he wrote to his former teacher at Neu Strelitz, enclosing a résumé of his whole life in the language spoken by Homer, insisting that even in his darkest moments he had been "uplifted by holy hexameters and the music of Sophocles." "I am intoxicated by this language," he wrote. "I must go to Greece, and live there! It surprises me that a language can be so noble! I do not know what others think, but it seems to me there must be a great future for Greece, and the day cannot be far distant when the Hellenic flag will fly over Sancta Sophia! And what amazes me more than anything else is that the Greeks, after three centuries of Turkish domination, still preserve their national language intact."

As always, his enthusiasms ran wild. Not content with reading Sophocles in the original, he must translate Sophocles into modern Greek. He must read everything that Plato wrote, every speech spoken by Demosthenes. He filled notebook after notebook with lists of words, sentences, conversations with himself, and long monologues. At night, in an inn in Nizhni Novgorod, he sat down and described in classical Greek the impression produced upon him by the famous fair. Then he went on to unburden his soul, writing a list of his own faults: his nervousness, his absurd addiction to money, the ruthlessness which he was the first to recognize, his strange desire to escape—to Mecklenburg, to America, even to the equatorial regions, where perhaps he might become like the natives who cared nothing for money, so long as there were bananas and oranges growing on the trees. All his most secret thoughts were written in Greek, a language so beautiful that he believed to the end of his life that it was spoken by the gods. But instead of calming his spirit, the Greek language only made him more wildly excited. He lived for those Sundays and those other days when, to escape from his wife, he traveled over Russia, from one fair to another, always with a traveling case filled with Greek books.

These Greek notes, written in thirty-five notebooks over a period of two years, contain his most revealing comments on himself. Here the stern moralist gives way to the Rabelaisian commentator, who was not above taking a pretty woman on his knee when he was traveling by stage-coach, or exchanging risqué stories with other businessmen at the great summer fair at Nizhni Novgorod, which he attended year after year. In St. Petersburg he was the man of property, sharp-tongued, with a shrill voice and a con-

suming ambition to make more and more money. At Nizhni
Novgorod he became human again, got drunk, frolicked
with women and behaved like all the other merchants who
kicked over the traces at the fair.

Increasingly, as time passed, he saw the world through
Greek eyes. He became a fanatic champion of Greek claims
to Constantinople, an attitude not calculated to endear him
to the Russians, who also claimed Constantinople. For some
months he searched for a Russian-speaking Greek, saying
that nothing would please him more than to have a Greek
in his employ. He found a tutor named Theokletos Vimpos,
a priest of the Greek Orthodox Church who was studying
in St. Petersburg. Vimpos was a warm friendly man who
spoke Greek with the purest of Athenian accents. The tutor
was one of the few who could penetrate Schliemann's reserve, and soon the iron-hard casing began to crack. With
the help of Vimpos, and a few other scholars who attended
the Sunday *soirées* given in the vast apartment, he began to
abandon the idea of escaping to some remote part of the
world. He told himself he was inescapably European, and
as soon as possible he would abandon his business and devote
himself to a life of scholarship.

So the weeks passed, while he fought within himself the
war of his own opposing natures. He was like a weather-
cock: one moment he was telling himself he dared not leave
his business, the next he was swearing by the almighty gods
of Greece that his life was senseless and miserable, and he
was the living example of a vile miser—no, it would be best
altogether to slip out of St. Petersburg and study in one of
the great university towns in Germany. But would he be
accepted there? He possessed no degrees, no formal training.
Then where? At such moments of doubt and indecision, he
would find himself backsliding again—he would have a
farm and devote the remainder of his life to scientific pur-

suits. In July 1856 he wrote to a friend that he was searching for a farm along the Rhine, but only a few weeks before he had written to another friend that he was determined to see the world, because he had seen so little of it, and he was beginning to think that he might make a career for himself as a writer.

The truth was that he did not know his own mind, or what he wanted, or what direction to pursue. In spite of some losses and a few bad debts he had made a second fortune out of the war, and he was aware of a mounting sense of guilt. He wrote in his Greek notebooks: "I am, I know, mean and avaricious. I shall have to give up being so mercenary. All through the war I thought of nothing but money." This was true, but he could hardly remember a time when he was not thinking of money. He hated himself, and approved of himself, and went about his business, hoping that the solution would come from somewhere outside himself, and none came, and so he fed his own misery.

He made plans to retire in 1857, but the financial panic which settled over Europe during the closing months of the year caught him just at the moment when he was about to abandon his business. He had, as usual, overextended himself. There were bills outstanding on London, Paris, Hamburg, and Amsterdam totalling 3,000,000 talers. Acting for himself, all his capital invested in trade, he saw himself ruined again. Foreign firms went bankrupt. His hair turned gray, and he was almost out of his wits with worry, trying to keep afloat. By juggling figures, by taking enormous risks, by superintending every aspect of his business, even the least important, he succeeded in keeping his business going. Actually, he had never been in any great danger. Yet the horror of that winter affected him deeply, and for months afterward hot tears would spring to his eyes as he remembered how he had kept awake through the long nights, pitting his financial skill against the skill of European bankers.

By the spring of 1858, when he realized that there was no longer any need for panic, with his fortune as secure as ever, he had decided the time had come to visit Greece. His relations with his wife had never been worse: they stared at one another coldly across the dining table and hardly exchanged ten words in a week. He had however begotten another child—"I stole it from her," he wrote brutally. When summer came, he decided he could bear her presence no longer and set out alone on a long journey of exploration through all the countries he had wanted to see, promising himself he would pay special attention to Athens and Ithaca, the island of Odysseus. Not Troy, but Mount Aetios on Ithaca, where Odysseus kept his palace, was the object of his dreams, perhaps because he saw himself as a wanderer like his hero, searching for a home.

First he went to Sweden and Denmark, having learned Swedish and Danish in 1854 for business purposes, but he stayed in these countries only a few days—they had little to teach him. Then he paid a brief visit to his father in Germany, and he was off to Italy. He was a little afraid of going straight to Greece, and decided upon delaying tactics. He would see what Egypt had to offer him before throwing himself with heart and soul upon the land which entranced him more than any other. As an ordinary tourist he sailed down the Nile on a *dahabiyeh* as far as the Second Cataract, learning Arabic during the journey. From Cairo he went by caravan to Jerusalem by way of the rose-red rock city of Petra, but he found little to interest him in Jerusalem, and soon by way of Smyrna and the islands of the Cyclades he was making his way to Athens. In later years he liked to remember that at some period during this journey he disguised himself as a bedouin, had himself circumcised, and penetrated the holy city of Mecca. But he makes no mention of the visit to Mecca in his voluminous diaries, and seems to have imagined the entire journey.

But he did not imagine Athens. He put up at the best hotel, climbed the Acropolis, and was supremely content. Athens was everything he had hoped for. That bright and glittering city possessed the power to hold his ghosts at bay. Through letters of introduction from Theokletos Vimpos he was able to meet Greek scholars, who complimented him on his perfect pronunciation and listened approvingly when he explained that he intended to spend some months on the island of Ithaca and perhaps compose a book on it. They offered him more letters of introduction.

He was about to leave for the island when he received a telegram from St. Petersburg announcing that he was being sued in the High Court by a businessman who had failed during the crisis of 1857, but instead of paying the sums due to Schliemann had decided to sue on the grounds that he had been defrauded. Schliemann was suffering from a fever. He sent telegrams to St. Petersburg asking whether the suit could be postponed, but the court permitted no delay. His career as an amateur archeologist came to an abrupt end as he hurried back to St. Petersburg, exchanging Greece for the miseries of an intolerable marriage and a court trial. For five more years he was to remain in Russia, safeguarding his fortune.

He won the trial; he won another child from Ekaterina; he won a third fortune; and he lost himself. He lost, too, his interest in languages, and Greece frightened him. To reach Athens he had made a long roundabout tour, as though not daring to confront the ultimate vision until he had steeled himself to the enchantments of other countries and other landscapes. Now, when he spoke about journeying abroad, he never mentioned Greece—he would go to China or South America. For nearly ten years the palace of Odysseus slept.

He was the businessman again, proud, imperious, sending off scathing messages to his agents, who bore with him only because he paid promptly and was regarded as one of the greatest importers in the world. In a delirium of high finance, he began to extend himself still further. Olive oil and indigo had been his staples; now he embarked on cotton and tea on a large scale. He quarreled with everyone. He quarreled with Ekaterina on the upbringing and education of his children. Sergey was turning into a bright boy, the apple of his father's eye. The second and third children, both as he said "stolen" from the mother, were girls. Natalya was born in 1858, and Nadezhda—the word means "hope"—was born three years later, the year when he made his most far-reaching deals. His business prospered. In 1862-63, in spite of insurrections in Poland which threw trading in Russia out of kilter, his net annual profit on indigo alone was $40,000,000, with 6 percent interest on the capital. This third fortune was the largest of all, and with this safely invested he could no longer pretend he would ever be in danger of penury.

He was always making final decisions which were never final. Now he decided he would settle down in Dresden with his wife and children, and live the life of a moneyed businessman in retirement, with properties and investments scattered all over the earth. He bought a house in Dresden, and then sent urgent messages to his wife to join him. She refused to come, reminding him that she no longer desired his embraces and he was perfectly free to choose a mistress. He threatened to return to St. Petersburg. "With the aid of the police and my own arms," he wrote, "I shall take my darlings away from my own home so that I can give them here in Dresden the German education which their mother denies them." So he wrote to a high government official, and he seems to have been surprised when he discovered that his demands were listened to without sympathy. His wife called him a tyrant, a despot, and a libertine, and he was all these. A graying unattractive millionaire, with a high domed forehead and watery brown eyes which lit up only when he was talking about money, he represented all that was most repugnant in Russian society. No one knew, or guessed, that this lost and bedeviled man would find himself in the end.

He did not find himself easily. Many years were to pass before he found the clue to himself. He did not know that to accomplish any act of any worth a man must submit himself to a higher authority, must submit completely and with awful humility, casting aside all the goods of this earth except those which assist him in the act of perfect submission. He knew indigo and cotton, olive oil and tea, and how much they were worth on the world's markets, but he had not even learned the beginner's steps in the art of living. So he wandered about in the quicksands, miserably aware that he was generally detested, with no close friends, a stranger to himself, hating himself, the prey of strange fancies. "How is it," he asked himself, "that I who have made three fortunes am so miserably unhappy?"

A heavy sum of money was owed to him by a certain Stefan Solovieff, and as soon as this money was paid in the winter of 1863, he decided to leave Russia. He sold his business, settled some money on his wife and children, and vowed he would never return. He had not the least idea what he would do. He seems to have gone traveling simply to drown his miseries, without plan, in a state of bewilderment. At odd moments it occurred to him to write impressions of his journeys, but he had no high opinion of his own writings. "All my scribblings collapse like a house without foundations," he wrote once, and in the same letter he speaks of himself as "one who will never remain anything else but a dabbler in scholarly pursuits." In his journey which took him round the world, he remained the dabbler, making his elegant, precise comments on the world as he found it. He was still a dilettante.

In April 1864 he was in Tunis, gazing open-mouthed at the ruins of Carthage. He made another trip to Egypt, and then went on to India, where his talent for languages failed him—he took no interest in learning Urdu or any of the Indian languages. He visited Ceylon, Madras, Calcutta, Benares, Agra, Lucknow, Delhi, and made his way to the foothills of the Himalayas. The heat and the noise of India frightened him, but Singapore pleased him and he was delighted with the short side trip he made to Java, before going on to China. It had been a long leisurely tour. He had high hopes for China. There at least were great scholars and men held learning in high repute.

Most of the time he was miserable in China. He complained of the food, the accommodations, the dust, the smells; and he especially hated traveling in the little two-wheeled carts. In his diary he mentions with approval only one person he met in China—the expatriate Englishman, Robert Thomas, who had been a missionary, but lost his faith and became a humble interpreter attached to the customs house at Cheefu. Schliemann liked him because he was a man who knew nine languages, speaking fluently in Russian, Swedish, German, French, Spanish, Portuguese, Italian, Japanese, and Chinese. Thomas learned these languages by writing out words and sentences and making stories from them. It was a method close to Schliemann's heart, and as he describes the impression produced by "this most humble and intelligent man," there is a touch of envy, a salute to an astonishing intellect, and a sense of his own righteousness. It seemed to Schliemann that Thomas could have bettered himself, if he had only applied himself more actively to making a fortune.

Soon he was on his way to Peking, which he reached on April 30, 1865, after an uncomfortable journey by two-wheeled cart from Tientsin. He hated every moment of the journey. He could neither sit nor stand in the cart, and made most of the journey sitting astride the lead-pole. It was evening when he reached Peking, and he was out of temper. He admired the huge stone walls surrounding the city, but once inside he was filled with horror. There were no hotels. He found lodgings in a Buddhist monastery, where he was asked to pay 12 francs for a room, but after prolonged bargaining he succeeded in reducing the cost to 6 francs. Everything about the room displeased him—the *k'ang*, the raised brick bed of northern China, the floor which had turned to mud because the monks had sprinkled water on it, the stools and the little tables. There were ten large scrolls hanging on the walls of the room, and for some reason it occurred to him to make careful measurements of them. They were covered with precise Chinese calligraphy, and he says in his diary that the scrolls contained extracts from the Confucian classics—an unlikely decoration for a Buddhist monastery.

But if he hated the room, he hated the lack of service more. He asked for food, but the monks assured him there was no food to be obtained. He slept soundly, exhausted by hunger, and at five in the morning he was awakened by his servant Atchon, who brought him a bowl of dirty yellow rice, a teapot filled with green tea, and a tea cup. Schliemann was almost out of his wits with horror. He could not eat rice without salt, and he could not drink tea without milk and sugar. He looked at the tea and came to the conclusion that the most ill-paid workman in Europe would have rejected it out of hand. Milk and sugar being unobtainable, he sent Atchon out to get rice salt, and being unable to maneuver the chopsticks he succeeded in finishing the rice by picking it out of the bowl with his fingers. Barbarous people! He wondered how they could live without knives and forks, milk and sugar!

At six o'clock he sent his servant out to procure horses, and he spent the day wandering through the most beautiful city on earth, hating everything he saw: the beggars, the rag-pickers, the decapitated heads on the execution ground, the idiotic funeral ceremonies, the whole Forbidden City, which seemed, from his vantage point on one of the towers on the wall surrounding the city, to be crumbling into powder because "the imbecile Manchus" had not the sense to keep up appearances. He visited temples, and swore under his breath at the priests who allowed the painted gods to crumble away. He observed that the silk gowns worn by the gods were all threadbare, and the paper windows were torn, and the temples themselves were being eaten away by climbing vines.

The young Empress Tzu Hsi was on the throne, and the Taiping Rebellion was still being fought in the Yangtze Valley, but his diary reveals not the slightest trace of any interest in the vast changes which were occurring in China. He spent only one day in Peking. Characteristically, he saw Peking as though it were already a buried city waiting to be excavated, and drew an astonishing portrait which agrees with no other account by contemporary chroniclers:

> Here and there I found the remains of white granite paving stones, and everywhere the ruins of ancient sewers, and the mutilated cornices of columns and pieces of sculpture half buried in the mud; and there were many magnificent granite bridges, but half of them were in ruins, so that it was im-

possible to pass over them—one had to make a detour. And all this debris of paving stones, these ruins of drains and columns and sculptures and bridges—all this only shows that Peking, now inhabited by a degenerate and bestial race, was once peopled by a great and inventive nation. Once there were magnificent clean streets with paving stones, great houses and splendid palaces, but now there were only hideous and dirty houses and the roads are more like vast sewers than the highways of a great capital.

So he raged, growing angrier every minute, while the rain fell, and his horse stumbled through the mud. He spent the whole day from six in the morning to seven at night riding through the desolate streets. He stored his observations in his capacious mind, made deductions from them, related them to one another, came to conclusions—and nearly all his conclusions were wrong. There never had been paved streets in Peking, nor stone sewers, and the "mutilated cornices" were probably carved tiles blown down by the wind. In all of Peking there were no granite bridges. He thought the shining palaces of the Forbidden City were in ruins, when they were merely invisible behind a green flood of summer trees. He had no understanding of, and no sympathy for, the Chinese addiction to shabby exteriors, to hide the exquisitely decorative interiors. It never occurred to him to blame the weather or his own weariness, or to ask questions; so he went on to the end, performing miracles of improvisation on the theme of the ruined city slowly sinking into the mud—if he had come on another day the dust would have been gold and all the yellow tiles would have been laughing in the sun.

His observations on Peking are instructive, for they show the manner of man he was: in love with ruins, seeing them even when they were not there, hasty in judgment, and not unusually inquisitive. A few years later, when engaged in excavating Troy, he would improvise theories in the same reckless way.

He was not thinking of Troy when he came to Peking. He was thinking of a far greater ruin stretching over hundreds of miles of mountain and desert—the Great Wall of China. Since childhood he had dreamed of climbing along one of the parapets of the Great Wall, and the long journey to China was only the preparation for the journey to the Great Wall. There, if anywhere, he told himself, he would find the secret of the ancient creative life which had long ago vanished from the earth. Accordingly, the next day, he set out with his servant and made his way to Koupa-kou, close to the Great Wall on the frontiers of Manchuria, which he reached two days later. He was in good heart. The sun was shining and he amused himself by wearing an Arab turban around his head, which attracted the attention of the villagers along the way, and he was delighted at the thought of coming into the presence of that majestic wall which wanders grotesquely along its irregular course for 1,400 miles. Everyone laughed when Atchon explained that his master had come all the way from Europe to see the wall—it was a great joke, and Schliemann beamed, happy to be in the presence of these wonderful, clear-eyed, generous people on the frontier, so different from the degenerates of Peking.

The sun was hot on his face and he was exhausted by the journey, but the wall tempted him. He called for volunteers, but even Atchon refused to climb up the jagged foothills. Schliemann decided to climb alone. According to his diary, it was a hard and dangerous expedition, which he would not have attempted if he had not been so overwhelmed by the sight of that gleaming wall wandering across the mountains until it vanished into the distance. He brought his measuring scale with him, and once he reached the wall he measured the size of the bricks—they were 67 centimeters long, 25 centimeters high, and 17 centimeters thick. He measured the height of the walls—they were 20 to 30 feet high, and the distance between the watchtowers was about 300 feet. He was sure the bricks dated from the Han Dynasty, about 200 B.C., although in fact they date from the Ming Dynasty, about 1400 A.D. He was almost delirious with joy after scrambling up to the top of the wall and seeing the foothills in the distance.

He remained in the tower most of the afternoon. It was not enough to have reached the wall; he wanted time to enjoy the spectacle of the small and shadowy world below him. He remembered everything he had read about the heroic defenders of the wall, who fought off invasions of the barbarians from Central Asia; and he remembered all the other great vistas he had seen in Java and from the Sierra Nevada. At last, when it was growing dark, he carefully detached a brick from the wall and with a piece of string succeeded in strapping it to his back; then he went slithering down the slope on his stomach. This was the first serious work of excavation he had performed, and he was understandably proud when he discovered that the brick was intact when he reached Kou-pa-kou. Thirsty, he shouted for water, and the peasants came hurrying up to him with bowls of water, and when he showed them the brick, they laughed at the thought of all the trouble he had been to to secure a solitary brick. "I am sure," he wrote later, "these generous and kindly people, who answered my call for water, have never smoked opium."

Some days later he wrote up his diary, describing at length everything that had happened on the journey. Nothing in the world, he said, had so moved him as the sight of the wall, now crumbling, once the bastion of China. In

words of elation and triumph he describes his emotions
as he gazed from his solitary tower at the world below,
and if he exaggerates his own prowess in mountain-climbing
—for he claims to have scaled the Himalayas and the sum-
mits of the Sierra Nevada—there is no doubt of the validity
of the emotion. Here, for the first time, the merchant prince
surrenders to the ardent archeologist:

> Standing on the volcanoes of Java and on the summits of
> the Sierra Nevada in California, on the high mountains of
> the Himalayas and the great plateaux of the Cordilleras in
> South America, I have gazed on magnificent vistas, but never
> on one so magnificent as this. I was astonished and stupefied,
> filled with admiration and enthusiasm, and I could not ac-
> custom myself to this miraculous wall, which had always
> excited me even in my earliest childhood. I saw it now be-
> fore my eyes a hundred times more glorious than I had seen
> it in my imagination. The more I gazed at this immense wall
> with its formidable crenellated towers seeking always the
> crests of the highest mountains, the more it seemed to me to
> be the work of a fabulous race of antediluvian giants.
>
> I knew that the wall was built about 220 B.C., but even so
> I could not bring myself to understand how mortal hands
> had built it: how it was possible for them to transport and
> put in place on those great jagged rocks those huge blocks
> of granite and the myriads of bricks. It occurred to me that
> the bricks must have been baked in the valley immediately
> below the wall. But to build such a wall, holding at bay so
> many invasions of the enemy in the north, needed the
> strength of Hercules himself.
>
> Today the Great Wall lies abandoned and neglected, and
> instead of soldiers in the crenellated towers there are only
> pigeons peacefully making their nests, and the harmless liz-
> ards multiply among the yellow flowers and violets which
> announce the coming of spring. No one can deny that this
> is the greatest work ever accomplished by the hand of man,

now to become the funeral monument of an age long since departed from this earth.

When Schliemann wrote these words, he was not yet certain what he intended to do with his life. The vision of Troy was still remote, and though he claimed afterward that not a day had passed since his childhood when he did not think of uncovering the buried city, it is likely that the discovery of Troy came about as the result of a slow process of crystallization. At about this time he was writing to friends, saying that it was always his ambition once he had secured a large fortune to set himself up as a writer. He would leave Russia and settle somewhere in Europe and cultivate his fellow-writers—he could think of no more agreeable occupation. It is possible that the journey to the Far East was simply the preliminary to his life as a writer, for many of the writers of his day entered upon their careers with accounts of their travels in strange countries. This diary, so carefully composed, the descriptive passages modeled closely on those of Ernest Renan, seems to have been intended as his first offering in the market-place. He possessed the gift of tongues; he had always admired writers; he had never yet failed to achieve his ambitions. Yet already in the opening pages of his first book, written at the age of forty-three, he was announcing the theme which dominated the last years of his life—crumbling ruins, cyclopean walls, the endless pageant of the buried past. What is surprising is that he should have announced the theme first in Peking and in a remote corner of China close to the Great Wall.

Once he had stood on the Great Wall, China lost all interest for him. He describes his journeys briefly and desultorily, with the air of a visitor amused by the strange customs of the barbarians. For some reason he paid particular attention to the bound feet of the women. "I have closely examined their feet many times," he says, "and I have not read any reports by European writers which describe accurately how they are bound." Thereupon he explains exactly how the three toes are forced back under the soles of the foot and how the peculiar waddling walk is accomplished. He is equally amused when he discusses the Chinese theater—the brocaded gowns, the high falsetto voices of the male performers, the strange masks and still stranger gestures. He seems to have been glad when the time came to leave China for Japan.

He was intoxicated with Japan, and all his best writing in the book he later wrote concerns the carefree days he spent there, though it rained most of the time and there were no friendly Englishmen like Robert Thomas to act as interpreter. He was on his own, enjoying himself. He attended *kabuki* plays, visited the public baths, admired the friendliness and silk kimonos of Japanese women, and was on the best of terms with ambassadors. He carried a curious red coral fob on his watch chain, and it pleased him when the women at the baths crowded round to examine it, and he admired their shamelessness. He liked the little inns where he stayed, the continual bowing, the air of gentle decorum which met him everywhere. To him Japan was delightful and mysterious, hardly credible, like a fairy tale, and he wrote about his brief experiences there leisurely, without haste, as though trying to recall the savor of every moment.

He arrived by luck during one of those brief periods of peace between the Mikado and the Shogunate. Only twelve years before Commodore Perry had sailed up the Bay of Yedo and presented his demands to the Emperor of Japan, without suspecting that there were two Emperors, and only the year before the combined British, French, Amer-

ican and Dutch fleets had bombarded Shimonoseki in re-
taliation against the actions of a local princeling, the
Daimyo of Choshu, who repeatedly fired on foreign ships
from his batteries along the coast. But Schliemann had no
interest in contemporary history. Japan unfolded before
him like a pageant, and he was delighted when he saw the
colorful procession of the Shogun passing along the great
imperial road called the Tokaido. He took careful notes of
the gaudy uniforms worn in that brilliant and barbaric
procession:

> First came the coolies carrying heavy luggage on bamboo
> poles, then a troop of soldiers in long white or blue blouses,
> black or dark blue trousers fastened at the ankles, blue socks,
> straw sandals and lacquered bamboo hats, with knapsacks on
> their backs, and carrying bows and quivers, swords and
> rifles. Their officers wore fine yellow calico, with sky-blue
> or white coats reaching to their knees and these were deco-
> rated with little touches of color as a sign of nobility. They
> wore blue trousers tied to the ankles, blue socks, straw san-
> dals and lacquered black hats, and they carried two swords
> and a fan at their belts. Their horses were without iron shoes;
> instead they wore straw sandals.
>
> After the officers came more coolies carrying luggage, and
> then came the higher officers on horseback with red hiero-
> glyphics on the back of their long white gowns, and then
> came two troops of lancers—then two pieces of artillery—
> then two more troops of infantry—then coolies carrying
> great lacquered chests—then lancers dressed in white, blue
> and red—then once again came dignitaries on horseback
> wearing white robes with red hieroglyphics—then a troop
> of soldiers in large white jackets followed by stableboys lead-
> ing four horses caparisoned with black hangings and four
> magnificent *norimono* (sedan chairs) black-lacquered, and
> behind these a standard in the shape of a fleur-de-lys in gilded
> metal.

At last there came the Shogun riding a beautiful brown horse without iron shoes, but with straw sandals like all the other horses. His Majesty seemed to be about 20 years old, with a fine face, his complexion rather dark. He wore a white gown embroidered in gold, and a hat which was gilded and lacquered. Two swords hung from his belt, and about twenty great dignitaries in white gowns rode beside him.

Never again was Schliemann to show such a passionate and feminine interest in the colors of things, and to write so accurately and delicately. He was so delighted by the procession that he returned the following day on horseback to look upon the scene where the procession had passed, and was surprised to find, not far from where he had been standing, three mangled corpses lying in the dusty road, so mutilated that it was impossible to tell whether they were soldiers or peasants. There they lay, sprawled out, terrible in their silent misery, and he could make nothing of it. The long and glittering procession of the Shogun, accompanied by nearly two thousand soldiers and retainers, had passed before his eyes, and he had not suspected that they marched over three mangled corpses.

Returning to Yokohoma, he made delicate inquiries. Had they been killed by orders of the slender, dark-featured Shogun, a sick man who was to die a year later? Why had they been left there? Why had they been trampled in the dust? At last he received an explanation which satisfied him. It appeared that no one at all was allowed to cross the road when the Shogun was setting out on a journey. Heralds were usually sent on ahead to clear the road. But it happened that a peasant had wandered inadvertently across the road just when the advance guard came up. An officer told one of his soldiers to hack the peasant to pieces, but the soldier refused. Thereupon the officer brought his heavy sword down on the soldier's head and then turned his attention to the peasant, who was soon killed. At that moment a senior officer rode up, and thinking the officer had gone mad, he bayonetted the officer who had already killed two men. So there they lay, a peasant, a soldier, and an officer of the Shogun's army, and the whole procession had passed over them. As Schliemann tells the story, we are aware of the authentic *frisson*, the quick barbaric horror of the thing, but he wastes no words.

From Yokohoma he went to Yedo, where he admired the great fortress-like bastions, the palaces, and the crowded streets. Yet from his account Yedo made no great impression on him—it was simply one more city on his itinerary, to be marked off after a few days' visit. By early September he was weary of Japan and ready to commit his impressions to paper, and so he boarded a small English ship called "The Queen of the Avon" and set off across the Pacific for San Francisco. With time on his hands, he wrote an account of his travels through China and Japan, a small book of 221 pages, which he published in Paris two years later under the title *La Chine et le Japon au temps présent*. It was his first book, and he was very proud of it, but it is of no particular value except for the light it throws on the author. The last entry in the book is a cry of triumph so disguised that it is meaningless unless we know his relationship to his wife.

A few days out from Japan, he calculated that he had reached the opposite end of the earth from St. Petersburg, and he noted: "On 7 September between 10.45 and 11 o'clock in the morning we passed latitude 43°9′ and longitude 149°42′27″ west—the antipodes of St. Petersburg." Apparently he did not trouble to consult the ship's captain. The calculation is inaccurate, and he was not as he thought at the other end of the earth from St. Petersburg.

Still the wanderer, still without a home, he stayed only

a few days in San Francisco and took ship to Nicaragua. He had no intention of making the trip through Panama again, and instead crossed Nicaragua and went on to Havana, where he bought some property. He stayed there for a few weeks, and then decided that Mexico might be worth a visit, but everything he saw in Mexico City discouraged him. At last, in the spring of 1866, he found himself in Paris with an apartment overlooking the Seine and the Cathedral of Nôtre Dame at the foot of the Place St. Michel. At the age of forty-four, he had decided what he wanted to be: he would become a philologist, a student of languages, going to classes at the Sorbonne, and in the intervals between attending lectures he would publish his book on China and Japan.

He had made three fortunes, visited half the countries in the world, sired three children by a frigid wife, learned twelve or thirteen languages, collected a vast library, but even now, grown gray and weary, he had no idea what he would do with his life.

The Search for Troy

France in the sixties of the last century was a country
which had surrendered to the bourgeoisie. Napoleon III
was on the throne—a sick and stammering Emperor who
rarely knew where he was going, and hardly cared. Around
the Emperor and the beautiful Empress Eugénie an elegant
court gathered, remote from the people and strangely
sterile. In those years all France seemed to be sleepwalking.
The most prosperous and intelligent people in Europe were
moving slowly towards the disaster of Sedan.

Schliemann, studying at the Sorbonne, was perfectly at
home in the France of the Second Empire. Wealthy, he
could indulge his whims, take a mistress, eat in the fashionable restaurants, and consort with the aristocracy. A

scholar, he could seek the companionship of other scholars. A businessman with huge investments in America, Cuba, Germany, and Russia, he could amuse himself by buying and selling property in Paris, thus proving to himself that he had lost none of the instincts of a merchant. He bought some houses in the Bois de Boulogne, and sometimes he would complain about the cost of plumbing and refurnishing the houses for his tenants. Why a multimillionaire should have troubled to become a house-agent, spending his time in long discussions on wallpaper, is only one more of the insoluble problems presented by that lonely and embittered man, who came to France in the expectation of being able to reap the fruits of his wealth and discovered only that he was regarded as one of the least prepossessing students at the Sorbonne, a man who seemed to go through the motions of life without any deep-rooted interests in living. There was no gusto in him. Like many men who retire from business, he discovered that retirement solved none of his problems.

As usual, he went about his life methodically: so many hours for study, so many for business, so many for amusement. He attended theaters and the races, and was welcomed in the salons of the great ladies. He met Ernest Renan, who seems to have accepted his fawning admiration with reserve, answering his letters politely but without enthusiasm. Since Paris is the spiritual home of all wanderers, he found solace in the city, but no sense of direction, and sometimes he longed for the bitter winds of St. Petersburg.

Above all, he longed for his children. He seethed with rage at the thought of Ekaterina keeping guard over them. He told her he intended to reopen his house in Dresden and welcome her with open arms. He would provide her with every luxury she desired—carriages, horses, jewelry, dresses from the most expensive *couturiers* in Paris—if only she would share her life with him. "I have become a true Parisian," he wrote, "and so when I come to Dresden our life will be pure happiness."

It never occurred to him that she refused to leave St. Petersburg because she could not bear the sight of him. In letter after letter he attempted to dazzle her with the inducements of his prodigal wealth, and on the rare occasions when she troubled to reply to his letters, she showed herself to be in complete mastery of the situation. She would not come, she would not offer herself to his embraces, and she would never permit the children out of her sight. He answered that if she came to him, they would live chastely together like brother and sister. He would make no demands on her. He loved her, and it was enough if he could only set eyes on her. He let his apartment on the Place St. Michel and bought a magnificent town house on the Bois de Boulogne, spending 40,000 francs on the furnishings, and promised her she could travel between his palatial residences in St. Petersburg, Dresden, and Paris as she pleased—they were all hers, and he had bought them only for her enjoyment.

When these inducements failed, he threatened to cut off her allowance and that of the children. "You have brought it upon yourself by your unreasoning and insane behavior," he wrote. "You yourself are responsible for the fact that the children are being disinherited. I swear to you that I have finally disinherited them. You have attained your ends. This is the last letter I shall ever write to you in this life."

There were many more letters. He pleaded, cajoled, demanded that she see the error of her ways, wept endless tears, and never realized that his letters only reinforced her decision to live her life apart from him. He told her that with one stroke of the pen he had canceled the inher-

itance amounting to a million francs each which he had
set aside for his children, "even though I would joyfully
have given my life to each and all of them." Ekaterina
remained unmoved. She had rich relatives, the house in
St. Petersburg, and the large sums he had settled on her.
Gray and balding, looking older than his years, Schliemann
continued to wear the disguise of a middle-aged student
at the Sorbonne.

Though he had promised to abandon business many
times, he never succeeded in keeping his promise. He read
the financial pages of the London *Times* every day, and
continually studied the money market. When he read that
American politicians were clamoring to pay off certain
bonds with paper money, he realized that the operation
would involve thousands of millions of dollars, the value of
gold would increase sharply, and the issue of paper money
would in effect form a repudiation of the bonds. He had
large American holdings. Afraid that his holdings would
depreciate, he decided to visit America.

He sailed for New York early in 1868, and as soon as
he reached Washington, he called upon the Secretary of
the Treasury, who explained that the American Government had no intention of repudiating the bonds. A little
later he called on President Andrew Johnson, as previously he had called on President Fillmore. "Johnson is
quite a simple man, about fifty-five years old," Schliemann
wrote later to a German friend. "I told him I had come to
pay my respects, and said I was pleased with his latest
message to Congress concerning Cuba. He told me that
Cuba had great leanings towards the United States, and the
time will soon come when the States will absorb the island."
It is unlikely that the President would have committed
himself in this way to a total stranger. Yet he was genuinely

pleased with his conversations in Washington—he felt that his land-holdings in Cuba were more secure than ever, and he was understandably gratified to learn that the bonds would not be repudiated.

He liked Washington, but New York no longer attracted him. On his previous visit he had admired the huge buildings, the broad streets, the air of frantic hurry and good fellowship he found everywhere. This time he examined New York through the eyes of a Parisian and saw only narrow ill-lit streets and confusion everywhere, the whole city still reeling from the effects of the Civil War. Like most Europeans he sympathized with the fate of the Southern States. "Today they are being treated like a conquered territory," he wrote. "They are under martial law, without political representation, without money, banks, or means of defending themselves."

At the same time he became passionately interested in the Negroes, visited their schools and listened to their spirituals, filling his diaries with long dissertations on their virtues. Then, just as suddenly, he lost interest in them. His consuming passion became the study of the American railway system. He rode on all the lines which reached out to the Great Lakes. Previously he found the American railways rather less than efficient. Now, after a thorough inspection, he was delighted with them. He noted that they were all paying a 10 percent dividend.

He noted other things: the price of indigo, the amount of grain exported, statistics about the development of Chicago during the past thirty years, the size of the buildings in Indianapolis, the value of timber at the current market rates. He was feeling his way back into the world of business, which he had never for a moment completely abandoned. Indianapolis pleased him. He came to know many

of the businessmen and important politicians, and sometimes the talk would turn to the divorce laws of the State
of Indiana, then undergoing revision.

Schliemann was not an American citizen, though he
sometimes claimed to have become a citizen while he was
in California, when that state entered the Union. But in
fact he had not claimed citizenship, and to divorce his wife
according to the state law of Indiana he would first have
to become a citizen. This he knew, and accordingly with
the help of his friends, who were not above stretching the
law a little, he made arrangements for becoming a citizen
the following year. He bought a house in Indianapolis and
an interest in a starch business there. He was in good
humor, looking forward to the time when he would be
free of Ekaterina for ever.

Throughout this winter journey to America he was in a
gay mood. He had ridden on the railroads with the feeling
of a director. He had made a number of profitable investments. He had met everyone in the government he cared
to meet except General Grant (who for some unexplained
reason had refused to see him), but everyone else was
impressed by the intelligent, incisive merchant, who had
made three fortunes and seemed on the verge of making
a fourth.

Outwardly debonair, he was seething with misery and
loneliness within. Gaiety crackles in his notebooks, but his
letters to St. Petersburg and Germany tell a different
story. He did not want to divorce Ekaterina. He told himself he was being forced to it, and he constantly sent her
imploring letters, accusing himself, admitting his faults,
promising to be more generous in future. On January 6,
which was Christmas Day in Russia, he was alone in a
Washington hotel room, close to tears and dreaming about
his three children, the Christmas tree, the presents, the

happy laughter. He was utterly miserable. He had sent no presents, because he was estranged from their mother, but now he was sorry. In his weariness and anger he told himself it would be worth $100,000 in American money to be among them. It was beyond everything, that he should be unable to share their joys and sorrows. Worse still, the next day was his forty-sixth birthday, and there was no one to share it with him. So he wandered about Washington like a ghost, not daring to tell his secrets to others, wearing his loneliness like a garment.

Sometimes the calm exterior he liked to show to the world cracked wide open. A friend had given him a letter of introduction to the Prussian Ambassador in Washington, and Schliemann presented himself at the Embassy. The Ambassador, Baron von Gerolt, welcomed him and asked his business. Schliemann replied that he was paying a courtesy call, and began talking about his life in Paris and the fortune he had made in St. Petersburg. Suddenly the Ambassador roared with anger, and shouted: "Well, why don't you go and call on the French Ambassador—or the Russian? The Russians don't have so many people here, but there are a lot of Germans, and I have no time——" Schliemann marched out of the Embassy in a raging temper, and when he left New York for France in February, his last letter written just before the ship sailed consisted of an insulting diatribe addressed to the Prussian, reminding him of the bleak reception he had given him, repeating every word the Ambassador had spoken, remembering every detail of the agony. His pride wounded, Schliemann flung a final taunt at the Ambassador: "I beg to inform Your Excellency that your insufferable treatment of me forms the only unpleasant recollection of my recent tour. I shall remember America as a place where everyone is highly cultured, charming and well-mannered—everyone except yourself!"

Then he was in Paris again, the chestnut trees in bloom and the war clouds looming on the horizon. He attended lectures at the Sorbonne and resumed his study of philology, went to the theater, amused himself by buying more houses and acting the part of landlord—he wrote voluminously on the subject of gas-burners and water closets—and it was not long before it occurred to him that he was being bored to death. The compass needle was still revolving frantically. He had no direction. There was nothing of any importance worth doing. Would he spend his life buying enamel baths and mirrors for his tenants?

Suddenly, in the middle of that restless spring, two things happened which changed the course of his life. They seem to have occurred simultaneously, shortly after his return to Paris. He attended some lectures on archeology at the Sorbonne, and he received a letter from his cousin Sophie Schliemann. She was a spinster, nearly fifty, and she wrote him an impassioned declaration of love. He answered coldly that he remembered the days they had spent together at Kalkhorst, but he had not the least intention of gallivanting with an elderly woman who had once refused to embrace him, or even to give him her arm. Injuries he had suffered when he was fourteen, thirty-three years ago, awoke in him; and he dismissed her in the same tone with which he dismissed the Prussian Ambassador. She had suggested timidly that she would love to travel with him. "Of course," he wrote to her, "I would think myself fortunate to travel with an experienced woman of the world, but to travel with a saint, and one far more suited to the cloister than the stage of this great world—this I would regard as the most tedious thing in the world!"

Sophie Schliemann, his childhood playmate, never received the letter, for she died on the day it was written. When he heard of her death some days later, he flew into a passion of grief. In Washington he had told himself he would give vast sums of money to share Christmas with his children. Now he told himself he would have done everything possible to save the life of his devoted cousin. The most famous doctors from Hamburg and Berlin would have hurried to her bedside. He himself would have watched over her, and perhaps by his very ardor saved her life. "There was nothing calculating, nothing sensual, in the love I possessed for this pure, true-hearted and angelic being. The love I had for her was purely platonic, of the most sublime sympathy." He asked for a photograph of Sophie's coffin, and raged because the letter was unstamped and addressed incorrectly, with the result that it was delayed. He told his sisters that he would have given a fortune to travel ten times round the world with her. If only he had known, he would have devoted the remaining years of his life to her. He accused himself of the utmost ingratitude because she had sent him a lock of her hair shortly before he left for America, and he had thrown it carelessly in his trunk. He retrieved it, and spoke of placing the hair in a gold case set with diamonds, which he would carry over his heart. "I shall do this as long as I live, for her beautiful hair has become the most sacred treasure of my life."

The death of Sophie Schliemann struck him where he was most vulnerable. He had loved her briefly and then dismissed her from his mind, but she was one of the few who had ever been close to him. She was the only girl beside Minna Meincke who had loved him for his own sake. Gay and impetuous, she was one of those girls who at the age of eleven or twelve look as though they will settle down quite early in their lives to a happy marriage, but instead choose to become spinsters. At long intervals in his life he had thought fondly about her. Just before his marriage to Ekaterina, he had written to his sisters, asking about her, hinting that he was thinking seriously of marrying her. But that was fifteen years ago, and he had no very clear impression of her. Quite suddenly she died, and just as suddenly she returned from the grave to haunt him.

He was a man without faith in religion, or any hope of an after-life. He believed that man was the measure of all things: with industry and acumen any man could make a fortune and enjoy the good things of the earth. But now he found that the old shibboleths were wanting. His grief over the death of Sophie was exaggerated and raw with self-pity; but there was a real despair in the hurried letters he wrote off to Germany, asking for details of how she died, a portrait of her, anything which would help him to remember her living. He learned with horror that she had spent the last six months of her life in penury. Then his misery knew no bounds, as he realized that with a small fraction of his fortune he could have eased her last days. The proud man, *homo superbus,* was compelled to examine his own motives. Why was he living? Why was he unhappy? Why was he always wandering around the world like a homeless beggar, friendless and alone, with no children around him, with no wife to comfort him? There must be some God somewhere, some hope of peace in the world.

Then there came to him, in that intolerable spring, the memory of Homer which had enchanted his childhood— not the *Iliad* with its tale of Troy besieged, but the *Odyssey,* the story of a wanderer who returns at last to his own home. He would go to Ithaca, where Odysseus found his Penelope in his own mountain stronghold high above the Ionian Sea. He would stand there, and somehow, by some miracle still unknown, he too would find his Penelope and there would be an end to his wandering.

Schliemann always gave the impression of a man of decision, who knew exactly where he wanted to go. He had a look of determination. He could add up sums at a prodigious pace, and make decisions on financial matters quickly, suddenly, with an intuitive grasp of complex dealings in merchandise. But in all other matters he was slow and halting, unsure of himself, pathetically aware of his own weaknesses. Nearly all the major turning-points of his life came about as a result of forces over which he had no control. He did not go to Greece because he believed in his own powers as an archeologist. He went because he was haunted by the ghost of Sophie Schliemann, because his wife refused him, and because at long last he had found a divinity so infinitely superior to him that it was no longer possible to withhold his entire devotion.

In his distress he turned to Homer, who had reigned over his childhood, and it did not surprise him that what he had been searching for had been close to him from the very beginning. The name of his god was Homer—not Homer the poet, nor Homer the master of a complex language which provided excuses for philological excursions, nor Homer regarded as the father of the Attic dramatists. What he yearned for was Homer the creator of a world so valid, so entrancing, and so truthful that a man could live in it and hold his head high.

When he made his way to Greece in the early summer of 1868 he had already decided to become an archeologist. He would unearth the towering castle on Mount Aetios, or "eagle's cliff," which Odysseus entered disguised as a beggar in rags on his return from his long wanderings.

To reach Ithaca, he went to Rome and Naples, and took ship to Corfu. He spent only a day on Corfu, the ancient Corcyra, which was perhaps Homer's island of Scheria, the abode of the Phæacians, where King Alcinoüs had his

splendid palace and his beautiful daughter Nausicaä entertained Odysseus. He could find no trace of Alcinoüs' palace,
but he found the legendary stream where Nausicaä had
washed her clothes and played with her handmaidens, and
after swimming naked in the stream he sought out the place
where Odysseus had been hiding in the bushes. It pleased
him to stand naked where the naked Odysseus had stood,
but no maidens came clamoring around him and there was
no wonderfully carved cart to take him to the palace.

The next day he took a steamboat to Cephalonia, the
largest of the Ionian islands, but its ancient capital had been
destroyed by the Romans, and he found little to interest
him there. Soon he had crossed the little strip of sea
which separates Cephalonia from Ithaca. He had been a
little dubious about the Homeric antecedents of the other
islands, but in Ithaca everything reminded him of Homer.
"Every hill, every stone, every stream, every olive-grove
reminded me of Homer," he wrote, "and so I found myself
with a single leap hurled across a hundred generations into
the glittering age of Greek knighthood."

From the moment he stepped foot on Ithaca he was like
a man enchanted. He must go everywhere and see everything. In spite of the heat—the thermometer stood at 120°
—he was deliriously happy. There were no hotels, but he
found lodgings with two elderly spinsters. He met a miller
with a donkey who offered to take him round the island,
which was shaped like a figure eight with a thin craggy
isthmus: on the isthmus, according to legend, was Odysseus' castle.

The miller, whose name was Panagis Asproieraka, knew
all the legends of Odysseus and pleased Schliemann by reciting them at great length. Sometimes Schliemann would
interrupt and ask: "Is that the harbor of Phorkys? Where

is the grotto of the nymphs? Where is the field of Laertes?"
But the miller was too full of his stories to answer these
questions, and Schliemann commented wearily: "The roads
were long, but so were the miller's stories." Yet he liked
the miller, and they got on famously together. He approved,
too, of the villagers—hard-grained peasants with a natural
nobility about them, neighborly and industrious, with honest eyes, worthy of their great ancestor Odysseus. Above
all, he enjoyed the prospect of uncovering the palace, and
so, after two days of exploration, he organized an expedition up Mount Aetios.

It was a small and inexpensive expedition, consisting of
four workmen and a donkey. Because it was the hottest
time of the year, they had orders to set out at five o'clock
in the morning. Schliemann would wake at four o'clock,
bathe in the sea, then drink a cup of black coffee and spend
the next two hours climbing up the mountainside. Once
there, he could look out over the wine-dark sea at the
mountains of the Peloponnesus, and sometimes it seemed to
him that he could see the whole of Greece.

The first day he found nothing of any importance, but
the day was saved when a peasant came and offered him
an ancient vase and a silver coin from Corinth with the head
of Minerva on one side, a horse on the other. The next
day he had the workmen pulling up the brushwood inside
the circuit wall, and he set them to digging in the northeast
corner. It flashed through his mind that here, on this very
spot, Odysseus might have built his marriage chamber—that
chamber of stone built around a long-leafed olive tree,
which had been made into a bed.

The workmen went on digging, but they found nothing
until three hours later, when they came upon the foundation stones of a building 3 meters wide by 4.75 meters long

and Schliemann was wild with excitement. He thought he had found the foundations of the marriage chamber. Then he found a semicircular stone covered with earth, carefully lifted it and continued digging. Four inches below the surface his pickax struck a delicate vase and smashed it to fragments. A little while later he found twenty more vases, some standing upright, others on their sides, and all of them containing ashes. He was sure they were human ashes. Then he found a sacrificial knife 6 inches long, a clay goddess holding two flutes to her mouth, and some animal bones.

There were no inscriptions, but his enthusiasm was now boundless and he turned to the workmen and told them that one of these funerary urns might very well contain the ashes of Odysseus. He wrote in his diary: "I believe these urns to be older than the oldest urns from Cumæ in the Museum at Naples, and it is quite possible that they contain the ashes of Odysseus and Penelope, or their descendants." The last words were perhaps a sop to his own incredulity.

He had made his first discovery, and his appetite for archeology was now whetted. For the first time he had stood on sacred soil and seen the mysterious past gazing up at him from the earth. Instead of a marriage chamber he had found the ashes of the dead; and he was overwhelmed with gratitude. Unfortunately this first easy success led him to believe in his innate ability as an archeologist, and all his subsequent diggings followed the same plan. There was always a "northeast corner." Intuitively, holding Homer in his hand, he would choose a spot where he thought there was some likelihood of treasure, and then he would order the workmen to dig. Only in rare cases could he explain why he had chosen the place. He worked by instinct and enthusiasm, feeling his way into the past, with result that he spent most of the remaining years of his life in fruitless digging. Twice he discovered great treasuries of gold, but these were the exceptions.

As the result of his first morning's digging he had twenty urns, a clay goddess, and a knife. In his excitement he forgot the heat and his raging thirst. Noon came. They had eaten nothing since the early morning. He decided it was time to break the fast, and wandered a little way from the summit to the shelter of an olive tree between the double walls. It struck him that perhaps here, on that very spot, Odysseus shed tears when he saw the dog Argus, which died of joy to see him home again. And then other thoughts occurred to him. Perhaps near here, or not very far away, the swineherd Eumæus had spoken the terrible words: "All-seeing Zeus takes away half the worth of a man when he becomes a slave." It is odd that, with so much of the *Odyssey* to choose from, he should have remembered these particular passages—slavery and the triumphant return, the two poles of his mind.

After a lunch of bread and wine, the workmen enjoyed their siesta while Schliemann resumed digging. He remembered afterward that the wine of Ithaca was three times stronger than Bordeaux, and he was a little drunk; but he found nothing more that day, and nothing the next. He made inquiries. He learned from these villagers with long memories that a certain Captain Guitara had discovered golden earrings and bracelets in 1811 and 1814, but no one knew where these treasures were. On the "Field of Laertes" he recited for them the last book of the *Odyssey*, translating the words into their own dialect.

The peasants clustered around him, surprised and delighted to see a foreigner who knew their legends so well that he could recite them from memory. As Schliemann recounts the story, it was almost the greatest moment of his stay in Ithaca:

> Their enthusiasm had no bounds, as they listened to the melodious language of Homer—the language spoken by their glorious ancestors 3,000 years ago. They heard of the terrible sufferings which the old King Laertes endured in the very place where we were all assembled, and they heard too of his great joy when he found again after twenty years the son he had thought dead. All eyes were bathed in tears, and as I concluded the song, men, women and children came up to me and embraced me, saying: "You have given us a great pleasure! We thank you a thousand times over!" Then they bore me in triumph to their town.

A few days later, having made no more discoveries, he sailed for Corinth, a lamentable place where there were no hotels and once more he had to pass a night in a dark bug-infested inn. He was up early the next morning, swam for half an hour in the sea, found a guide, a donkey, and two soldiers for escort, and made his way south to Mycenae, which made no deep impression on him, though he measured the walls and admired the Lion Gate.

He had left his guide and the escort in the village of Charvati, and when he returned in the afternoon he found them fast asleep: to wake them he had to squirt water on their faces. He told them he wanted to proceed to Argos, but they told him it would be quite impossible to reach Argos that evening. "I had no desire to stay in this village, the poorest and dirtiest I ever saw in Greece—no spring water, no bread, no food, only some brackish rainwater." By cajoling the guide and giving the soldiers small presents, he was able to continue the journey and reached Argos. Perhaps because he was exhausted by the long ride, the heat, and the miserable inn, he had little to say about the place, though he noted that it had been "the greatest and most powerful city in ancient Greece, famous for the love of its inhabitants for the fine arts, especially music." This reads like Baedeker, and is not very convincing. He is more illuminating when he discusses the rich, sweet wines of Argos —he found them *ausgezeichnet*.

The next afternoon he wandered off to Tiryns, the great fortress stronghold with its immense walls, but he was not particularly attracted to it, and the two pages devoted to Tiryns in his journal are concerned with philological questions. Weary of ruins, and still more weary of his escort, he walked alone to Nauplia, glad to be once more by the seashore, where it was cooler and there was no need to ride about on a donkey without a saddle. In later years he was to make great discoveries at Mycenae and Tiryns, but his first glimpse of them was disappointing.

Nauplia refreshed his spirit. Here was a hotel, good food, a rest from wandering. And here, while he was waiting for a ship to take him to the island of Hydra, a strange incident occurred. During the afternoon he was walking in the main street when he saw five men shuffling through the dust with chains round their legs. They were evidently prisoners on leave of absence from the local prison. One of these prisoners, seeing that Schliemann was carrying some books, approached him and asked to borrow a book or a newspaper. The man was a heavy-set dignified peasant, with handsome features, and Schliemann immediately gave him a book. The prisoner expressed his gratitude and examined the book carefully, holding it upside down. Puzzled, Schliemann said: "Can you read?" "Not a word," the prisoner answered, "but I shall soon learn." The other prisoners came up. Asked why they were wearing leg-chains, they explained that they were good peasants from the hills, had been arrested without cause, and were suffering from the perfidy of the police. They spoke gently and bravely, and Schliemann approved of their devotion to reading. He learned later that they were all murderers, and would soon be executed.

A few days later he sailed to Athens, where he renewed his acquaintance with Theokletos Vimpos, the man who taught him Greek in St. Petersburg. Vimpos was now Bishop of Mantinea and a professor at the University of Athens. For a few days they were inseparable, and then in August Schliemann set out for Troy by way of Constantinople. The Russian consul obtained a guide and two horses for him.

As he wandered over the plain of Troy he was in high spirits. It was soft rolling land; there were clumps of spruce and oak; the water was sweet and the air was like wine. At Bunarbashi, long believed to be the site of Troy, he found a huddle of small houses inhabited by Turks and Albanian Greeks. The walls were black with mosquitoes, the people were poverty-stricken. When he asked for milk to slake his thirst, it was given to him in a jug which had not, he thought, been cleaned out for ten years. The impertinence of the villagers and the stupidity of the guides annoyed him, but he was pleased to see the storks flapping their wings on the roofs of the houses, because they reminded him of Ankershagen. He wrote in his journal: "Storks are very useful— they eat snakes and frogs."

He had dreamed of a Troy of white marble, majestic and permanent, gleaming in an eternal noonday of the imagination. At Bunarbashi he found only filth, rubbish heaps, miasmas rising from the surrounding marshlands. He was not inclined to look favorably on Bunarbashi, ten miles from the sea. Homer speaks of the Achaeans making seven or eight journeys a day from the seashore to the site of Troy. Schliemann felt sure that the hill of Hissarlik at the western end of the valley was a more likely site. This was an opinion he shared with Charles Maclaren, an English scholar who wrote *A Dissertation on the Topography of Troy* in 1822. Frank Calvert, an Englishman who acted as American vice-consul at the Dardanelles, shared the same view. He owned half the hill. With the Austrian consul, Von Hahn, he had done some preliminary digging. Convinced that he had found the site of Troy, he wrote a report on his finds in the *Archeological Journal* and invited the British Museum to begin large-scale excavations. On the eastern slope of the hill Calvert had discovered the remains of a palace or a temple formed of great blocks of hewn stone. He wanted the British to have the honor of discovering Troy, but nothing came of his proposals. He was convinced that he had discovered Troy, while his brother Frederick, who owned a 5,000-acre estate near Bunarbashi, was equally sure he had discovered Troy near his vineyards. Frank Calvert had already begun his excavations with two ditches dug across the hill. Schliemann simply followed in his footsteps.

As Schliemann concentrated on Hissarlik, everything began to fall into place. The approaches, the shape and size of the hill, even the evidence from the pathetic ditches dug by Calvert proved that Hissarlik was Troy. To find the ruins of Priam's palace, all that was needed was to remove the top crust of the hill. As he imagined it, the citadel was on the hill, while all around it stretched the wide-flung city, as Athens lies below the Acropolis. There would be ruins buried in the earth all around the hill, while the hill itself would contain the marble palaces, the treasures, and the bones of the heroes. On August 21, less than two weeks later, he was back in Constantinople, busily discussing his theories with Frank Calvert.

He was in a mood for quick action. Vast plans, sudden

resolves, furious onslaughts against the hill—he would enter into battle at once with the ghosts of the past. Calvert, whose mind moved more slowly, was a little amused by Schliemann's wild enthusiasm. A calm, quiet man, he suggested that it was already late in the season for digging, and it might be better to wait for the following spring. There would have to be careful preparations, a *firman* permitting the excavations from the Turkish Government, among other things. Calvert generously promised not to stand in the way. Half the hill belonged to him; he could, if he had wished, have bargained with Schliemann, but it seems never to have occurred to him. In all his dealings with the vice-consul, Schliemann seems to have been a little dazzled by the Englishman who assisted him at every opportunity, asked for nothing, and behaved in all matters unlike the merchants who always demanded the best possible terms. Without Calvert's help there would have been no discoveries at Troy.

Troy had become Schliemann's obsession, but there was one other matter preying on his mind—his forthcoming divorce from Ekaterina. Friends in Indianapolis had promised him a divorce in the following spring. Accordingly he proposed to be in America in the spring, and as soon as the divorce papers were signed, he would return to Troy. Meanwhile he decided to spend the fall and winter in his apartment in the Place St. Michel, writing an account of his six-week tour through Greece.

The book, which he called *Ithaka, der Peloponnes und Troja,* falls between many stools. The antiquarian, the philologist, the archeologist, the historian, the businessman, and the excited child quarrel among themselves. There are whole pages and even chapters which read like the dreariest doctoral dissertation, but here and there the spark shines through. The gods, who endowed him with wealth and intuition and the knowledge of many languages, unfortunately gave him no sense of style. Too often he writes like a banker. His schoolmaster at Neu Strelitz had described him as "a diligent worker, but often lacking clarity of thought." There is little clarity in the book, and only too many signs of diligence in the long philological discussions. But occasionally ideas bubble up from the remote depths of his capacious mind.

He makes no attempt to conceal himself: his desire for glory, his acquisitiveness, his unsmiling contempt for nearly everyone he meets, and his rejoicing whenever he encounters another wealthy banker in his travels. When he describes how he recited the twenty-fourth book of the *Odyssey* to the worshipping peasants of Ithaca, it is almost impossible to believe that it happened in exactly that way. Yet it is easy to believe that he possessed genuine sympathy for the shackled prisoners he met in Nauplia. He was a man at odds with himself, and the book shows it. He parades his knowledge, quotes the authorities who bolster his arguments and neglects sometimes those who oppose him, and runs every philological conundrum to the ground. Where Homer and Strabo conflict, he pours scorn on Strabo; and setting himself up as the champion of Homer, he ascribes intolerable prejudice to anyone who would dare to find the least topographical inaccuracy in his cherished poet. His fundamentalist belief in the divinity of Homer emerges clearly from this book, together with the fundamentalist's combative temper.

This book, so oddly put together from his journals and scraps of philological learning, was to be his passport to fame. He wrote it hurriedly in English, then translated it into German and sent it off to his Leipzig publisher, who printed 750 copies at the author's expense. How deeply he regarded his role as author can be seen from the letter he wrote at the beginning of November to his thirteen-year-old son Sergey:

> I have been laboring day and night over my archeological work, for I really have the hope of achieving some small reputation as an author. I am a member of the Geographic and Archeological Society here, and I read them some thirty pages of the book—it gives me great joy to tell you that my remarks were greeted with enthusiasm.
>
> If this book is successful, I will spend the rest of my life writing books, for I cannot imagine a more interesting career than the writing of serious books. Writing, one is always so happy and content and at peace with oneself, and then when a writer emerges again into society he has so many thousands of things to say—the fruit of his long researches and meditations—and so he can amuse everyone. And everyone looks up to writers and welcomes them, and even though I am only an apprentice at the game, I have ten times as many friends as I want. . . .

In fact he had almost no intimate friends, and nearly all his letters contain concealed pleas, little despairing cries, for friendship and understanding. Greece had warmed him, but he was still a remote, faintly intimidating figure, who took offense easily, cared little for the feelings of others, and possessed a ludicrously high opinion of himself. Ernest Renan was the lion of Paris society, and Schliemann hoped fervently to follow in his footsteps, without possessing any of Renan's grace and ease. As his letter to his son indicates, he knew little enough about the burdens and rewards of authorship.

Above all, Schliemann was driven by the desire to be honored and respected; the rewards which the world offers to dignitaries meant a good deal to him. Nothing would please him more than to be addressed as "Herr Doktor," and one of his chief reasons for staying in Paris was the doctorate he hoped to obtain from the Sorbonne. Unfortunately, the curriculum at the Sorbonne was so arranged that he was unable to see himself as anything more than an occasional student, and so he applied to the University of Rostock. Asked what thesis he proposed to submit, he suggested an account of his career written in classical Greek. This extraordinary dissertation—perhaps the most astonishing in the annals of the university—was accepted. Schliemann wrote his history of himself, received his doctorate, and was always annoyed if he was not addressed by his title.

So November and December passed, while he wrote his brief autobiography and his book on Ithaca, the Peloponnesus, and Troy. Meanwhile his enthusiasm for excavating the hill at Hissarlik was waning. Alone in his Paris apartment, with the cold winter fog creeping up from the Seine, he was no longer the wild enthusiast he had been. It would be an expensive undertaking, and might take years, many years. Also, he knew nothing about the arts of excavation. How does one go about it? How many workmen would he need to employ? How much would it cost? How does one protect oneself against bandits? What kind of hat does an excavator wear?

All these problems, and many more, were troubling him when he wrote to Frank Calvert toward the end of December 1868, enclosing a list of nineteen questions and requesting an immediate answer. In these questions, which are reproduced here as he wrote them, we see the tentative beginnings of the work which was to engross him for the remaining years of his life:

1   When is the best time to begin the work?
2   is it not advisable to begin as early as possible in Spring?

3   I am very susceptible to fever; is there much apprehension of same in Spring.

4   what medicines have I to take with me?

5   Must I take a servant with me? or can I get a very trustworthy one in Athens? Probably it is better to have a faithful Greek who speaks Turkish.

6   Have I to take a tent and iron bedstead and pillow with me from Marseille? for all the houses in the plain of Troy are infested with vermin.

7   Please give me an exact statement of all the *implements* of whatever kind and of *all the necessaries* which you advise me to take with me.

8   Do I require pistols, dagger and riffle?

9   Is there no obstacle on the part of the landowners to excavate the artificial hill?

10   Can I get labourers enough, where and at what wages?

11   How many can I employ? Is it better to take Greek(s) or Turks?

12   In how much time do you think I can dig away the artificial mountain?

13   at what cost?

14   you suggested to dig first a tunnel! But I am sure this is not practical, for if the hill really consists of ruins of ancient temples and walls, the cyclopean stones will impede the tunnel being made.

15   What has led you to conclude that the hill is artificial?

16   You indicate the dimensions as 700 feet square; a Frenchman would understand you 26½ feet long and as much in breadth; but I think you mean 700 feet long and the same in breadth, which—in the french mode of calculating, would make 490,000 square feet. But in my book I have stated the length and breadth with 233 metres, which would make about 54,000 square metres.

17   What is the high of the artificial mount to be taken away?

18   I think the best plan is to take a credit on Constantinople banker, who adds to it a firm in the Dardanelles so that

I am not bothered and can take out at the Dardanelles
what I require.

19 What sort of a hat is best against scorching sun?

This long list should be read carefully, for it shows his
hesitations, his hopes, his fears, and his curiously wayward
approach to the whole subject of excavations. He seems to
be appalled by the enormity of the task before him, and
astonishingly ignorant. Frank Calvert replied immediately
in a sensible letter full of cautious advice and gentle remon-
strance. He had studied archeology and read widely in the
works of Layard, who discovered Nineveh, and he explained exactly how the trenches should be dug and the
best season for digging—between early spring and summer
—and where laborers could be obtained, and how much
they should be paid.

As for Hissarlik: "Part of the artificial hill is my property
and as I have already informed you, you have my consent
to clean it out." He promised to use his influence with the
other proprietor to permit the excavation of the whole hill,
and expected no serious difficulties. Knowing Schliemann's
predilection for tea, he pointed out that few luxuries were
obtainable in the Dardanelles, and though there was coffee
and sugar in abundance, he had better bring tea leaves with
him. He corrected Schliemann's mathematics, explained
there was no real need for pistols and daggers—those romantic implements were not so dependable as guns—and he
suggested that Schliemann would be wise to rent one of the
houses in the village of Ciplak, whitewashing it and destroying the vermin with insect powder. Finally he suggested
that the best hat to wear against the heat of the sun was a
white muslin turban, like those worn by the Turks.

Still contemplating Calvert's letter, Schliemann went off
for a holiday in Germany, visiting Fürstenberg where he

had been a grocer's assistant, and Rostock, for the presentation of his doctorate. His book was in the hands of his publishers, and there was little at this stage that he could do to prosecute the excavation of Troy, especially since his presence was needed in Indianapolis. So off he went to America. He hoped to get the divorce immediately, but there were inevitable delays. He had suggested important alterations in the laws, but these were rejected by the state legislature. Weary of hotel life, he bought a house in the fashionable district of Indianapolis and settled down to await the final decree. He filled his house with black servants and a black cook, employed five lawyers, and amused himself while fighting the case by writing long letters to acquaintances all over the world. On April 14 he wrote to Calvert, saying he feared he would be unable to obtain the divorce before June: consequently digging would have to be abandoned until the spring of the following year.

On the same day he wrote to Renan a strange little letter, half in English and half in French, describing an incident he had observed in New York concerning an eight-year-old merchant who was selling books on a streetcar. The boy went down the streetcar shouting: "Two cents each for the books!" Then he whispered to each of the passengers in turn: "But *you* shall have three for five cents!" Afterward he went around the streetcar again, picking up the books or taking money, and Schliemann talked to the boy, who said his father had died the year before, leaving a sick wife and six children, and so the boy was trying to support the family. Schliemann was impressed and gave him a dollar, but the gift was rejected. "I will not take your money unless you accept sixty books from me," the boy said, drawing himself up to his full height. "I am a merchant, not a beggar!" Schliemann was deeply impressed, took the sixty books, and made a little speech. "May this dollar," he said, "be the foundation-stone to your earthly fortune, my boy! May you one day become a great banker, the pride and glory of this great country, which, with such characters as yours, is bound to eclipse all the empires emblazoned in history!"

There is nothing improbable in the story, with its troubling reference to "a great banker, the pride and glory of this great country," but one would like to know what Renan thought of this typical Horatio Alger story. Unfortunately there are no records of Renan's reply.

In his usual way Schliemann kept himself busy in Indianapolis. His starch factory was progressing well. He studied the money market, wrote lengthy reports about business to Schröder, polished up his Arabic—he wrote a short treatise on *The Arabian Nights Entertainment*—and sent to the Convention of American Philologists meeting in Poughkeepsie a lengthy dissertation on the art of learning languages quickly. Troy was temporarily forgotten; he was writing enthusiastic letters on the subject of the Northwest Passage and the discovery of the North Pole, and promising to give financial assistance to prospective explorers. And while the divorce was still under study, he was preparing in the most extraordinary way to find a bride to replace Ekaterina.

He had decided upon a Greek bride, because he liked the sound of the language, especially when spoken by women. But how to find one? He could, of course, return to Greece, make inquiries, and search diligently for a suitable wife, but an easier way occurred to him. In February, as soon as the unbound sheets of his book on his Greek travels arrived, he sent two copies to his friend Theokletos Vimpos: one copy was for Vimpos himself, the other for the library of the University of Athens. He enclosed a check for 100 francs drawn on Paris to pay for the binding, adding that if there was any money left over, it might be spent for the benefit of the poor of Athens.

Then, abruptly, he turned to the subject which absorbed him completely. Would Vimpos please send him the portrait of a Greek girl—any girl, so long as she was beautiful. He would especially like one of those portraits which hang in the windows of photographers' shops; and with this photograph in his letter-case, Schliemann was sure to be immune from the danger of marrying a Frenchwoman, for everyone knows that French women are dangerous. He began the letter hesitantly, almost reluctantly. Half way through, he felt in a mood to make his supreme request—would Vimpos please choose a bride for him. Her qualifications? She should be poor, beautiful, an enthusiast for Homer, dark-haired, well educated, and the possessor of a good and loving heart. The ideal was Vimpos' sister, but she was already married. Perhaps he could find an orphan, daughter of a scholar, compelled to earn her living as a governess. Schliemann concludes his letter by saying that there was no one in the world except Vimpos to whom he could entrust the secrets of his heart, and he encloses another 100 francs for the poor of Athens.

Vimpos was not in the least outraged by the letter. He went about Athens, collected photographs of desirable young Athenian girls, and sent them to Indianapolis. Among these photographs was one of Sophia Engastromenos, a pretty dark-haired girl with a delicate oval face, large eyes, and thick curving eyebrows. It was the face of a girl of quite unusual beauty, very serious but capable of lighting up with quick childish smiles. Schliemann had twelve copies of her photograph made, and sent one off to his father with a brief note saying he knew he would be happy with her, but he had decided not to marry her unless she was enthusiastic about learning. If all went well, he would go to

Athens in July, marry her and then bring her to Germany.

He did not reach Athens in July because the divorce proceedings were held up. He had nothing to fear. He had become an American citizen in March, and it was therefore only a question of waiting patiently for the time when the papers were signed. At last, toward the end of July, his divorce was granted. He hurried to New York and took the first available ship across the Atlantic. He was still not sure whether he would marry Sophia, for he wrote to a friend from the ship: "Thank God, there are great possibilities of choice in Greece, and the girls there are as beautiful as the pyramids of Egypt." It is unlikely that Sophia would have been pleased to be compared with a pyramid.

He arrived in Greece in August on the eve of the Feast of St. Meletius, the patron saint of the little church near the country villa of the Engastromenos family at Colonus, slightly more than a mile northwest of Athens. Colonus was the birthplace of Sophocles and the scene of the mysterious disappearance of Oedipus—"White Colonus," says Sophocles, "fed by heaven's dews, the place where the clear-voiced nightingales sing amidst the wine-dark ivy." There was no place more auspicious. The moment Schliemann reached the little town he found himself looking upon the celebration of an ancient rite, for the girls were carrying garlands to the church.

Sophia was not an orphan, nor was her family particularly poor, nor had she ever been a governess. Her father was a draper, with a shop and town house in Athens, a solid handsome man who won the cross in the War of Independence. Sophia was in the church, standing on a stool and hanging up garlands when Schliemann arrived at the house in the company of Theokletos Vimpos. In the church there was the cry: "The German has come!" He had not been expected so early in the day. Sophia jumped off her stool and hurried into the house to change her dress. The whole family was there—father, mother, sisters, brothers, cousins —and they were all sitting round the table, gazing at the strange German with the sad smile and the gold-rimmed spectacles, nearly bald, with a heavy gold watch-chain hanging over his waistcoat.

At last Sophia came into the room, wearing a white dress, with ribbons in her hair, very demure. Wine and cakes were being served. Sophia sat down at the table with her eyes lowered. Schliemann was talking about his travels all over the world in impeccable Greek. Suddenly he turned to Sophia and asked her three questions. The first question was: "Would you like to go on a long journey?" Sophia answered that she would. The second question was: "When did the Emperor Hadrian visit Athens?" Sophia gave the exact date. The third question was: "Can you recite passages of Homer by heart?" Sophia could, and did. The examination had been passed with flying colors.

During the next three days Schliemann haunted the country villa. He spent his days there, retiring to his hotel only in the evening. Sophia knew she was being watched closely, but she showed no nervousness. She played with her sisters and cousins, helped to prepare the table, and sometimes vanished into the cellar where they kept their casks of oil, butter, and olives. There were so many relatives in the house that Schliemann had to slip a message into her hands to see her privately.

Once when they were alone, he said abruptly: "Why do you want to marry me?"

"Because my parents told me you were a rich man," Sophia answered simply.

Schliemann was hurt to the quick and strode off in anger to his hotel. He had thought the girl possessed a natural nobility, and she had answered like a slave. He wrote on his hotel notepaper:

> I am deeply pained, Miss Sophia, at the answer you have given me—one worthy of a slave, and all the more strange because it comes from an educated young woman. I myself am a simple, honorable, home-loving man. If ever we were married, it would be so that we could excavate together and share our common love for Homer.
>
> The day after tomorrow I shall leave for Naples, and per- haps we shall never meet again. But if you should ever need a friend, remember your devoted
>
> HEINRICH SCHLIEMANN
> Doctor of Philosophy,
> Place St. Michel, 6, Paris

This letter, with its confusions and self-appraisals unre- solved, was written in white-hot anger and despatched by hotel messenger. Sophia was overwhelmed. While the whole family insisted that she compose a letter to allay the German's wrath, and called in one of her uncles, a govern- ment official, to help her, she seems to have known exactly what to do. The letter she wrote shows no evidence of any assistance. She wrote on cheap notepaper hurriedly bought from a local store:

> Dear Herr Heinrich: I am so sorry you are going away. You must not be angry with what I said this afternoon. I thought that was how young girls should speak. My parents and I will be very happy if you will come and see us again tomorrow.

Schliemann was relieved, but determined to punish her. He wrote more letters and received more letters in exchange, until he felt assured of her affection. It was as though he could not trust himself to confront her. Six days passed before he relented, and then only because the seven-teen-year-old girl wrote in her round careful handwriting a proposal of marriage, and against such a proposal he was defenseless. He had arrived in Athens late in August, and on September 24 they were married.

Schliemann wore a frock coat, Sophia wore a white dress and bridal veil wreathed with flowers from Colonus, and all her relatives attended in Greek national costume. Then there was a feast which lasted late into the evening, and that night the bride and groom drove to Piraeus, the port of Athens, and waited until three o'clock in the morning before they could board the ship for Naples. Sophia insisted on bringing her dolls with her, and Schliemann was in no mood to argue. She had won her first victory, and she was to win all the others.

Beautiful and childlike, moving with an easy grace which she never lost even in old age, Sophia dominated him by appearing never to dominate him. She loved him to dis-traction, with the violence of the young in love with the old, yet never completely understanding him. Reserved and cold even in the presence of his intimate friends, he loved her passionately, delighting in her quick changes of mood, her laughter, and her profound seriousness, which was always like the seriousness of a child. During the honey-moon he wrote: "She has a kind of divine reverence for her husband."

It was true; but the words should not be allowed to stand alone, for he too possessed a kind of divine reverence for this wife, who had been given to him so unexpectedly and against all odds. To the end of his life he worshiped her; and though they quarreled, and sometimes the old habits of intolerance were renewed in him, her own quiet gaiety was proof against his pride, his self-esteem, his overweening vanity. In her company he was warm and gentle. The miracle had been accomplished; and sometimes he would find himself looking at her with the expression of a man bewildered by his own good fortune.

It was a strange honeymoon. Naples, Pompeii, Florence, Munich—always the hurried journeys through the museums, with Schliemann delivering in his high-pitched voice a running commentary on all the works of art, until Sophia could have cried out in agony, and loved him all the more for it. People stopped and stared at the elderly professor—he was forty-seven, but looked ten years older—and his young wife, both so serious, so intent upon the study of art. In the evenings he would ask her to recite two hundred lines of Homer, and often she would fall asleep before she was finished. She had awakened the pedagogue in him.

He was determined to mold her closer to his heart's desire, and he insisted that she become a linguist—she would learn German and French, one language a year, and surely that was not demanding too much from her! Then he took her to Paris and installed her in the vast apartment overlooking the Seine and the Cathedral of Nôtre Dame. It was a cold winter. She missed her relatives. Her husband dressed her in the latest fashions and made her wear a chignon, but when some Greek girls came to visit her, she tossed the chignon away, got down on her knees and showed them her dolls.

She hated Paris—the fog coming over the Seine, the cold, the dampness, the knife-edge winds blowing up the Place St. Michel. She was bored by the society he cultivated, the visits to the Geographical Society, the continual talk about Troy, Mycenae, and the islands of the Greek archipelago, where hitherto unknown treasures might be buried. Schliemann's mind moved like the intricate mechanism of a watch, never still, for he was still searching for a theater of operations and was desperate for the opportunity to prove himself.

By the end of January he was restless again, planning to return to Troy, but about this time he learned of the death of his daughter Nadezhda and was prostrated with grief. Once again he was haunted by ghosts. He accused himself of complicity in her death: he would have done everything in the world to save her, the best doctors would have been sent to her bedside, why had he not been informed before? It was a familiar story: the millionaire caught in the toils of grief, telling himself he would have fought against death itself with his gold, if only he had been given the opportunity. He thought of rushing to St. Petersburg to comfort his remaining children, and might have done so if Sophia had not fallen ill.

She grew pale and listless, but the doctors could find nothing wrong with her. She was studying too hard—he had decided she should learn German and French simultaneously, and could not understand why she was so slow. Sometimes he took her to the circus, where she enjoyed herself, but more often she was taken to the theater. Sitting upright in a box, wearing diamonds, listening to speeches she could barely understand, she was bored to tears. When she fell ill, the doctors could find nothing wrong—perhaps it was no more than the fever of homesickness.

In the middle of February, with Sophia no more than a ghost of herself, suffering from unaccountable fits of weeping, Schliemann decided to take her to Athens and make his way to Troy. Calvert had promised to obtain a *firman* to permit the excavations from the Turkish government, but no *firman* had arrived. On board the steamer "Niemen" bound from Marseilles to Piraeus he wrote to Calvert on February 17, 1870, with his usual impatience:

Please inform me by the first opportunity whether you have got now the firman, for in that case I would like to commence the excavations at Hissarlik at once. I think the early season can be *no* impediment to do so, for the weather is warm and delightful here and it can hardly be different in the Troad. I would wish to begin work at once, the more so since I have later on other important things to attend to.

Thus, if you have got the firman, please give me once more a list of the implements and instruments required, for in the hurry with which we left Paris I have forgotten to copy same from your letter of last winter . . .

When Schliemann reached Athens, there was no *firman* awaiting him. He had thought of making some excavations at Mycenae, but a party of seven Englishmen had been killed by bandits not many months ago, and the Greek government frowned on archeologists who wandered alone into the interior. In despair, Schliemann decided to pass the time until the *firman* arrived by sailing in a sailboat among the islands of the Ægean Sea.

It was an unhappy adventure. He knew nothing about sailing boats, and the Greek sailor who accompanied him seems to have been incompetent. He visited Delos, where Apollo was born, and Paros, famous for its marble quarries, and Naxos, which was sacred to Bacchus, but he was most attracted to the small island of Thera (Santorino). He reached Thera after drifting for four days in a storm, living on bread and water. It was the most southerly of the small islands scattered about the Ægean Sea, and had an important history: from this island in 631 B.C. the Greeks had sailed to colonize the rich province of Cyrene in Africa. It was a volcanic island, and Schliemann was delighted with the strange cliffs formed of layers of lava in different colors— red, black, yellow, white and brown. These cliffs, seven hundred feet high, were "a terrifying and awesome spectacle." He liked the islanders and was able to buy from them some recently discovered Stone Age vases found under three layers of lava, and then he made his way back to Athens, hopping from one island to another.

In the past his good fortune was sometimes announced beforehand by a great thunderstorm. So it had been when his ship foundered off the island of Texel; and then again in mid-Atlantic the thunder of Zeus roared overhead and not long afterwards he made a fortune in California. So now, returning to Athens, he may have believed that the four-day storm which hurled his small sailing ship onto the shores of the island of Thera was a sign of the good fortune waiting for him in Troy. No *firman* had arrived from Constantinople, but there was nothing to prevent him from visiting the Troad; nothing to prevent him from employing workmen; nothing to prevent him from wielding a pickax. Alone, without help, leaving Sophia behind in Athens, he decided to take Troy by storm.

The Gold of Troy

When Schliemann came to Troy, he was traveling a well-trodden road. Other and greater men had worshipped at those crumbling altars, overgrown with thorny scrub and decaying trees. There was no mystery—or only a little mystery—about the site. For generation upon generation men had wandered along the inhospitable Phrygian coast to seek refreshment among the broken towers and moldered stones of the city where Helen was kept captive and the ten-year war was fought.

Xerxes, King of Persia and most of the world, had paused there, if we can believe Herodotus, during his march through Asia Minor on his way to Greece. He climbed up to the citadel, sought out the knowledgeable inhabitants of the place, and listened to their stories of the siege. Then he sacrificed a thousand oxen to the Trojan Athena and ordered his priests to pour libations of wine to the spirits of the great men of old. That night all the Persian troops who had gathered there felt a ghostly dread coming out of the earth, but they could put no name to it.

For the Persians and for others Troy was a place of strange terrors, of mingled myths and nightmares. Like all battlefields it was haunted by ghosts screaming for vengeance. Xerxes called himself the avenger of the crime. According to the Persians, it was the fall of Troy which made them the hereditary enemies of the Greeks.

But when the Greeks came to Troy, they saw it as the place where they had triumphed over Asia. So when Alexander crossed the Hellespont on his way to make war on Persia, he ran oiled and naked around the tomb of Achilles on the promontory of Sigeum, and donned some of the arms preserved in the Temple of Athena, and made grandiose plans for embellishing the city.

Julius Caesar, hunting Pompey over land and sea, arrived on the Rhoetian promontory and wandered about the ruins of the city burned forty years before by a Roman expeditionary force. All he found was the enveloping forest, rotting oak thickets growing over the palaces of kings and the temples of gods. He was crossing a stream which meandered through the sand when someone said: "This is the famous river Xanthus!" He stepped on a patch of grass, and someone cried: "This is where they brought Hector's body! Be careful not to offend his ghost!" And when he came to a pile of loose stones, someone plucked his sleeve and said: "Do you not see the altar of Hercaean Jupiter?"

Caesar had seen nothing, only ruins and the surrounding darkness, but he knew he had come to a sacred place, and

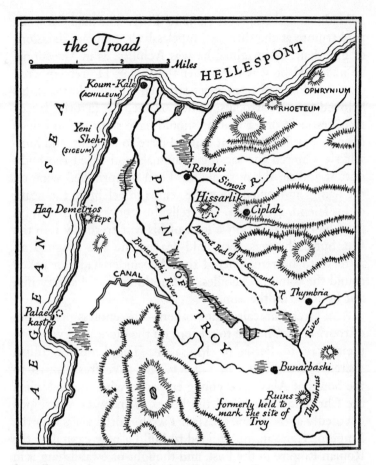

feared the ghosts. So he hastily erected an altar of turf, burned incense on it, and prayed to the gods who guarded these sacred ashes, asking prosperity for himself and vowing to rebuild the shattered walls until they gleamed and sparkled as before. And then remembering Pompey he hurried off to Egypt, so impatient to kill his enemy that he sailed past all the wealthy cities of Asia and did not pause until he reached Alexandria.

Madmen and emperors came to Troy. The mad Caracalla paid tribute at the shrines. Hopelessly lost among delusions of grandeur, he imagined he was Achilles, as in Macedonia he imagined he was Alexander the Great. He remembered that Achilles had been grief-stricken by the death of his beloved friend Patroclus; so he poisoned his favorite freedman Festus in order that he should have someone to grieve over, and ordered a great funeral pyre to be built, and himself slaughtered the sacrificial animals and lifted the body onto it and set the pyre alight. Then he sprinkled wine on the flames and called upon the winds to celebrate the death of his friend. Herodian, who tells the story, adds that in his grief he tried to cut off a lock of his hair to throw into the fire, but as he was very bald-headed, he was laughed at. Afterward he remembered that Alexander had run naked round the tomb of Achilles, and nothing would satisfy him but he must do the same.

And after Caracalla came others—the endless procession of tourists determined to set foot on the sacred soil while on their way to Persia or Jerusalem. The Emperor Julian visited Novum Ilium in 124 A.D. and gave fresh burial to the bones of Ajax. The young emperor, who laughed when the Christians worshiped the bones of martyrs, worshiped devotedly at the shrine of Ajax. Two hundred years later the Emperor Constantine decided to build a new capital of the Roman Empire in the East, and thought of establishing it in Troy before finally deciding upon Byzantium. Then for a few more years the Trojans secretly offered sacrifices at the ancient altars, but with the coming of the Christian emperors the city lost its importance.

For fifteen hundred years it had guarded the approaches to the Dardanelles. Now grass grew in the streets, the walls of temples and palaces collapsed, and soon there was nothing but a huge mound of thistles and grass. The Anglo-

Saxon chronicler Saewulf, who passed close by the shores of the Troad about 1100 A.D., says the ruins of Troy were scattered over many miles; and two hundred years later Sir John Mandeville, that mysterious traveler who may never have visited the East, says that nothing remained, for Troy was completely destroyed.

Though destroyed, Troy remained. No other city except Jerusalem had such power to kindle the imaginations of men. Virgil and Homer kept it alive during the Renaissance; and Italian scholars dreamed of the day when they too could walk along the roads where Achilles strode, "as high as a mountain." The English, like the Romans, sometimes thought they were the descendants of the Trojans, claiming that the original name of London was Troynovant, the "New Troy." In the *chansons de geste* Troy was a living city, all the more luminous because it was a city of the imagination.

In 1870 there seem to have been only two people—Frank Calvert and Heinrich Schliemann—who believed firmly that Troy was a real city; that its walls, its palaces, even the furniture and literature of the Trojans, lay buried in the mound at Hissarlik. Charles Maclaren, the brilliant archeologist, who had proved to his own satisfaction as far back as 1822 that Troy was to be found at Hissarlik, was dead; the consensus of scholars was that Troy was at Bunarbashi, and few people believed that anything would be gained by excavations at Hissarlik.

Frank Calvert had neither the money nor the inclination to make a complete excavation of the mound. The eastern part of the mound belonged to him, the western part belonged to two Turks living at Koum-Kale.

Schliemann was convinced that the more important discoveries would be made in the western part, overlooking the sea. Characteristically he decided to attack the part belonging to the Turks, leaving for some future occasion the exploration of the part belonging to Calvert. He said later: "I was so sure of finding great buildings, and then too I hoped they would pardon my audacity when they saw the treasure—*j'espèrais qu'ils me pardonneraient mon audace à la vue de ces trésors.*" From the very beginning his eye was on the buried treasure.

On April 9 he dug the first trench with the help of ten Turkish laborers from the nearby village of Remkoi. The workmen were paid 10 piasters a day. Schliemann stood over them with a pistol in his belt, a riding whip in his hand. The first spadeful of earth was dug on the northwest corner of the hill at a place which roughly corresponded in Schliemann's mind to the position of the Scaean Gate. After an hour's digging, 2 feet below the surface the workmen came upon the remains of a wall. Schliemann was excited. The workmen worked hard, and by sunset they had uncovered the foundations of a building 60 feet long and 40 feet wide.

The next day, with eleven more workmen, he began digging at the southeast and southwest corners of the building which was slowly emerging before his eyes. At last the flagstones were revealed. They were covered with 2 feet of earth and detritus formed through the ages— sheep dung, the remains of plants, and atmospheric dust. There were no potsherds; only this thick coating of earth. Then he dug below the flagstones and found exactly what he had expected to find: cinders, calcined matter, evidence of fire. There was so much burned matter and it was arranged in such an orderly manner that he came to the conclusion that altogether ten wooden houses had perished in the flames before the last stone house was built on their ruins. Among the cinders he found a coin, bearing on one side the image of the Emperor Commodus and on the other the image of

Hector, the son of Priam, the great general who commanded the Trojan forces. In Schliemann's eyes the coin, which bore the inscription *Hector Ilieon* ("Hector of Troy") was the most auspicious sign of all.

For two days Schliemann dug around this building, but on the third day, fearing that the Turkish proprietors might arrive at any moment, and in haste to discover more profitable remains, he started on two long trenches, one from east to west, and another running due north. By slicing across the top of the mound he hoped to form a general picture of the buried city, just as a man drawing lines at right angles across a small village and examining all the objects encountered in the path of these lines might reasonably be able to form a rough sketch of the entire village. Somewhere these lines would cut through the main street, the mayor's office, the post office, the fire engine shed.

Schliemann's plan was perfectly sound, but he had hardly begun these new excavations when the Turks arrived, to discover a small army of excavators on their land. Schliemann explained through an interpreter that he was doing work of scientific importance, that he wanted nothing for himself, and that he was honoring Turkey by his presence. Alarmed and baffled, the Turks argued that he had no right to be there, and asked him to leave. Schliemann took them over the property, cajoling, pleading, making long speeches about his discoveries which would soon be hailed by archeologists all over the world—he had already discovered part of the wall of the temple of Pallas Athena, innumerable bones, tiles, boars' teeth, signs of a conflagration.

The Turks were more interested in the heavy blocks of stone he had unearthed. They intended to build a stone bridge over the Simois, and these blocks exactly suited their purpose. They agreed to let Schliemann continue digging the two long trenches on condition they were allowed to use the stone for the bridge. He paid them forty francs, and they went off smiling.

Throughout his life as an excavator Schliemann had the habit of giving heroic names to his discoveries. He had found an immense wall, and instantly named it the temple of Pallas Athena. A little while later, while digging deeper in the north trench, he discovered below twenty-two layers of cinders the terra-cotta bust of a woman, and instantly named it the bust of Helen of Troy. Supremely self-assured, never hesitating to make grandiose claims, he rarely permitted himself the luxury of the slightest doubt. But sometimes doubts crept in.

The more he thought of his encounter with the Turks, the more convinced he was that he was at the mercy of forces beyond his control. By paying them forty francs and promising them the use of the stone for the bridge, he had obtained a temporary truce. But what if the truce were broken? What if the Turks insisted on their rights? He had tried to bargain for the land, but the price they demanded was exorbitant. They had demanded the use of the stones for their miserable bridge—it was the worst kind of sacrilege. How to deal with them? How to obtain full rights over the land? He was still debating these questions when, on the afternoon of April 21, the Turks returned, said they now had enough stones for their bridge, and ordered him to stop digging.

Schliemann had no weapons against this ultimatum. He could not fight them on their level, but he could fight them on other levels; and that night, in a mood that curiously mingled resignation, despair, and vast hopes for the future, he wrote off a series of letters outlining what he had done and the problems he faced to friends in Germany, France,

Athens, and Constantinople. To a powerful friend in Germany he wrote:

> I have uncovered the ruins of palaces and temples on walls of much older buildings, and at the depth of 15 feet I came upon vast walls six feet thick and of most wonderful construction. 7½ feet lower down I found that these same walls rested upon other walls 8½ feet thick. These must be the walls of the Palace of Priam or the Temple of Athene.
>
> Unfortunately there has been continual unpleasantness with the two Turks who own the land, and they will probably make me put an end to my work tomorrow. Meanwhile I intend to go to all possible lengths to buy the land, and shall not rest until I have uncovered the Palace of Priam.

For the moment there was nothing he could do. Bowing to the inevitable, he paid off his workmen and returned to Athens, where he hoped to receive permission to dig in the ruins of Mycenae. He would spend a few weeks in Mycenae, and then, with the *firman* from the Turkish government and the mound of Hissarlik in his possession, he would resume digging in the Troad.

Everywhere he turned there were obstacles. The Greeks refused to allow him to dig at Mycenae, claiming that the surrounding territory was infested with bandits. Frank Calvert had only just recovered from a serious illness and was in no condition to assist him. Sophia was still ill. Schliemann wrote an account of his ten-day adventure in the Troad for the *Kölnische Zeitung*, openly admitting that he had excavated the mound without the permission of the owners, and he was surprised when he learned that the Turkish authorities had read the account and disapproved of his activities. There was nothing for him to do but bide his time in Athens.

He hated his inactivity. He could not understand why

Frank Calvert was so unhelpful. He offered to pay £100 for the land owned by the two Turks, adding tactlessly that if Calvert could buy it cheaper the difference would be his own profit. To Schliemann it was all very simple: once the land was in his possession the excavations could go on, and he was perfectly prepared to spend three months every year for five years cleaning the rubbish away from the palaces buried in the mound.

The weeks passed, with Schliemann oppressed by the misery of frustration. He bombarded Frank Calvert with letters, begging him to intercede with the Turkish government, waiting as always "with immense anxiety your kind information on this head," but there was little Calvert could do—little he had inclination to do. The Turks were outraged, in no mood to offer assistance to a man who dug huge trenches across Turkish property.

Summer came. It was too hot for digging on the plain of Troy, and Schliemann set out for Paris and the cultivated conversation he missed in Athens. He had big investments in property—more than 200 people lived in the buildings he owned—and it pleased him to look over his property from time to time. One day in the middle of June when Paris was empty, he received a letter from Sergey in St. Petersburg. The boy said he was not progressing well at school.

Schliemann replied in French in a letter so filled with frigid boasting that he gives the impression of a man on the verge of insanity. He wrote:

> It was very sad to hear you have not been progressing. In this life one must progress continually, otherwise one becomes discouraged. Try then to follow the example of your father who, in all the positions he has occupied, has always proved how much a man can accomplish provided he has a fierce energy. I performed miracles during the four years

1842-1846 in Amsterdam. I did what no one else has ever done and no one else could ever do. Then I became a merchant in St Petersburg, and no merchant was ever so accomplished or so prudent. Then I became a traveler, but not an ordinary traveler—I was a traveler *par excellence.* No other merchant in St Petersburg has ever written a scientific work, but I wrote one which was translated into four languages, a book which became the object of universal admiration. Today I am an archeologist, and all Europe and America are dazzled by my discovery of the ancient city of Troy—that Troy which the archeologists of all countries have searched for in vain for two thousand years . . .

I did what no one else has ever done and no one else could ever do. . . . These boasts arose from weakness. They are cries of despair, uttered in loneliness and misery, as he sought in vain for the purposes of his own life. He had hoped to lay bare the legendary city of Troy, but two obscure Turkish peasants whose sheepfolds lay across the mound of Hissarlik had simply ordered him off their property, as though he were a common trespasser. They had no right to do it! He, Schliemann, had unearthed the buried city, that city which was his by right of discovery. Had he not promised to spend a hundred thousand francs on the excavation, for the sole purpose of enlightening the scholars of the world? He possessed property all over the world. Then why should a small hill in a corner of Asia Minor be refused to him? Why had these Turks in baggy trousers defiled his city by removing the sacred stones to build a bridge? Just before leaving Hissarlik these same peasants had demanded £100 for the damage he had caused, but this, of course, he refused to pay.

On July 19, 1870, Napoleon III declared war on Prussia, and Schliemann was still in Paris, burning with resentment against those two peasants who by this time had probably forgotten his existence. He wrote to Frank Calvert from Boulogne-sur-mer, where he fled shortly after the declaration of war, begging him to see that no stones were removed from the palace walls he had unearthed—surely there must be some way to prevent those peasants from destroying a work which had survived for thirty centuries?

At the end of August he wrote to Safvet Pasha, the Turkish Minister of Public Instruction, a long, imploring letter, saying that he had never hoped to find any treasures. No, this was not the reason why he had dug at Hissarlik. On the contrary, he had acted out of "the pure and disinterested love of science," with only one desire—to prove that the city of Troy lay beneath the mound. He enclosed a copy of *Ithaka, der Peloponnes und Troja*. He threw himself on the mercy of the Turkish government. Surely they would realize the importance of his researches. Surely they would not blame him for having made, in the wild enthusiasm for Homer which overcame him when he found himself at Hissarlik, a few unimportant excavations which nevertheless proved the existence of Priam's palace and the great wall surrounding the city.

"I worked in rain storms as though it were summer. I thought I had lunched and dined when I had eaten nothing all day, and every little piece of pottery which I brought to light was for me another page of history!" He begged His Excellency's pardon for having acted high-handedly, and offered to wait upon His Excellency at any time, if only there was some slight hope that the excavations might be allowed to continue. There was no reply. The inscrutable Safvet Pasha confronted the inscrutable Schliemann across the whole length of Europe, and neither gave an inch.

If Schliemann had not written this outrageous letter with its pious sentiments and florid appeals to "our common mother Science, to whom both of us owe our lives, which both of us adore with the same enthusiasm," the story of the discovery of Troy might have been very different. The letter, for all its denials, convinced Safvet Pasha that Schliemann was looking for buried treasure, and when Schliemann arrived in Constantinople at last in December, the minister greeted him affably, promised him every kind of assistance, proclaimed his total belief in the blessings of science, and did everything he could to prevent the excavations from continuing. Schliemann was left with the impression that it was only a matter of a few days before he would be in full possession of Hissarlik, with a *firman* from the Turkish government permitting him to excavate to his heart's content.

While waiting in Constantinople, his mind absorbed by the approaching fall of Paris and the problem of obtaining title to the mound at Hissarlik—with great difficulty Frank Calvert had obtained from the two Turks a verbal promise that they would sell their land for 1,000 francs— Schliemann received a letter from his wife full of dejection and despair. He could be cruel to those he loved. He answered that she had no reason to despair. If she would only count her blessings—her husband who worshiped her, her position in life, her house in Athens and all the good simple people who were devoted to her, while in France two million men, women, and children were dying of starvation, with enemy shells falling on their defenseless houses, with not a crust of bread to eat and not a stick of firewood to warm them. If she would only think about more important matters! He had visited Safvet Pasha. He had been greeted cordially. The long-wished-for *firman* had been promised, and in a few days would be safely in his hands. He would go to Hissarlik in a few days, buy the land, and then he would have to return briefly to Paris, but she should not think of the dangers of the journey. He went on:

You should fall straightway on your knees and thank God for all the blessings He has showered on you, and you should ask His pardon for permitting yourself in these days of strain to forget the bounty He has poured over you.

You forget, too, that I have learned Turkish during my involuntary stay here. I have been studying the language for the past eighteen days, and I assure you I speak and write it fluently, and already I have a vocabulary of 6,000 words.

A week passed. There was still no word from Safvet Pasha. On January 8, 1871, Schliemann wrote a formal request for permission to continue the excavations. Ten days later he was summoned to the Ministry of Public Instruction. There he learned that Safvet Pasha had telegraphed the governor of the Dardanelles granting permission for the excavations to continue and at the same time ordering that the land be bought *on behalf of the ministry*.

Schliemann was violently angry. "I told him in the plainest language what I thought of his odious and contemptible conduct." He explained that for two and a half years he had done everything possible to acquire title to the land. He had been actuated by the purest scientific principles. All he had ever wanted to do was to prove that the Trojan War was no fable, that Troy had actually existed, but it was a question of cutting through a whole mountain at enormous expense, and it was intolerable that he should not be allowed to possess that little spit of land, which he was perfectly prepared to pay for.

An Englishman, the director of the National Museum, was present at the interview, and Safvet Pasha seems to have been confused and ashamed by the outburst. He did his best to calm Schliemann by saying that everything was perfectly in order. Of course there was nothing to prevent him from going to Hissarlik and buying the land and continuing his excavations "as long as he submitted to the regulations of the Ottoman Empire concerning any treasures which are discovered."

At this new turn in the discussion, Schliemann overflowed with gratitude. He evidently assumed that he had been granted everything he asked for. He thanked the minister cordially, and promised to mention the minister's name in his forthcoming book on his excavations at Troy. It is possible, and very likely, that Schliemann had completely failed to understand what the minister was saying. It is also possible that he deliberately misinterpreted the minister's words. He had shouted and threatened. In the Turkish fashion Safvet Pasha had attempted to quiet him, saying that Schliemann was a man of good sense, and of course everything was possible to him. Among these face-saving gestures and hesitant smiles Schliemann appears to have detected approval and genuine sympathy, and it never seems to have occurred to him that he was being politely dismissed. To the end of his life he maintained that at the meeting on January 18 he received a verbal promise which gave him full authority to buy the land and continue the excavations.

Three days later, in the pouring rain, he reached Koum-Kale, a little village on the Trojan plain. He was soaked to the skin and exhausted by the journey. There he learned that the minister had telegraphed orders for the purchase of the land on January 10, and title to the land was transferred to the minister two days later. At once Schliemann demanded to be taken into the presence of the Governor of the Dardanelles. He asked whether the minister had countermanded the order. "No, the order stands." the Governor replied. Feeling betrayed, in a raging temper, Schliemann returned to Athens.

If the Turks thought they had seen the last of him, they were mistaken.

Schliemann was a man who rarely changed his ideas. He had long ago convinced himself that the land belonged to him by right of conquest. Had he not left his irrefutable mark on it? Then, too, he had learned that the minister had paid 600 francs for the land, while he himself was prepared to offer 1,000 francs. Surely the land should go to the highest bidder! If they were refusing to give him the land, it was because they held science in disrepute, because they were barbarians, because they feared his towering eminence as an archeologist, whose fame resounded through Europe —he was prepared to use all arguments, on all levels, in order to outwit them. Like a blustering child, he was prepared to strike back in all directions.

His first attack took the form of a long letter to Wayne MacVeagh, the American Ambassador to the Sublime Porte, begging for the Ambassador's intervention and enclosing 4,000 piasters—3,000 piasters to pay for the land, and 1,000 piasters for the Ambassador's trouble. In this letter Schliemann describes his interview with Safvet Pasha, painting himself as a knight in shining armor and the minister as an incompetent fool who had forgotten to countermand an order after promising to do so. He wrote:

> What is certain is that His Excellency Safvet Pasha gave me the field at Hissarlik and authorized me to travel to Hissarlik and purchase it formally, and therefore it follows that if his word is sacred the place belongs to me at the price of 3,000 piastres, which he paid for it. I am therefore taking the liberty of enclosing 4,000 piastres with the request that you pay 3,000 to His Excellency, and I would beg you to accept the remaining 1,000 for the costs attendant upon this petition. He knows that everything I have stated is true, and he will not for a moment hesitate in agreeing with my demands.
>
> This is not a question of a commercial transaction. It is a

question of resolving the most important of all historical problems, and every step you take in this affair will be applauded by the entire civilized world.

There was method in Schliemann's madness. There were to be many more letters to officials in Constantinople. He would show himself in all his disguises: gentle, severe, charming, intolerant of all opposition. Little by little he would break down all opposition, and in the end his will would prevail.

Meanwhile there were more urgent matters to attend to. That winter Paris was ringed around by the heavy guns of the army of the Crown Prince of Prussia. Schliemann was concerned about the fate of his property. He had a deep affection for his apartment on the Place St. Michel, which contained his library and a small collection of archeological treasures from the Far East, Ithaca, and Thera, and among them was the vase containing the ashes of Odysseus. There was nothing for it but to return to Paris.

Armed with a letter of introduction from the Prussian Ambassador in Athens, he left hurriedly for Munich, acquired more letters of introduction, went on to Strasbourg where he interviewed Count Bismark-Bohlen, the governor-general, and then to Versailles where he attempted to acquire from the hands of Bismarck himself a safe-conduct into the besieged city. But Bismarck and President Jules Favre, who had already concluded a form of armistice, had agreed that no one should enter Paris until peace was restored.

Characteristically Schliemann regarded all laws which impeded his progress, even martial laws, as intolerable abuses of freedom. For five francs he bought a false passport written out in the name of the postmaster Klein of Lagny. Schliemann was forty-nine, but looked sixty; the photograph on the passport showed a man about thirty years old. Inevitably, as he made his way through the German lines, he was regarded with suspicion. Three times he was detained for examination. He said later that he might have been put up against a wall and shot, but he remembered the German mania for titles, and by addressing every lieutenant as general and every simple soldier as full colonel, he succeeded by flattery in passing through the lines unscathed.

News reaching Athens suggested that Paris was in ruins, but it was not so. As he walked around the city, Schliemann discovered that all the familiar buildings were still standing—the Pantheon, the church of St. Sulpice, the Sorbonne were untouched. His apartment at 6 Place St. Michel, and the house he owned next door, were exactly as he had left them. Tears rolled down his cheeks when he entered his library—"such tears as would have sprung to my eyes if I had come into the presence of a child resurrected from the dead." Oddly enough, the house at 5 Place St. Michel had received a direct hit, and he found himself thinking of that day when all the warehouses except his own at Memel had been destroyed in the flames. Once more a divine purpose had protected him. It was spring, and the chestnut trees were in flower, and Paris on the eve of the Commune was as beautiful as ever. He wrote to his friend Gottschalk, a businessman in Würtemberg:

> By day the face of Paris has changed so very little. There are just as many people on the streets as before: only there are few carriages, because most of the horses have been eaten. It is at night that Paris is sad, the only light in the streets coming from miserable oil-lamps. Because there is no gaslight the theaters are open during the day. All the museums and libraries except the Sorbonne are still closed. To my great delight the College of France opens its doors tomorrow. Among the hundreds of untruths I heard about

Paris there is the one that the trees everywhere—in the streets, in the gardens of the Tuileries, in the Parc Monceau and the Champs Elysées—have been cut down. Let me assure you that not a single tree has been cut, and you may wander through the Bois de Boulogne for days before coming upon any trees cut down, and these are usually near the fortifications . . .

When the Communards were in possession of Paris, Schliemann was still there. He had faith in France, and little faith in Germany under the monarchy—he agreed with Victor Hugo that Germany would become a republic in time, and that she had power to invade other countries was of very little interest, since she would herself be invaded in her turn. He passed the time quietly in his study, contemplating the war from a distance.

He wrote to Frank Calvert suggesting that something might be gained by a meeting between Safvet Pasha, the American Ambassador, and himself—surely the opportunity must not be allowed to lose itself in the chancelries of the Sublime Porte. He remembered that treasure had been found at Hissarlik, and this not far from the place where he had dug his first trench. The treasure, which consisted of 1,200 large silver medals of the period of Antiochus the Great, was perhaps one of the factors which weighed heavily with the minister. In that case Schliemann would demonstrate his pure disinterestedness. He offered to give all the gold and silver treasure he discovered to the minister, and every coin. He offered to permit two watchmen from the ministry on the site of the excavations. Only one thing he refused: he would not dig unless he was given title to the land:

I will even give him double the value of the precious metals I may find, for I have no other object in view than to solve the mighty problem of Troy's real site and am ready to sacrifice for its excavation years of my life and a vast amount of money, but the field must be my property and as long as this is not the case I will never think of commencing the excavations, for if I dig on Government ground I shall be exposed to everlasting vexations and trouble . . .

Never previously had he promised to surrender all the treasure he discovered to the ministry and in addition pay double the value of the precious metals. He was speaking like one possessed of illimitable largesse, who cared nothing for the treasure once it was dug out of the earth, but in fact he was still determined to seize the treasure, and keep it. Against the duplicity of the Turks he was prepared to employ the greater duplicity of a skilled merchant, and the cunning of Odysseus.

In those days he thought often of Odysseus. In a sense he had modeled himself from childhood on that cunning wanderer. Sophia was pregnant, and he had already settled the name he would give to his unborn son—Odysseus.

Paris was in the hands of the Communards. Undaunted, Schliemann simply walked through the German lines with his false passport. He reached Athens in May, in time for the birth of his child. He had always imagined it would be a boy. Instead it was a girl, and he called her Andromache after the beautiful wife of Hector.

In June, a month after the birth of Andromache, he hurried to Constantinople and presented a new offer to Safvet Pasha. This memorandum reveals the temper of the man—his Odysseus-like cunning, his highly developed sense of his own importance, and that quality which the Jews call *chutzpa*, which is neither nerve nor gall, but the finest flower of these. He denied that he had any hope of finding treasure; this, indeed, was the last thing on his mind. If, however, any treasure was dug up, he offered solemnly to divide it between himself and the Turkish government. He made no claim on the land, and asked only that he be provided, in the name of the Grand Vizier, with the protection which would be afforded to any foreigner in a remote part of Turkey. He wrote:

I have the honor to submit to Your Excellency a proposition which is very close to my heart concerning excavations I hope to undertake in the Troad, near the Dardanelles, with the aim of determining, if possible, the true site of the palace of King Priam.

I have already made some small excavations at Hissarlik, and I believe I have found the palace which formed part of the ancient city of Troy. The difficulties I there encountered on the part of the two proprietors have been happily resolved now that Your Excellency has bought the property.

I do not expect, Your Excellency, to find any treasure there. Such hopes vanish in the light of the far-distant epoch we are dealing with. My task, then, will be limited to archeological tests based upon the writings of Homer. If by chance it should happen that I come upon ancient objects of value which would be of interest to the Imperial Museum, I would be happy to divide them, one half for the Museum, the other half for my collection, to remunerate me for the expenses I have undertaken. The equitable division of the treasures should take place in the presence of a representative of the said Museum, and I should be permitted to take my share out of the country.

I am not asking Your Excellency for any financial assistance in making these excavations, for I myself shall assume the entire financial burden. However, I request Your Excellency to furnish me, as soon as possible, with a *firman* from His Highness the Grand Vizier addressed to His Excellency the Governor of the Dardanelles, so that I may be protected during my researches and excavations, and the same protection shall be given to the historic buildings brought to light as a result of my work.

This letter, written with the help of Wayne MacVeagh, the American Ambassador, and John Brown, the sympathetic and learned Secretary to the Embassy, resolved all the outstanding problems. Shrewdness and guile lay concealed within it; poison was mingled with honey; and Schliemann himself had no intention of keeping to the letter of the agreement. But now at last there was a face-saving agreement which satisfied both parties to the dispute.

Schliemann was in London on August 12, 1871, when a sealed package arrived from the American Embassy in Constantinople. The package contained the *firman*. The same day, anxious to start digging, Schliemann wrote to Frank Calvert, saying that he hoped to start work at the end of September: "Pray, write me to Athens whether *the fever are then over* and what the average weather is in the Dardanelles in October."

Once more there were delays. On September 27 he arrived with his wife in the Dardanelles, only to learn that there was some doubt about the wording of the *firman:* it was not clear whether it referred to the hill at Hissarlik, and no permit had reached the local authorities from Achmed Pasha, the governor of the Dardanelles. Also, the *firman* as written ordered him "to respect the walls of the ancient and celebrated city," and he wondered what would happen if he broke through any of the cyclopean walls.

He had already established his headquarters in the village of Ciplak. Everything was ready. He had chosen his foreman, the workmen had been hired, wheelbarrows and baskets had been assembled, spades, picks and axes were being unbundled—all that remained was to break through the last vestiges of red tape. He sent an urgent message to Brown, followed it with another three days later, and at last, on Wednesday, October 11, he was able for the first time to attack the hill with the full protection of the Turkish government. Beside him as he worked was a Turkish official, Georgios Sarkis, an Armenian by birth, a former second secretary of the Chancery of Justice of the Dardanelles, "the eyes and ears of the government," to act as a perpetual watchdog and to see that no treasure was taken from the earth without the Turkish government being aware of it.

Schliemann had brought only eight wheelbarrows from France, and accordingly he started work the first day with eight workmen. The next day, seeing that work was progressing rapidly, he employed thirty-five, and on the following day he employed seventy-four. He paid each workman 9 piasters. The wages were paid out by Nicholas Zaphyros Jannakis, a colorful Greek who entered Schliemann's service shortly after his marriage. Jannakis, who came from the village of Remkoi and knew all the local dialects, acted as bodyguard, cook, cashier, and general factotum. Schliemann trusted him implicitly and always called him by his proper name, though it was his invariable custom to give his other servants names out of Greek mythology. Wherever Schliemann was, Jannakis was sure to be somewhere near; and whenever there was some local official to be bribed, Schliemann would leave it to Jannakis, who paid out the bribe money from the gold coins he always carried in his belt.

The rains came, and they were still working. As usual, Schliemann was in a hurry; he hoped to uncover the whole of Priam's palace in six weeks. Even in the rain the workmen worked from six in the morning to six at night. There was a thirty minute rest for breakfast at nine o'clock in the morning, and an hour and a half for lunch in the early afternoon. No one was allowed to smoke except during meals— Schliemann had a theory that smoking reduced a man's energy and powers of concentration. He was a hard taskmaster as he superintended the digging, cursing the rains and the interminable Greek feast-days which held up operations. Three times in the course of a month there were such heavy storms that digging had to be abandoned; on those days he wrote out his reports.

But there was little to report: a few coins and calcined bones, huge walls, and some strange phallus-shaped objects which seemed to belong to a period long before the Homeric Age. On the morning of October 30 he began to dig up hundreds of these objects—lance-heads of green stone, curious objects shaped like fiery mountains, and *phalloi* of hard black diorite, some striped with white and all of them beautifully polished. Among these were boars' tusks and boars' teeth.

He could make nothing of this. It was the last thing he expected to find. And day by day these objects were being unearthed. He began to find little clay models which resembled owls, and it occured to him that they might represent the owl sacred to Pallas Athena. Homer spoke of "owl-faced Athena," but since Athena was the virgin protectress of Athens, scholars assumed that the term meant that her eyes had the brightness of owls' eyes and she could see in the dark. He had hoped to find treasure, the painted walls of a palace, perhaps a great funeral chamber; instead there were these little black glistening *phalloi*, painted owls, and tiles with an owl's head sketched on them, and here and there traces of molten copper.

Most puzzling of all were the terra-cotta shapes which resembled small spinning tops, sometimes with two holes bored into them, which he found at a depth of ten feet. He thought of the heavy stone *phalloi* he had seen in the Indian temples, representing the male principle, and it occurred to him that the *carrousels* or tops represented the female principle. But what in heaven's name were they doing in the palace of Priam?

All of his discoveries that winter puzzled him. Owls, of course, were sacred to Athena and appeared on Athenian coins, but these owls seemed to derive from an age beyond history. He thought he had discovered some relics from the Stone Age, and wrote off a discouraging letter to James Calvert, the brother of Frank Calvert, begging for advice. Calvert replied that there was nothing peculiarly astonishing in these finds. The Greeks made no painted pottery until the sixth or seventh century, and such abstract shapes had been found before. "You must not be discouraged by the supposition that you are working in a barbarous period," he wrote. "Go ahead!"

So, more puzzled than ever, Schliemann continued to dig, finding more and more *phalloi* and spinning tops, which strangely resembled the shapes of the funeral mounds dotted over the plain of Troy. He found obsidian knife-blades so sharp they might have been used for razors and small terra-cotta boat-like objects which reminded him of the canoes he had seen in India. Perhaps all these objects derived from India. He was convinced that the startling, lifelike *phalloi* had some remote connection with Vedic India. But there were also faint inscriptions which seemed to be Egyptian, and here and there he came upon clay tiles with swastikas cut into them, and these puzzled him as much as the *carrousels*.

He went on working. On November 16 he was excavating one of the walls formed of huge blocks of wrought and unwrought stone, and for three hours sixty-five workmen were engaged in clearing a single door-sill with block and tackle. They were still at work on the wall the next day. November 18 was a Greek holiday, when the men refused to work, and Schliemann occupied his time writing up his journal. He was a man who rarely expressed himself with humility, but he was so puzzled by the obsidian knives, the spinning tops, the *phalloi*, the swastikas, and the occasional spidery inscriptions that he entered a general plea for assistance in elucidating his finds. It was his custom to send copies of his journal to scholars abroad, and in his characteristic fashion he invited those "who desire further enlightenment in these matters to write to me at my address in Athens, where I shall be spending the winter."

The bitter north wind was sweeping across the plain of Troy. Huddled in his greatcoat and wearing a sun-helmet, he decided to superintend the excavations until the last possible moment. But on November 24, after two days of violent storm, he abandoned all operations and returned to Athens, where he spent part of his enforced holiday assembling notes for a treatise on the swastika. Unlike the Nazi swastika, the true swastika moves from right to left, and there is hardly any place in the world where it has not been found. They are seen on ancient Chinese carvings, on the pulpit of St. Ambrose in Milan, on a Celtic funeral urn found in Norfolk, England, and in the *Ramayana* the ships of King Rama bore it on their prows. He carefully assembled a vast number of references to swastikas and seems to have contemplated a book on the subject, but he was still engrossed by the thought of uncovering Priam's palace and refused to wander from his appointed path, and so the book was left unfinished.

Much of his time was spent in rewriting his journal, which appeared in five instalments in the *Augsburger Allgemeine Zeitung*, later reprinted in his book *Troianische Altertümer* (Trojan Antiquities). Ernst Curtius, the distinguished Hellenist, after reading the early reports, pronounced against Hissarlik in favor of Bunarbashi, and

Schliemann roared with anger. He admitted that the lower city of Troy probably extended along the valley and perhaps reached as far as Bunarbashi, but only a fool would assume that the palaces were anywhere else but at Hissarlik.

In spite of the *phalloi* and the *carrousels* he was still convinced that he had discovered the ancient city. Great scholars like Ernest Renan, Max Müller, and Longperier might believe that Troy was a completely imaginary city, but for himself he was convinced of its reality. In March 1872, just before setting out for his fourth expedition to Troy, he wrote from Athens: "I have an unshakable faith in Homer. If I succeed in bringing to light the palace of Priam, the acropolis of ancient Troy, my discoveries will produce an immense sensation all over the world, and admirers of Homer will come in their hundreds of thousands to admire the sacred relics of those historical times." That they did not come in their hundreds of thousands was no fault of Schliemann's.

He embarked on his fourth attempt in good heart. From Schröder's in London he received a present of sixty wheelbarrows and a large number of excellent English spades and pickaxes. With his wife he returned to the Dardanelles at the end of March and resumed digging on April 5.

There was the usual trouble with the workmen. There were so many rainstorms and so many Greek festivals that in the first two weeks he obtained only eight days' work from them. Some days he employed 100 workmen, other days 126, and he calculated that he was employing an average of 120 at a cost of 300 francs a day. Three weeks after digging began, most of the workmen mutinied when he found them smoking and ordered them to stop. Worse still, the few workmen who remained at work were being stoned by the rest.

Schliemann acted promptly. He dismissed almost his entire work-gang and spent the night rounding up replacements so successfully that he had 120 new workmen working for him the next day. Because work was progressing slowly, he increased the workday by an hour. Work now started at five in the morning and ended at six in the evening. Yet he was still plagued by the unaccountable and baleful influence of the Church—during the Greek Easter no work was done for six days. He tried to bribe the men back to work, threatened them with obscure punishments, taunted them with laziness, and got nowhere. There were still no great discoveries. Occasionally there were moods of black despair, when he felt like a man committed to the task of honeycombing a mountain to no purpose.

In May there were more feast-days. Once again he attempted to bribe the workmen with higher wages, but they only answered: "If we work, the saint will strike us." On those days he sometimes visited the workmen and prescribed remedies for their diseases. The local doctors were usually Greek priests, whose prevailing remedy was the bleeding-cup. Schliemann had a horror of blood and of bleeding, and he especially detested the bleeding of children —one could always tell when children had been bled repeatedly because there were deep wrinkles around their lips. For himself, he thought the sovereign remedy was salt water, and wrote: "I never bleed anyone, and prescribe sea-bathing for almost all diseases."

One day a girl covered with ulcers was brought to him. The whole of her left eye was ulcerated; she suffered from fits of coughing and could hardly walk. His remedy was a dose of castor oil, frequent sea baths, and some simple exercises to expand her chest. Two weeks after receiving the prescription, she made the three hours' journey

from her village to Schliemann's camp at Hissarlik, threw
herself down at his feet and kissed his shoes. She told him
she had regained her appetite after her first bath in the sea.
There was no hope for her left eye, but most of her ulcers
were cured, and for years afterwards he liked to tell
the story of the girl from the village of Neo-Chori who had
been cured by sea water.

Summer came. The heat roared out of the sky, and the
nights were thunderous with the croaking of frogs in the
marshes. It was the time when small brown vipers, thin as
whips and very dangerous, scuttled out of the ruins. Schliemann learned that the villagers drank a concoction of snake-
weed found on the Trojan plain, and for safety's sake he
followed their example.

But he was not a man who played for safety. He was
always taking risks. He cut deep trenches across the
mound, and was surprised when the walls sometimes collapsed and his workmen were buried under the rubble—
by a miracle no one was ever seriously injured. He was
always climbing about the excavations with the agility of a
monkey. He labored all day, and worked on his notes
through the night.

Yet he knew nothing about scientific archeology, a
science which was then in its infancy. Emile Burnouf, the
director of the French School at Athens, had to reprimand
him for his carelessness. It was not enough to dig *phalloi*
and *carrousels* and broken pieces of pottery out of the
ground: the exact positions must be recorded, the date,
the time, the circumstances, all these must be entered into
the day-book. "You must take care to report these things
accurately," he warned, "or else you will never be able to
come to definite conclusions on your wonderful discoveries.
Tenez bien compte de cela!" Those last words suggest an

impatient schoolmaster. Schliemann was an obedient pupil. He took far greater care of his records, labeled everything, and came to realize at last that accurate records were almost the most important part of the excavation.

And still very little was coming to light. Huge walls, occasional marble slabs with long dedicatory texts, all very late, and a few huge jars and some delicate black pottery— this was almost the sum of his discoveries. Of King Priam, Prince Hector, and Achilles there was no sign.

Suddenly on June 18, 1872, he discovered a monumental relief of Apollo riding the four horses of the Sun. Though small, it was a brilliant work—the horses modeled lightly but with great skill and vigor, the god crowned with a spiked diadem with ten long rays and ten shorter ones, his golden hair flowing free. It was a late rendering, perhaps Ptolemaic, but Schliemann was immensely pleased with it and immediately set about smuggling it out of the country with the help of Frank Calvert, on whose part of the mound it was discovered. Then for years it graced the garden of Schliemann's house in Athens.

As summer advanced and still there was no sign of Homeric Troy, his moods of black despair returned. At enormous expense he had cleared a large terrace on the northern slope, and revealed a stone tower; but increasingly doubts entered his mind. The work was easier now, for the British Consul at Constantinople had sent him 10 handcarts and 20 more wheelbarrows and he had a whole armory of digging implements—6 horse-carts, 108 spades, 103 pickaxes, 24 iron levers—but though the work was easier, Schliemann himself was losing hope.

He paid his workmen five centimes for anything they discovered, and came to the conclusion that they were forging clay goddesses and *carrousels*. The workmen

feared him and showed little liking for him. Though he had
an excellent memory, he could never remember their names.
They reminded him of people he had seen in the past, and
he gave them new names—this one was "doctor," that one
"the monk," another "the dervish," another "the schoolmaster," because he reminded him of a schoolmaster he
had known in Germany.

That summer for the first time Schliemann complained
of weariness and sickness. The old fire was burning low.
He began to talk of surrendering his *firman* to a well-
endowed archeological society or to a foreign government,
and spoke bitterly about the drain on his resources. For
days on end there were dust storms, so that the workmen
could hardly see. The wind, driving down from the north,
exhausted them. In July came "the pestilential miasma,"
which in Schliemann's view arose from the decomposition of millions of dead frogs, and with the miasma came
fear. He feared the snakes which fell from the rafters of
the house he had built on one of the cliffs of Hissarlik; he
feared scorpions; he feared the workmen.

Sometimes he would wander off to a neighboring village
and forget his loneliness in conversation with a Greek shop-
keeper, Constantinos Colobos, who was born without feet,
but who had learned Italian and French and could recite
pages of the *Iliad* by heart. He enjoyed his discussions with
the old man, but there were few other relaxations in that
"lonely and miserable wilderness." On August 4, when
he was already suffering from marsh fever and was about
to give up for the summer, he found his first treasure.

At first sight the treasure was not calculated to throw
him into ecstasies. It consisted of three gold earrings and
a gold dress-pin. Nearby was a skeleton. He pronounced it
the skeleton of a young woman, and was sure she died

during the burning of Troy. "The color of the bones," he wrote, "leaves no doubt that the lady was overtaken by fire and burned alive."

He worked on, hoping more treasure would come to light, but though he found some more *phalloi* and "a very pretty bird's egg made of fine marble," there were no more important discoveries. There had been no rain for four months. For days on end the mound of Hissarlik was hidden by clouds of dust. Suddenly there were thunderstorms and the whole mound seemed to turn into mud. He gave orders to abandon the excavations for the season, and with his wife he returned to Athens. He was a sick man. His three foremen, his bodyguard, and his wife were all suffering from fever.

In Athens he recovered his health, and he was well enough a month later to pay a brief visit to the Troad with a photographer. Burnouf had asked to see a plan of the palace of Priam, and noticing some inaccuracies had suggested that a better plan could be drawn with the help of photographs.

When Schliemann reached Hissarlik he found that the watchman was calmly selling huge stones from the walls to the villagers. Some of the stones went to build houses in the Turkish village of Ciplak, others to build a belfry in the Christian village of Yeni Shehr. Schliemann was almost out of his wits with anger. He dismissed the watchman and had another installed in his place. He insisted that the new watchman be armed with a musket. With the photographs and new plans he returned in triumph to Athens.

As usual, Schliemann was planning to do a hundred things at once. When he felt discouraged by the excavations at Troy, he would remember the other places which had not yet felt the excavator's spade. He wrote to the Greek government a memorandum in which he offered to excavate both Mycenae and Olympia at his own expense, provided that he could keep the finds until his death when they would become the property of the Greek nation, and he offered to leave 200,000 francs to build a museum which would bear his name. The offer was rejected, and he began to talk wistfully of abandoning Athens for ever and living in Paris.

But Troy held him. When he heard that his *firman* from the Turkish government had been canceled on the grounds that he had exported nearly all his finds, he became still more attached to Troy, and bombarded all his acquaintances in high places to intervene with the Turkish government. As soon as he received unofficial permission to continue his excavations, he was back at Hissarlik. He told friends he proposed to start digging on March 1, but he was already at work on January 31. The ice-cold north wind was blowing. He caught a cold. There were more thunderstorms and a plague of church festivals. In March an unexpected enemy appeared in the shape of a merchant from Smyrna who engaged 150 villagers to dig up liquorice roots, paying them 12 to 23 piasters a day—a sum considerably above that which Schliemann was paying. Schliemann cursed, but there was nothing he could do. He wrote in his journal:

March 15, 1873. The nights are cold, and the thermometer frequently falls to freezing point in the morning, but during the day the sun is beginning to be oppressively warm, the thermometer frequently reading as high as 72°. The leaves are beginning to burst on the trees, and the Trojan plain is covered with spring flowers. For the last fortnight we have heard the croaking of millions of frogs in the surrounding marshes, and during the last eight days the storks have returned. The misery of life in this wilderness is increased by the innumerable owls who build their nests in the holes in the walls I have excavated: there is something mysterious and horrible in their screeching; it is unbearable, especially at night.

He had built a small stone house and a wooden house on the cliff. The stone house, built in the autumn of 1871, had 2-foot thick walls which could keep out the bitter cold winds, but he decided to give this house to his foremen, who had not enough blankets. Schliemann himself occupied the wooden house. The wind penetrated the cracks in the walls. One night toward the end of March he awoke at three o'clock to find the room full of dense smoke and one wall already in flames. In one corner of the bedroom there was a stone fireplace resting on wooden boards, and evidently a spark had ignited the wood. The north wind was blowing fiercely. Shouting to Sophia to run out of the building, he threw water from a bath onto the burning wall, and later the foremen, who had been awakened, helped to put out the flames with earth.

In a quarter of an hour it was all over, but for days afterward he shivered at the thought of how he had been within an inch of losing his books, papers, and antiquities, and how if he had slept only a few moments longer Sophia might have perished. And once again in his journal he complained of weariness, the hopeless fight against the perpetual north wind, the huge cost of employing an army of workers—he was still employing 160 workmen—and the church feasts which reduced him to abject misery, for he was sure he was on the eve of important discoveries. He found some delicate black pottery, a copper lance-head, more *carrousels*, all shattered and worth nothing.

In April the wind dropped, and the whole plain was covered with yellow buttercups. Now the workmen slept in the open under the cloudless skies. Schliemann was calmer than ever. He seems to have had a strange premonition that he was close to a great discovery. On April 16, he found a paved street and nine enormous earthenware jars as tall as a man. Such jars had never come to light before, though similar jars would be found later in Cnossus. In May he was hot on the trail. He uncovered two gates 20 feet apart, which he immediately named the Scaean Gate, and the large building behind the gates he called Priam's palace. There were more vases with owls' heads and vast amounts of rubble.

He was content. He had found what he had hoped to find, the long years of labor nearly at an end. He announced that he was preparing to publish his discoveries —there would be 200 plates and 3,500 engravings. True, Hissarlik was a small mound, and people would say that Homer never envisaged a small city when he spoke of Troy; but the wide gate, the palace walls, the cyclopean breastworks, the innumerable pieces of black pottery, the great jars, and the thousands of artifacts proved that Schliemann had discovered the citadel of Troy. His joy was short-lived. Sophia heard that her father was dying. She hurried off to Athens, only to learn that he was already dead. From his house on the cliffs of Hissarlik, Schliemann wrote the gentlest of all his letters:

> Comfort yourself, my dearest, with the thought that after a short while we shall all join your wonderful father. Comfort yourself with the thought of our dear daughter, who needs her mother and will never have any joy in life without her. Comfort yourself with the thought that your tears will never bring your father back to life, and that good, courageous man—far from the sorrows and cares of this life—is now enjoying the purest happiness beyond the grave, and is therefore happier than we who remain behind to weep and lament him. If you cannot master your grief, then come back

to me by the first steamboat and I will do everything I can to assuage your grief. There can be no excavations without you. With tears of joy I pray you will soon come back to me.

A few days later Sophia hurried back to him. She knew where she was wanted. He was lonely without her. She was the emblem of all his success in life, and when he wrote that there could be no excavations without her, he meant that he could not excavate in good heart or with hope of success unless she was by his side.

Summer was coming on, the buttercups were dying, and soon the whole plain would have the burned-out black appearance which came with summer. Schliemann was folding up his tent. He wrote to his son Sergey that he would bring the excavations to an end in the middle of June and then take his wife and daughter to some bathing place in Central Europe for a much-needed rest. He was pleased with his four months' work. He had discovered the walls of Troy and the site of the palace, excavated 250,000 meters of earth, and obtained enough antiquities to furnish a whole museum.

The letter to Sergey was written on May 30. On the same day he wrote to Frederick Calvert, who had an estate at Thymbria near Bunarbashi only a few hours' walk away, a letter of a different temper altogether. It was a letter written in fear and trembling, smuggled past the guards at night. In all his life Schliemann never wrote a more dramatic letter nor one so intimately connected with his fondest hopes and dreams:

> I am sorry to inform you that I am closely watched, and expect that the Turkish watchman, who is angry at me, I do not know for what reason, will search my house tomorrow. I, therefore, take the liberty to deposit with you 6

baskets and a bag, begging you will kindly lock them up, and not allow by any means the Turks to touch them.

In the six baskets and the bag was the golden treasure of Troy.

In his published writings Schliemann never revealed the exact date on which the treasure was discovered. We know the hour and the place—it was about seven in the morning, and the place was a deep cut below the circuit wall close to Priam's Palace. He may have discovered the treasure on May 30, the day he wrote his hurried note to Frederick Calvert, or a few days earlier.* On May 31 he wrote in his journal his first account of the treasure, adding that he had not yet had time to examine his finds or even count them—by this time they were out of his possession and safely in the hands of Frederick Calvert.

From three separate accounts written at different times, it is possible to piece together the story of his discovery. It was one of those hot May days, with the whole plain smoking with bright yellow dust. Eight days previously he had discovered a large silver vase with a small silver beaker inside it. Not far away he found a copper helmet; the helmet itself was shattered, but the characteristic horns (*phaloi*) were intact. For days he worked on, hoping to find more treasure.

He was sure there must be more treasure nearby. Accordingly, he divided his workmen into many groups and sent them digging in different places on the mound. By scattering them and losing them in the long trenches and

---

* In *Troja*, which he published ten years later, Schliemann says "the treasure was found at the end of May, 1873." This is the only definite statement he ever made about the date of the discovery. Emil Ludwig, in *Schliemann of Troy: The Story of a Goldseeker,* says the discovery was made "on a morning in the middle of June, one day before the termination of the work," but this is clearly wrong.

corridors which honeycombed the mound, he felt sure that if he discovered any large cache he would be able to smuggle it unobserved to his own house on the cliffs. In particular, he was anxious that the Turkish representative on the scene, Amin Effendi, should not be present when he discovered the treasure.

Schliemann, his wife, and a handful of workmen were digging along the circuit wall close to the Scaean Gate when Schliemann suddenly noticed at a depth of 28 feet "a container or implement of copper of remarkable design." Peering through the dust and rubble he was able to make out that the container was about 3 feet long and 18 inches high, and that there were two helmet-shaped objects on top of it, and something which resembled a large candlestick. The container was broken, and he could see some silver vessels inside it. Above all this were some reddish and brown calcined ruins from 4 to 5 feet thick, as hard as stone, and above this again were the huge fortification walls, 5 feet broad and 20 feet high.

He had found treasure, and now there was the question of preserving it from the cupidity of the Turks. None of the workmen had noticed it. Sophia was beside him, and he turned to her and said: "You must go at once and shout '*paidos!*'"

Paidos was a Greek word meaning "rest period."

Sophia had not yet seen the treasure, and was amazed at the thought of ordering a rest period so early.

"Now, at seven o'clock?" she asked.

"Yes—now! Tell them it is my birthday, and I have only just remembered it! Tell them they will get their wages today without working. See that they go to their villages, and see that the overseer does not come here. Hurry, and shout: '*Paidos!*'"

Sophia did as she was told. It was her task to call out

the rest periods, and so she climbed up the rickety ladders which led to the platform. Soon the workmen were drifting away, pleased at the opportunity of an unexpected holiday, and a little troubled, because there had been no such holidays before. Amin Effendi was especially puzzled, because he was usually well-informed about holidays.

When Sophia returned all the workmen had gone, and Schliemann was attempting to dig the treasure out with a pocket knife. The fortification wall, composed of earth, rubble, and heavy stones, was threatening to fall, but at the sight of so much treasure he lost his fears. He turned again to Sophia and said: "Quick, bring me your big shawl!'

Once again Sophia had to make the journey up the step-ladder to the upper platform and to the house. She returned with an enormous scarlet shawl, heavily embroidered, such as Greek women wear on feast-days. The treasure was poured into the shawl, and together they carried it back to the house.

As soon as the door was locked, the treasure was spread out on the rough wooden table. Many of the pieces had been packed into one another. Such treasures gleam freshly behind glass cases in museums, pale yellow, with a curious lifelessness, but when they were found they had a wonderful glowing reddish color. The treasure consisted of a copper shield, a copper cauldron, a silver vase and another of copper, a gold bottle, 2 gold cups, and a small electrum cup. There was a silver goblet, 3 great silver vases, 7 double-edged copper daggers, 6 silver knife blades, and 13 copper lance-heads. At the bottom of the largest silver vase there were 2 gold diadems, a fillet, 4 gold ear-drops, 56 gold earrings and 8,750 gold rings and buttons, most of them very small.

The most astonishing were the diadems, one of them consisting of ninety chains, forming an elaborate gold headdress with leaf- and flower-pendants and long tassels hanging down at the sides. Persian and Roman diadems were simply jeweled bands worn round the head; the Trojan diadems were formed of innumerable gold rings entirely covering the forehead. Nothing like them had been seen before, and none have been discovered since.

Trembling with excitement, Schliemann held them up to the light and then placed them on Sophia's forehead. To the end of his life he seems to have thought they were the diadems of a queen, though they are more likely to have been those of a king. He heaped necklaces around her neck and put the gold rings on her fingers, until she shone with barbaric splendor. At last, after so many years, the obscure son of a Mecklenburg clergyman was standing in the place of kings before a woman arrayed like a queen.

He was sure he had found the treasure of King Priam, hidden secretly in the wall when Troy was already in flames. At the last moment, he thought, they had been stowed away in a wooden box, and there was no time even to remove the key. What he thought to be the key was later shown to be a copper chisel, and there was no evidence that the treasure was ever enclosed in a box.

Much was, and remains, mysterious about the finds. The gold vessels were of superb workmanship, but the tiaras, wonderfully impressive at first sight, proved to be of primitive workmanship, built up with coils of wire and thin gold sheeting. None of the rings were engraved. The beautifully modeled gold sauceboat was a masterpiece of design, but why should it have been found among knife blades, arrowheads, and strange little terra-cotta idols? Not only gold and silver had been stored in the wall. There was some crudely carved ivory and shaft-hole hammer axes of semi-precious stone, but there was also a little lead figurine of a woman with a swastika scratched on her pubic triangle. Idol-worship and barbarism went hand in hand with artistic refinement. Was this the Troy of Homer, or of some earlier, more barbaric age?

Schliemann was perfectly certain that he had unearthed treasure belonging to Priam, and in the following weeks he liked to speak ironically about how he had found "the treasure of King Priam, that mythical king, of a mythical city, who lived in a mythical heroic age." It was his way of saying that the discovery of the treasure had proved that Priam was real, and the city was real, and the heroic age was supremely unmythical. The gold was there to prove that Troy was real.

He was a man tormented by gold, and never more tormented than when he found himself in possession of the gold and was afraid of being discovered. He had not completely succeeded in hiding his discovery. Rumors were flying across the Trojan plain. Amin Effendi called at his house, and said angrily he was sure something was being kept from him. The watchman demanded permission to search the house. In the name of the Sultan he ordered Schliemann to open all his chests, even the wardrobes. Schliemann's only reply was to throw him out of the house.

That night, or the next night, the treasure was taken to Frederick Calvert's house at Thymbria and a few days later smuggled out of the country.

For a few more days Schliemann peered and probed at the foot of the wall, but no more treasure was discovered. On June 17 the excavations were abruptly terminated. The workmen were paid their wages, and a priest came to bless the desolate mound, now riddled with corridors and trenches like a battlefield. Announcing that he would return to Athens and never set foot on Troy again, he left quietly, taking with him only a few of the objects he had gathered, for the rest had been sent on ahead. On June 19 he was in Athens, and that day he set about writing the first of the long series of letters in which he celebrated his discovery.

He was on fire with enthusiasm and excitement. He had made "the greatest discovery of our age, the one which all men have been looking forward to." For the first time this strange man who boasted continually had cause for boasting. Against hope, against reason, against all the evidence he had discovered Troy. *Ubi Troia fuit.* He had only to hold up the shimmering golden diadems, and who would dare to disbelieve him?

But the gold treasure remained a liability, and the habit of secrecy, which he had fostered so carefully at Hissarlik, was not easily put aside. While he was writing to all the learned societies in Europe that he had discovered the treasure—the letters sometimes read like proclamations—he was busily arranging to bury the treasure in the earth. Sophia's relatives were brought into the conspiracy. All over Greece strange objects wrapped in straw were being concealed in stables, barns, and farmyards. A wickerwork basket was dispatched to an uncle living in Eleusis. The treasure itself vanished shortly after Schliemann weighed and described minutely each object. Neither the Greek nor the Turkish governments would be able to lay hands on it.

Schliemann remained in Athens when Sophia went off to Ischia, for a long deserved holiday; and some weeks later a trusted servant was sent to tell her by word of mouth where each object had been buried.

Schliemann was caught on the horns of a dilemma. He wanted fame, which is impermanent, and the treasure, which was the most permanent of all things. The treasure was a weapon he could use against governments, particularly the Greek government. He had only to announce that he would bequeath this treasure to any one of three or four governments, and he knew he would be received with open arms and allowed all the facilities he needed for excavations. As soon as he returned from Hissarlik, he quarreled with the Greek government. He let it be known that he possessed the treasure and would give it to Greece, but they must give him full permission to excavate at Mycenae and Olympia. They had refused his offer before. They refused again, apparently because they were afraid of trouble with Turkey.

Trouble came in August when the Turks had had time to make a few elementary inquiries and to read the dispatches which Schliemann had sent to the *Augsburger Allgemeine Zeitung*. Schliemann learned that Amin Effendi was to be punished because he had failed to keep close watch on the excavations. Punishments of officials in the Ottoman Empire sometimes ended fatally, and once again Schliemann found himself on the horns of a dilemma. He would not return the treasure. He would not return to Turkey to intercede for the official. But at least he could write a letter "in the name of humanity and of sacred justice," pointing out that Amin Effendi was completely innocent:

> If he was unable to keep watch over everything that happened, that was because there were always five works of excavation proceeding at any one time, and by heaven, no one has yet been born who can multiply himself five times and keep watch over five works simultaneously.
>
> I found the treasure while Amin Effendi was working on another part of the mound altogether, and if you had seen the despair written on the poor man's face when he learned from other workmen about the treasure, and if you had seen

his tearing rage when he came rushing into my room, ordering me to open all my chests and wardrobes in the name of
the Sultan, you would have had pity for him.

No one ever watched over my excavations more relentlessly than Amin Effendi, but a man must be an archeologist
himself before he can survey the work of one excavation,
and his only fault was that he was not an archeologist. . . .

It is not a convincing letter. There are hesitations and
ambiguities, such as might come to a man defending himself when he knows he is in the wrong. In his one-sided
fashion Schliemann argued that when his *firman* was re-
voked, he was left free to do as he pleased. "The Turkish
government," he wrote, "broke our written contract in
the fullest sense of the word, and I was released from every
obligation."

But the Turkish government had permitted him to continue his excavations and no doubt expected from him its
fair share of the objects he removed from the earth. Schliemann's instinct was to regard any agreement with governments as though they were commercial agreements.
The Turks asked him privately to send a part of the
treasure as a token offering to the Imperial Museum in
Constantinople. Schliemann answered that he would send
nothing, and in the same letter requested permission to return to Troy and dig for three more months, promising
that everything he discovered in those three months would
be given to the Museum.

Once again, as so often in the past, Schliemann found
himself riding a storm. His weapons were guile, cunning,
patience, loquaciousness. He could, and would, use every
trick of the market place to preserve his gains. Dissatisfied
by the attitude of the Greek government, he began to think
of immigrating to Italy. Palermo and Naples were both
excellent sites for an archeologist, and he was soon making

tentative approaches to Italian museum officials: he would build a museum to house his treasures, provided he was given a free hand to dig as he pleased.

Meanwhile his fame was increasing. Gladstone, the British Prime Minister, heard of his discoveries and was impressed by them. Max Müller, the distinguished orientalist, wrote an article on them. In Germany the battle between the defenders and the opponents of Schliemann was already launched. Through the fall and early winter Schliemann completed his book *Troianische Altertümer*, which consisted largely of his Trojan journals interspersed with photographs. Simultaneously he made a French translation, and sent both copies to his publishers.

With the book finished, he was restless again. The right to excavate in Olympia had been officially granted to the Prussian government. He was outraged, but there was nothing he could do about it. He decided to make a preliminary survey of Mycenae. There, if anywhere, he thought he would be able to repeat his successes at Troy.

With his contempt for governments and permits, he embarked on the expedition secretly with Sophia, informing no one. He engaged workmen on the spot and in five days dug thirty-four small trenches on the acropolis, discovering only a few unimportant pieces of shattered pottery. Long ago, in his book *Ithaka, der Peloponnes und Troia*, he had stated his belief that there were graves dating from the heroic age within the citadel wall at Mycenae, and the most important result of this brief visit was to reinforce his belief. He suspected the existence of a mortuary dome chamber near the famous Lion Gate, and still another one a little further away. He could not explain why he was so sure the tomb chambers were there, and he seems to have sensed them, as he sensed the presence of gold at Troy. He spoke of digging a single shaft just beyond the Lion Gate. This shaft, he thought, would reveal the mausoleum of the Kings of Mycenae—Thyestes, Agamemnon, and all the others. Already he possessed the ashes of Odysseus and the treasure of Priam; the discovery of the royal graves at Mycenae would crown his career.

Unfortunately he had no business to be in Mycenae at all, and as soon as the Greek government heard that he was digging there, orders were sent by telegram to the prefect of Argolis to prevent him from putting a spade to the earth. This telegram was followed by two more. The first said that everything Schliemann had dug from the ground must be confiscated, and the second said that his luggage must be examined.

These tasks were entrusted to the police chief at Nauplia, who visited the house where the Schliemanns were staying, discussed the matter calmly over coffee, and was shown a basketful of broken pottery. It was the opinion of the police chief that such potsherds could be found in any village lane and in all ancient cities, and wrote to his superiors: "I found nothing of importance, and so I let it pass."

When Schliemann returned to Athens he found the government up in arms against him. He had been an object of suspicion ever since his discoveries at Troy. The police chief, the prefect of Argolis, and the mayor of Mycenae had shown themselves incompetent. "By their actions," wrote the Minister of Education, "they have proved that the soil of Greece is defenceless, and any unauthorized person can do as he pleases with it, in complete disregard of the laws."

Schliemann, who had discovered nothing of any real worth, simply bided his time. He had fallen in love with Mycenae. As soon as a favorable opportunity occurred, he would send a memorandum to the Greek government, offering to dig at Mycenae at his own expense, giving everything he found to the government, reserving for himself only the right to report and describe his finds. The favorable opportunity occurred two months later; and the same minister who had characterized him as a thief and an enemy of Greece solemnly signed the agreement.

He had decided to start digging at Mycenae on April 21, and he was making arrangements for the journey when the Turks instituted proceedings against him for half of the treasure. The trial, which was fought through the upper and lower courts, lasted a year, and exhausted his patience. He had to remain in Athens. By court order, policemen came to his house and searched for the treasure, and found no trace of it. He refused to say where the treasure was hidden, he refused to answer the questions of the prosecutor, he refused to make a settlement. He was determined to fight the Turks to the bitter end, and at the same time he sent a stream of messages to Constantinople, demanding the right to continue his excavations at Hissarlik, as though there were no quarrel between them.

In that strange year from April 1874 to April 1875, perhaps the strangest he ever lived through, he quarreled with everyone. He quarreled with the police, who dogged his footsteps. He quarreled with his own lawyers. He quarreled with the Greek government, and he quarreled with his critics. In Germany particularly doubts were being cast on the value of his discoveries at Hissarlik, and he replied to these criticisms with unaccustomed acerbity. Why had the Prussian government been given the concession to dig at Olympia? He was outraged. Had he not offered to dig there at his own expense—those words which are repeated in so many of his letters—and give everything he found to the Greeks? He appealed over the heads of his ministers to King George of Greece. "I have come to Greece for the sole purpose of serving science," he wrote, "and I brought with me *my own honorably acquired fortune.*" He underlined the last words, as though an honorably acquired fortune was itself a passport to royal protection.

To placate the government and to put himself in good standing with the Athenians, he offered to remove at his own expense the Venetian Tower, built in the Middle Ages on the Acropolis. The tower spoiled the view. No one liked it, but no one had troubled to remove it. The tower was 80 feet high, and the Venetians had built it out of slabs of marble from the Acropolis, and now the owls had their nests in it. How better could he serve Greece than by demolishing an eyesore? He estimated that it would cost £465 to pull down the tower, and when the Greek government accepted his offer, he was delighted. Then for many days he stood on the Acropolis, superintending the destruction of the old tower, as pleased with himself as if he were excavating for gold.

When the courts adjourned for the summer, he slipped out of Athens and made a quick tour of northern Greece, visiting Orchomenos, where he made some excavations six years later. He was so convinced of the importance of that ancient city that he offered to finance an exploration to be undertaken by the Greek Archeological Society. Then he was in Athens again, fighting critics and lawyers, demanding from the Greeks the right to excavate at Olympia, from Safvet Pasha the right to return to Troy, from the King the right to speak in the name of science and to excavate where he pleased. It was a year of patient improvisation, of somber reflections, and of sudden sallies against his enemies, and when it was over he was exhausted. The trial aged and embittered him, and once more he began to speak of abandoning Greece forever and settling in southern Italy.

At last the long trial came to an end. Schliemann had

played his cards skillfully. The Greek judges found in favor of the Turks and ordered him to pay an indemnity of 50,000 francs. Since he valued the treasure of Priam at a million francs, he had in effect won the trial. As a gesture of friendship he sent five times the amount of the indemnity to the Imperial Museum at Constantinople. He also sent seven large vases and four sacks filled with stone implements.

Having won his victory, he was in a mood to enjoy his growing fame. Gladstone had written him an affectionate letter of greeting, and his warmest admirers were in England. Accordingly he set out for England in the summer of 1875, taking Sophia and Andromache with him. He stopped in Paris to address the Geographical Society, but he made so many vast claims that his speech was greeted coldly; and when it was over, no one came up to congratulate him, and there were no flocks of visitors at his house on the Place St. Michel.

In London he was lionized. Gladstone eulogized him. All through July he was being wined and dined in the best circles. He had installed Sophia and Andromache in Brighton, and complained that he was only able to tear himself away from London once or twice a week to visit her. From London he wrote to Gauthiot, the secretary of the French Geographical Society:

> Here the meetings of the learned societies are crowded when I address them, everyone applauds me, and everything I say is published. The Court demands my presence, and all the foreign princes and princesses send me invitations and listen to my remarks with interest—everyone wants to have the name of the discoverer of Homeric Troy in their autograph books. Soon I shall be leaving this charming society, where everyone heaps honors on me and offers me much kindness, to return to Paris—where I was regarded as a traitor!

He spent only a few hours in Paris. The Queen of Holland invited him to The Hague. There was a reception in his honor, attended by all the dignitaries of the Kingdom. The Queen gave him a private audience, and for long hours he pored over the Egyptian objects in the Leyden Museum in her company. He had two excellent reasons for admiring the Queen: she had a passion for archeology, and she spoke seven languages fluently. He wrote to Felix Ravaisson, the Conservator of the Louvre:

> Her Majesty is always inviting me for breakfast, lunch and dinner. She has read much, and is gifted with a quite extraordinary memory. I believe I could even persuade her to do some excavations in Asia Minor, the Greek Archipelago or in Italy, but of course I shall limit myself to advising her and not take part in them.

Then he went off to Copenhagen for a week of prowling round the museums, happy to discover among the Stone Age weapons some curious similarities with those he discovered in Troy. He went to Rostock to deliver yet another speech on his excavations. The Italians welcomed him on his return. He announced that he intended to settle in Naples for the rest of his life. He spent some weeks at Alba Longa, where some funeral urns had been excavated recently, but it was not a promising ground. He had no better luck on the island of Motyë off the west coast of Sicily, where there was once a Carthaginian settlement; and though he examined the ruins at Segente and made some preliminary diggings, he found nothing to warrant a prolonged stay. At the end of October he was writing: "I do not know where to turn. For Troy it is too soon, and if I return to Greece I shall have to fight their continual explosions of jealousy."

All his fame had come from Troy. Abruptly leaving Naples at the beginning of December, he made his way to Constantinople, interviewed Safvet Pasha in the Ministry of Public Instruction, and demanded a new *firman*. Safvet Pasha was dubious. He promised, however, to use his good offices, on condition that Schliemann faithfully keep to his promise of offering everything he discovered to the Imperial Museum.

In April 1876 the *firman* was sent to him, but by this time he was engrossed in the thought of uncovering the royal graves of Mycenae. He knew how to time his excavations. "For Troy it is too soon. . . ." He wrote up his reports on the small and scattered excavations he had made the previous year—there was only a handful of Carthaginian arrowheads to show for the weeks he had spent at Motyë—and immersed himself in the study of Mycenae.

More and more Mycenae attracted him. He could not have Olympia, and he had discovered all he could reasonably hope to discover at Hissarlik. There remained Mycenae, which the ancients believed to have been founded by Perseus, the son of Danaë and Zeus, who appeared to her in a shower of gold. There, if anywhere, he would find treasure.

The Golden Masks

In Schliemann's day the traveler approaching Mycenae in summer saw the plain of Argos all yellow and white with stubble and dust, and the once-great fortress city was no more than a rubble of stones on one of the foothills, guarding the pass between two mountains nearly 2,500 feet high. These blue and barren mountains have something threatening about them—ponderous and sharp-edged, with power in their heavy outcrops and huge shoulders. The mountains still threaten and the wolves still howl in the foothills, but much has changed. Today the plain is well-cultivated, there are good roads through it, orchards flower between tobacco and cotton fields, and there is barley in the foothills. Still, even today, Mycenae is a menacing place as it lies huddled in the shadow of the bleak hills, commanding all approaches.

Mycenae is an ideal site for a city dominating the plain of Argos and the sheltered bay of Nauplia 9 miles to the south, and appears to have been inhabited from prehistoric times. Here about 1700 B.C. a powerful king built gigantic ramparts around an early Bronze Age city and erected a new palace. No one knows the name of the king, or where he came from. The entrance to the city was a paved highway flanked by two bastions. Deep within the bastions there stood, and still stands, a great Lion Gate of massive and imposing construction, once closed by a double wooden door, with an enormous lintel crowned by a relief of two lionesses face to face. Once through the Lion Gate and beyond the walls which are 16 feet thick the visitor comes upon a circular terrace. In Schliemann's day this was covered with rubble and the detritus of the ages, and beyond this lay the tumbled ruins of palaces and private houses, all weather-worn and covered with lichens. On the slopes of the ridges and in the surrounding valley lay the ruins of the lower city. This windswept hilltop was a wild and desolate place, rarely visited except by plunderers. For centuries nothing had changed. In the second century A.D. Pausanias visited the place and found the same bare wilderness and pastureland interspersed with slopes and precipitous cliffs. It was even then a ruin lost in the corner of the plain, dark and ominous and crumbling away.

Once it was a large and prosperous city with broad streets, carriage roads, and shining pathways. A powerful king ruled from the citadel, armies poured through the Lion Gate, and there were great treasuries of gold. Both Homer and Sophocles speak of Mycenae as being "rich in gold." Pausanias says the city was founded by Perseus, who

Heinrich Schliemann in St. Petersburg

Heinrich Schliemann in middle age

Sophia Schliemann

Wearing the diadem of Troy

Shortly after her marriage

(F. A. Brockhaus, Leipzig)

Golden beaker found in treasury of Troy

Apollo riding his chariot, found by Schliemann at Troy

Gold cup and gold beaker

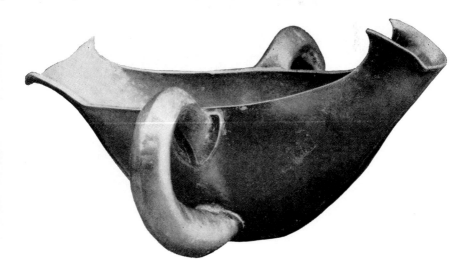

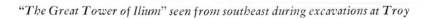
"The Great Tower of Ilium" seen from southeast during excavations at Troy

Schliemann's own photograph of the treasure shortly after its discovery

Gold crowns from the shaft graves at Mycenae

The Beautiful Mask

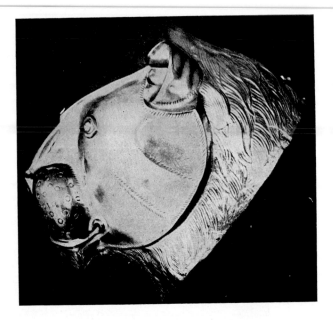

Golden mask in the form of a lion's head from Mycenae

Heroic mask from Mycenae

Heroic mask from Mycenae

Head of a bull in silver and gold from Mycenae

The Cup of Nestor from Mycenae

above and right:
Gold cup and gold beaker
from Mycenae

The Lion Gate at Mycenae at the time of Schliemann's excavations

Tiryns at the time of Schliemann's excavations

Schliemann in old age

gave it its name either because he lost his scabbard-cap (*mykes*) there, or because he found mushrooms (*mykes*) at a spring which later came to be called the Perseia. In fact no one knows the origin of the city's name. Schliemann thought it must come from *mykithmos* ("bellowing") since the plain of Argolis was renowned for its oxen. It was a guess, as good as any others, and he did not insist upon it.

The dynasty founded by Perseus was peaceful, but the following dynasty, founded by Atreus, was soaked in tragedy. When Atreus learned that his wife had been seduced by his brother Thyestes, he killed two of his brother's sons and placed their flesh before the father at a banquet. Told that he had eaten his sons' flesh, Thyestes vomited what he had eaten, overturned the table and ran off, calling down curses upon all the descendants of Atreus. Then he consulted the oracle and was told he could destroy Atreus only by begetting a son by his own daughter Pelopia. One night when he was sacrificing, a girl approached him and he seduced her without knowing he was seducing his own daughter. The words of the oracle came true. The child, born of this midnight encounter, grew to manhood and murdered Atreus. Then Thyestes ruled for a while, only to be followed on the throne by Agamemnon, the son of Atreus.

The curse uttered by Thyestes lost none of its fatal power. While Agamemnon was fighting at Troy, Aegisthus, the child of Thyestes and Pelopia, made love to Clytemnestra, the wife of Agamemnon. The guilty lovers waited for the coming of Agamemnon. They sent a watchman to the seashore, to signal the coming of the ships laden with captives from Troy. Across the plain an unsuspecting Agamemnon rode in his chariot at the head of his armies. When he reached Mycenae a banquet was served, and at the banquet or in a nearby bathroom he was murdered by his wife and her lover.

Agamemnon dead, the curse still hung heavily over the house of Atreus:

> . . . and sang within the bloody wood
> Where Agamemnon cried aloud,
> And let their liquid siftings fall
> Upon that stiff dishonored shroud.

So T. S. Eliot and the Greek dramatists depict those times when a curse was like a physical thing, palpable in the midnight air, continuing for ever like ripples when a stone is flung in a pool. Agamemnon's death did not put an end to the curse. His children, Orestes and Electra, murdered Clytemnestra and her lover Aegisthus. Orestes came to the throne, and with him the curse which had devoured the family of Atreus may have lost its power.

Homer, Aeschylus, Sophocles, Euripides all tell the story of the murder of Agamemnon. For the Greeks the fall of Troy and the fall of the house of Atreus were the great heroic tragedies on which their spirits fed. They regarded Mycenae and Troy as equally sacred: both were places haunted by the presence of great heroes. Having uncovered Troy, Schliemann was simply following the logical path when he turned his attention to Mycenae. In Troy he had found the treasure near the main gate leading into the city. He had the feeling that at Mycenae, too, he would find treasure near the main gate.

He had few clues to work on. There were legends and traditions, but few of them were clear and some were misleading. The most authoritative statement about the tombs of the heroes was made by Pausanias:

In the ruins of Mycenae is a fountain called Perseia and the underground buildings of Atreus and his sons, where their treasure is buried. There is the tomb of Atreus and there are also tombs of those whom Aegisthus murdered on their return from Troy after entertaining them at a banquet. There is the tomb of Agamemnon and that of his charioteer Eurymedon, and of Electra, and one of Teledamus and Pelops—for they say Cassandra gave birth to these twins and while they were still infants Aegisthus killed them with their parents. Clytemnestra and Aegisthus were buried a little outside the wall, because they were thought unworthy of burial within it, where Agamemnon lies and those who were killed together with him.

Schliemann, who had read all the available books and plays about Mycenae, pondered these words, learned them by heart, and came to regard them with the same reverence with which he regarded the words of Homer. When Pausanias wrote, 1,300 years had passed since the fall of Troy. Pausanias was simply recording local traditions. Schliemann was inclined to accept these traditions for the same reason that he accepted the traditions concerning Henning von Holstein. He had implicit faith in stories about buried treasure.

The more Schliemann pondered the words of Pausanias, the more he became convinced that previous commentators were in error. According to them, the tomb of Clytemnestra lay outside the city walls, while the tombs of Atreus and Agamemnon and those who died with him lay inside the city walls. But it occurred to Schliemann that even in the time of Pausanias the city walls had been reduced to rubble. He argued that Pausanias meant that the tomb of Agamemnon was to be found inside the walls of the Acropolis, not the city walls which could be traced across the surrounding countryside. With this belief, and fortified by the knowledge that the treasure of Troy had been found near the main gate, he set to work in August, 1876, with sixty-three workmen in the neighborhood of the Lion Gate. This time he was not allowed to work alone. Three officials from the Greek Archeological Society watched every movement he made.

Schliemann had always hated being watched, and he especially hated the presence of the officials. Beyond the gate huge stones blocked the passageway. He set his workmen to removing the stones. The officials objected. Schliemann replied that they were interfering with his plans. As usual, he had divided his workmen into groups and hoped to confuse the officials by working on several projects at once. In the relentless heat, with huge clouds of dust pouring over the ruined city, Schliemann's temper was easily aroused, and the officials usually brought their complaints to Sophia, who did her best to quiet them, not always with success. As the work went on, and more workmen were employed, and Schliemann threatened to level more walls, they objected to Schliemann's highhanded operations more violently. Stamatakes, the chief representative of the Greek Archeological Society on the spot, wrote to Athens:

> He is eagerly demolishing everything Roman and Greek in sight, in order to lay bare the cyclopean walls. Whenever we find Greek or Roman vases, he looks at them in disgust, and when these fragments are put in his hands, he lets them fall to the ground. He treats me as though I were a barbarian. If the Ministry is not satisfied with me, I beg to be recalled, for I remain here at the expense of my health. After spending the whole day until 9 P.M. with him at the excavations, I sit up with him until 2 A.M., entering up the finds. I allow him to take some things which he wants to study to his own

rooms. For all these kindnesses which are permitted to him, Schliemann expressed himself to the Mayor as very well satisfied.

The government, however, had taken note of Schliemann's methods at Troy and was determined not to be caught napping. Stamatakes was instructed to see that (a) no walls were pulled down, (b) the excavations should no longer take place over several areas, but should be concentrated at one place at any given time, and (c) the number of workmen should be limited to a reasonably manageable figure. Stamatakes himself would be held responsible for any infringement of these regulations.

The new rules were easier to announce than to enforce. Accompanied by the prefect of Nauplia, Stamatakes delivered the message to Schliemann. They approached him hesitantly and took pains to speak with an almost excessive politeness. Schliemann completely lost his temper. He appealed to the prefect to have Stamatakes dismissed. He said it was intolerable that he should have to work with such a man. Stamatakes said something about carrying on "according to the law and the agreement you have signed." Schliemann answered hotly that it was not a matter of agreements. No one else understood what needed to be done, and he was being plagued by absurd officials, who were completely unaware of his, Schliemann's, sacred duty to reveal an ancient civilization buried deep in the earth. He would employ every device of modern science to protect and preserve this ancient civilization, but it was necessary for him to work in perfect freedom. Away with the officials!

While Schliemann blazed with anger, and Sophia remained in the shadows, the prefect of Nauplia solemnly read out the dispatch he had received from Athens. The tall, slender Stamatakes confronted the small and wiry

Schliemann: the responsible official who owed a duty to
Athens, and the archeologist who owed a duty only to the
past. The air was electric. Schliemann's face had turned
bright red, as it always did when he was angry, and he was
muttering to himself. The workmen had stopped working.
Occasionally there would come from one of them, a stout,
heavily-built buffoon who had been elected mayor of the
local village, an ironical remark uttered in a stage whisper.
All the time the prefect of Nauplia continued to read out
the edict.

At last, the reading over, Schliemann turned on his heels,
barked out an order to the workmen to continue digging,
and paid no more attention to the officials. The workmen
obeyed him, but slowly, with no heart in the work, frightened by the bright glare in his eyes. And that evening
Schliemann wrote one more of a long series of letters to
the minister, and not trusting the post office to deliver it,
he asked Sophia to leave the next day for Athens. She
would deliver the letter herself to the minister, and await
his reply.

So the work went on, with Schliemann and Stamatakes
at each other's throats. There were brief reconciliations,
fervent declarations of affection, sudden bouts of hatred.
Schliemann had refined the art of employing delaying
tactics. His letter to the minister was a masterpiece of
subterfuge, in which he proclaimed his undying love for
Greece, his dedication to archeology, and his belief that
the minister's dispatch to the prefect of Nauplia was written in a moment of aberration. He added that he no longer
possessed the least desire to excavate in a country where he
was treated with such contumely.

The Greek and Turkish governments possessed large
files full of similar letters. They recognized his tactical
skill, and were in a position to take his threats seriously: if

he wished to leave Greece, they would do nothing to prevent him. But Sophia had no desire to leave Greece, and she was an accomplished actress, always at his side, employing all her charm and all her wiles to defeat the adversary. Soon Stamatakes, usually so reserved and scholarly, was referring to the slight Athenian girl as "that inhuman monster." He recognized that she had a full share in organizing the careful plans by which Schliemann maintained full liberty of action in spite of orders from the government.

While Schliemann was threatening to leave for America, Stamatakes was threatening to resign. He spoke of the intolerable burdens that were laid upon him, the unbelievable rudeness of Schliemann, his obstinacy, his cunning, his devilish habit of making life insufferable for everyone around him. Sophia bided her time. Whenever the air grew thick with threats and counter-threats, she would watch her opportunity, and then at a moment chosen by herself she would enter the fray and speak a few calming words. In the body of a girl there was the mind of a mature woman. Schliemann, who rarely gave credit to others, was unstinting in his admiration of her cunning. Was she not Penelope, and was he not Odysseus?

The work went on, but nothing of great moment was being discovered. Curiously, they found no Roman or Byzantine coins, like those found at Troy. Below the ruins of the Hellenic city they found splendid archaic vases painted with geometric patterns and terra-cotta goblets bearing a strange resemblance to Bordeaux wine glasses. There were the usual clay figurines of goddesses painted bright red. There were knives, buttons, clay animals, arrowheads not unlike those he had excavated at Motyë, hundreds of *carrousels* made of a beautiful blue stone, combs, needles, shattered fragments of crystal. There were millstones and hatchets, and pieces of bones which Schliemann believed to be parts of Mycenaean musical instruments. It was beginning to look as though he was fated to repeat the same experience he had suffered at Troy—innumerable *carrousels*, innumerable *phalloi*, innumerable little clay goddesses, nothing of very much significance.

At last in the fourth or fifth week the workmen digging south of the Lion Gate came upon two tombstones, each about 4 feet high, made of sandstone and bearing designs in relief in a technique resembling primitive wood-carving. One showed a hunter in a chariot pursuing deer with a hunting dog running beside the chariot-wheels. The other showed another chariot with the horse led by a naked soldier armed with a broadsword.

Schliemann thought he saw some resemblance between the style of carving on the tombstones and the style of the famous lions on the Lion Gate. He noted that the tails of the horses, dog, and deer were unusually thick and long, and though the chariots were only briefly sketched in, he came to the conclusion that they faithfully reflected the chariots used in the time of the Trojan wars. A few more fragments of tombstones appeared in the following days. A still more important discovery was a solitary gold button. With gold and tombstones, Schliemann felt he was hot on the scent.

He had found the tombstones within the great circular space beyond the Lion Gate, and as he continued to work there he became increasingly puzzled by what he discovered. All around the circle he found stone slabs arranged to form a nearly continuous ring of benches. This suggested that the circle represented the open-air meeting place where the nobility would be summoned by heralds to listen to proclamations; and perhaps too it served as a dance floor and a place where the poets celebrated their kings. Orators would stand there; prizes would be given there; and here too the sacred symbols of power would be periodically shown to the people.

These places were holy ground and were usually connected with the dead heroes, and sometimes the tombs of kings would lie beneath the stones. Such a place was called the *agora*, and though holy, was used as a market place. Euripides in the *Electra* speaks of the people of Mycenae being called "to the *agora* to see the wonderful lamb with the golden fleece," the golden lamb being a symbol of royalty. Pausanias said that the heroic tombs were within the *agora* of Megara. Pindar, too, speaks of the heroes being buried in the *agora* on the island of Thera. Schliemann began to believe that the tombs of the heroes would be found within that ring of stone.

For some reason which he never made clear, he did not at once begin to excavate within the circle. South of the circle lay a gigantic house with seven large windowless rooms; and thinking this was the royal palace, he decided to excavate here in earnest. The early finds were disappointing: the inevitable *carrousels* of blue stone, the inevitable hatchets and axes, the inevitable scraps of painted pottery. The great discovery was a vase some 12 inches high, on which an ancient artist had depicted a procession of soldiers marching off to war. They are painted dark red on a light yellow ground. Here for the first time we see the equipment of the soldiers who fought in the wars before Troy, and what is surprising is the liveliness of these quickly sketched portraits and their curious air of modernity. They march out of an ancient past, but we would recognize them if they came into the room.

It is worth while to pause and study these soldiers, for it is likely that the Homeric heroes wore a garb similar to theirs. They wear horned helmets with plumes fluttering from the crests. Similar horned helmets appear on Egyptian reliefs representing battles between the Egyptians and "the people from the lands of the sea." They carry long spears to which wine bottles are attached, and heavy semi-circular shields. They wear small breastplates like gorgets over their coats of mail, which are fastened at the waist by a belt, perhaps of metal. The coats of mail reach only to their thighs, which are protected by tassels, probably of mail. They wear stockings, which may also have been of mail, though Schliemann was inclined to believe they were made of cloth. On the paintings the helmets are dotted over with white points, and Schliemann suggested that the artist intended to represent the luster of bronze. It is more likely that the helmets were made of leather and dotted with metallic spikes such as are found on a small fragment of another warrior vase which Schliemann discovered a few days later.

Schliemann was puzzled by the horns (*phaloi*) on the helmets. "It is altogether inexplicable to me what they can have been used for," he wrote, "and there is no word in Homer which might be interpreted so as to indicate their existence on a Homeric helmet." For once Schliemann was caught napping, for Homer refers to them clearly enough in the third book of the *Iliad* in the description of the duel between Menelaus and Paris: "Menelaus drew his silver-

Heinrich Schliemann • "Faith and dreams led him on his journey, and he was not so very far from the Homeric heroes whom he had adored ever since he was a child"

and the walls of Troy several times in a day. So he dug at Hissarlik, and found first nothing but Stone Age relics, including some very explicit sexual symbols. Then at last he uncovered a great treasure of silver and gold, and this brought fresh problems, for it had to be concealed both from the workmen, who would try to steal it, and from the Turkish Government, who would try to confiscate it. As to how he did so and went on to greater triumphs at Mycenae, I must leave it to Mr. Payne to tell you.

This is more than a deeply interesting book; it is an inspiring one. It is the story of how a single ideal—a devotion to the heroic age of Greece—can not only overcome every kind of difficulty and danger, but transform and redeem its possessor. Without his passion for Greece, Schliemann would have been only an unpleasant sort of Horatio Alger hero; with it, he has become one of the benefactors of our culture.

BOOK-OF-THE-MONTH CLUB, INC.
345 Hudson Street, New York 14, N.Y.

Printed in U.S.A.

The Gold of Troy

A Report by BASIL DAVENPORT

Reprinted from the Book-of-the-Month Club News

WHEN I was a child I supposed the Greek myths had no more reality than the story of Cinderella. I well remember the joy with which I learned that there was indeed a labyrinth in Crete and a palace of Agamemnon at Mycenae and, best of all, that in what is now Turkey there was a ruined city of Troy, where a treasure had been found that the finder called the Treasure of Priam. Later I was profoundly excited, as everyone who sees them must be, by the sight of the golden death masks found at Mycenae— masks which, as *The Gold of Troy* says, "show the hero at the moment after he has become a god." When I saw this book, the story of Heinrich Schliemann, explorer of Troy and Mycenae, I seized upon it with eager expectation. And I found even more than I expected.

For Schliemann's own life, as I discovered, is one that no novelist would have dared to invent. During his boyhood in Germany he was denied anything more than an elementary education, and worked long hours as a grocer's clerk. To escape from this life he needed money, and

Head of a bull in silver and gold from Mycenae

to gain money he needed knowledge. So, between the ages of 20 and 24, he learned seven languages: French, Spanish, Portuguese, English, Italian, Dutch and Russian; he would not allow himself to learn Greek, it seems, until he was a rich man, for fear he would find Greek so fascinating that he would have no time for anything else. He made four fortunes, three of them in Russia as an importer, one in the California gold rush, where he just happened to be, called there to settle the estate of a deceased brother. He was obviously a man of iron determination and extraordinary ability, but he does seem also to have had amazing luck. This luck ultimately stood by him when it came to winning a wife. He was diffident with women; when he first considered marriage with a Russian girl, he tried unsuccessfully to get his sister to visit her and send him, in effect, a report on her, such as he was accustomed to get from his agencies abroad.

Apollo riding his chariot . . . found by Schliemann at Troy

His cha as his li the h 7 l Troy, he deter would look 41, he was sti with his life, and becoming a philolog. be became an excavat dentally.

Yet the excavations are, rig heart of Robert Payne's book. have the perennial fascination of any victorious struggle against odds. Schliemann's archaeological work was carried out in the face of all kinds of difficulties—the dishonesty of his workmen, the objections of local landlords, the opposition of the Turkish Government, and "a plague of church festivals" which delayed the digging. Working as he did in the 19th century he had of course no knowledge of modern archae-

His first marriage was unhappy, but after it ended in divorce he wrote to a Greek Orthodox bishop in Athens and asked him to suggest a Greek wife—one who was pretty, dark-haired and an enthusiast for Homer. Against all probability this second marriage was singularly happy; one of the proudest moments in the life of the poor grocer's boy was when he hung his beautiful wife with the jewels of prehistoric kings.

ological techniques, and no guide except the writings of Homer, for whose literal inerrancy he had a reverence that sometimes becomes comic. But the guidance of Homer proved sound. There were two possible sites for Troy, two hills called Bunarbashi and Hissarlik. It was the general opinion that Bunarbashi was the likelier; but, said Schliemann, Bunarbashi was too far from the sea, for Homer's warriors come and go between the coast mounted sword, swung it backward, brought it down on the horn of the enemy's helmet, and then the sword broke into pieces and dropped from his hand." The purpose of the horn was to receive the blow of a sword, but there may have been other purposes: to avert the evil eye, to reinforce the warrior's virility, and to give him the feeling that he had an extra eye. There were two-horned and four-horned helmets, and sometimes the *phaloi* were curved like goats' horns.

But though these curved and pointed horns provide an important clue to the bearing of the soldiers as they march away from the slim-waisted woman waving to them on the left, there are more important clues. The plumes seem to be feathers, not horse hair. The thick belt corresponds to the Homeric *mitre*, a broad band of metal which protected the lower abdomen. We know that Homeric leggings were sometimes provided with silver ankle-clasps, and ankle-clasps seem to be indicated here. Even the long noses, large eyes, and neatly trimmed beards are what we might expect. These soldiers are related to those who fought hundreds of years later against the Persians, and they march with the same dancing step. In the most extraordinary way this broken vase illustrates the ancient history of Greece.

So the months passed, and of worthwhile discoveries there were only the four fragments of tombstones found on the *agora* and the warrior vase. With about 125 workmen Schliemann had worked from morning to dusk under the scorching sun. Clouds of hot dust roared across Mycenae. His eyes were inflamed, his temper was short, and he was continually fighting the officials, who were more interested, he thought, in leaving everything *in situ* than in uncovering the past.

Visitors came, but there was little to show them except

potsherds and beads and painted figurines. The Emperor of Brazil, Dom Pedro II, rode up from Corinth to examine the excavations. Schliemann was delighted to have so distinguished a visitor, and gave him a great dinner in the underground tomb called the Treasury of Atreus, which had long been known and therefore offered little prospect for excavation. Schliemann spoke of discovering treasure. He would repeat at Mycenae his famous discoveries at Troy. The Emperor smiled. He had been warned by the Greeks of Schliemann's boasts. He expressed interest in the tombstones, and was a model of politeness. Handsome, skeptical and unassuming, the Emperor astonished Schliemann by his knowledge of archeology, praised him highly, and spoke of "the invaluable contributions you are making to the understanding of ancient civilizations."

Flattered, Schliemann presented the Emperor with pieces of painted pottery; and he was a little surprised a few days after the Emperor's departure to learn that Police-captain Leonidas Leonardos, who had carefully watched over the Emperor's safety during his visit, had received the miserable sum of forty francs as an imperial gift to be distributed among the police force. The police were saying that the captain had received a thousand francs and embezzled all except forty. There was an inquiry, and the captain was dismissed from his post.

Schliemann, who knew the man well, was outraged. He telegraphed to the prime minister in Athens, without effect. Learning that Dom Pedro was in Cairo, Schliemann telegraphed the Emperor:

> When you left Nauplia, Your Majesty gave 40 francs to Police-captain Leonidas Leonardos to distribute among the police. In order to slander this worthy man, the mayor of Nauplia maintains that he received 1,000 francs from Your Majesty. Leonardos has meanwhile been dismissed from his

post, and I am having the greatest difficulty in saving him from prison. As I have known him for many years and regard him as a most honest man, I beg Your Majesty in the name of sacred truth and humanity to telegraph to me the exact amount you gave the Police-captain.

Dom Pedro was a weak man, but he could be generous on occasion. He telegraphed that he had in fact given the Police-Captain forty francs, and soon to Schliemann's delight Leonidas Leonardos was reinstated.

Summer came to an end, and the rains came beating down on the *agora*, turning the rubble into mud. The work went on. About the middle of October Schliemann was digging deep in the *agora* when he came across a tomb 20 feet long and 10 feet broad cut out of the slope of the naked rock. Robbers must have plundered the tomb, for he found only some stone slabs and a scattering of gold buttons and ivory horns, which may have been decorations for the mortuary chamber. Then he dug a little further south toward the center of the circle, and at a depth of 15 feet he reached a layer of pebbles. Below this lay three bodies thickly covered with clay and what seemed to be the ashes of a funeral pyre. Through the clay came the glint of gold.

With the treasure in sight and the government officials peering over his shoulder, Schliemann once more knew the powerful agitation which came over him when he discovered the treasure of Troy, and once more he turned to Sophia for assistance. He was too nervous and too excited to uncover the bones himself. Sophia curled down in the hollow and stripped the clay off the bodies with a small pocketknife.

There were five golden diadems with each body. Five golden crosses with the arms shaped like laurel leaves lay on one body, five on the second, and four on the third. These diadems were unlike the elaborate gold-chain diadems found at Troy; they were made from thin sheets of gold hammered with decorative circles and bosses. Where the diadems of Troy showed extreme sophistication, even though the design was simple, the Mycenaean diadems were curiously unassuming, and their simplicity was disarming, suggesting the raw nakedness of power.

Scattered about the shaft grave were small obsidian knives, fragments of painted vases, and a silver cup. Schliemann thought he saw evidence of fire and afterward spoke at considerable length of how the bodies must have been burned or roasted. He thought the pebbles at the bottom of the tomb somehow provided ventilation for the funeral pyres, and it was his belief, shared later by Dörpfeld, that it was the Mycenaean custom to roast the flesh off the bones. He could make out the shapes of the skeletons, but they had suffered from moisture and soon crumbled. The treasure of Mycenae now consisted of fifteen diadems and fourteen golden crosses.

Schliemann now decided to explore the side of the grave-circle furthest away from the Lion Gate. At a depth of 9 feet he found some skeletons and near them were obsidian knives, but there was no treasure. He was a little puzzled, but went on digging. If the first grave was disappointing, and the second gave up only a handful of treasure, the third treasure which he came upon after digging only a little way below the skeletons showed a dazzling and unexpected richness of ornament. Here was God's plenty, the whole chamber crammed with objects of gold which shone with a reddish luster.

By this time most of the workmen had been sent away, and a ring of soldiers guarded the treasure chambers. Once more Sophia curled herself among the skeletons and the gold, carefully removing the soil which still covered the royal tombs. She worked patiently and slowly, afraid of destroying the delicately chased patterns on the thin sheets of gold. As in the second grave there were three bodies; one of them wore a gold crown with more than thirty gold leaves surmounting it. These leaves were lightly fixed to the crown, and they must have trembled and shimmered when the king wore it. There were eight more diadems, and six more crosses of gold, some of them double crosses and very ornate. There were gold necklaces and goblets and vases and wine jars, some with golden lids attached by fine gold wires. There was a golden flower on a silver stalk. There were shining spheres of rock crystal which may have been the pommels of royal swords.

But the most surprising discovery was an enormous number of stamped golden disks—he counted over seven hundred of them in this tomb-chamber alone. Some were shaped like leaves, others like butterflies, octopuses, stars, and sunflowers, and there were some with purely geometrical designs. Schliemann came to the conclusion that they were miniature copies of shields, but it is more likely that they were symbols of the enduring life which the dead were expected to lead throughout their underground existence.

Together with the gold disks were a large number of gold plaques, rarely more than an inch across and not unlike the miniature gold plaques which have been found during excavations in Persia dating from the time of Cyrus and Xerxes. With extraordinary liveliness the artist has modeled a strip of gold foil into the shape of lions, griffins, cuttlefish, deer, eagles, and swans. These, too, were perhaps ornaments sewed onto the robes of the dead.

Schliemann thought he had found in the third grave three skeletons of women, and he pointed to the smallness of the bones and of the teeth, but it is just as likely that they were men, a king and two princes arrayed in their panoply.

A dagger was found among the bones; and two scepters of silver plated with gold.

With the third grave opened, Schliemann set about excavating the rest of the *agora*. Wondering where to dig next, he remembered being struck by the appearance of the dark soil to the west of the third grave. The soil was almost black, markedly different from the soil elsewhere in the *agora*. He dug down to a depth of 15 feet, but found only potsherds. Nine feet further down he discovered what he thought to be a circular altar 4 feet high with a round opening, reminiscent of a well. He felt sure it was an altar raised in honor of the dead heroes who must be buried below, and perhaps gifts were poured through this altar for the dead. The royal graves of Sumeria have clay funnels through which offerings are poured, but they had not been excavated in Schliemann's time and as usual he was forced to rely on his own guesses. The altar still puzzles scholars, but Schliemann's original guess was right. He dug a further 3 feet below the altar and found another tomb filled with treasure. There were five bodies smothered in gold and jewels. Three of them wore masks of gold, and near the head of the fourth lay a strange twisted mask in the shape of a lion's head, which at first Schliemann thought to be a helmet.

Of these four masks one was so crumpled that it had almost lost the shape of human features. By gazing at it for some minutes, Schliemann thought he could make out a youthful face with a high forehead, a long Greek nose, and a small mouth with thin lips. This mask possesses no character. But two of these golden masks are the glory of the fourth grave. They possess power and authority, and a terrible beauty. Death is marked on them, but there is no hint of repose in those awesome features. In character they are completely unlike the serene masks painted on wood which appear on the coffins of the Egyptian pharaohs, and evidently they serve a different purpose. The artist has not attempted to depict them as they were in life, for they wear the unmistakable signs of death. Schliemann thought they were portraits. "There cannot be the slightest doubt that every one of them represents the likeness of the deceased," he wrote. "Had it not been so, all the masks would have represented the same ideal type."

But if they are portraits they are so simplified that they have almost entirely lost those features by which they would be recognized in life. They are reduced almost to abstractions. In one the hollowness of death is conveyed by two bulbous eyes which appear to be bursting out of the face, and in the other the heavily ridged forehead and the tightness of the compressed lips suggest the agony of death. Like the gold masks of Peru, which are extraordinarily similar, they represent not so much portraits of dead men as portraits of death, sculptured and molded by an artist who has transferred to a thin sheet of gold his own terror before the sight of a decaying corpse. An unearthly beauty shines through the masks. We see these kings or princes as they were many hours after their deaths, through the eyes of an artist who made no attempt to reveal them exactly as they were, for otherwise he would have shown them in greater detail and with a more human aspect. Almost they are godlike. It seems to have been the artist's intention to suggest the divinity in the dead rulers, who carried into the grave the mysterious power they exercised during their lives. These masks can be interpreted as portraits of kings at the moment of dissolution when they became gods.

One looks at these masks with awe and a sense of failure. All through Western history artists have grappled with death and attempted to depict it, but rarely with the success of these unknown artists at Mycenae. Here, at the very beginning of our civilization, death is depicted fearlessly, with immense power and simplicity.

Yet no one knows the precise purpose served by these masks. Neither Homer nor any other Greek writer refers to death masks of any kind. We know that the masks were wrapped round the faces of the dead, and perforations near the flattened ears show how they were held in place by means of threads. Unfortunately the skulls of the five bodies were in such a state of decomposition that none of them could be saved, and we do not know their exact position when they were found. We have the masks; we have all the jewelry scattered around the bodies; but we know too little about archaic Greece to be able to envisage the scene when the bodies were laid in their rock tombs.

When Schliemann first discovered the lion mask, it was flat and broken, and some small pieces appeared to be missing. Assuming it was a helmet, he laid it aside. Later he examined it more closely, made out the lion's eyes, ears, and muzzle, and pronounced that it was a mask and therefore worn over the face. Later kings wore lion's heads as helmets with the muzzles resting on their foreheads, as we see on the coins of Alexander the Great. It is possible that the lion mask was a helmet after all.

Even Schliemann was baffled by the wealth of treasure in the fourth grave. The masks formed only a small part of the treasure. Two of the bodies wore golden breastplates, another wore a crown with dancing leaves, and there were eleven massive gold goblets. One of these had two delicate doves chased on the handles, exactly like Nestor's gold wine cup in the *Iliad*, which was "studded with gold pins and decorated with two golden doves." There were ornamental golden belts and ribbons, a gold garter, a gold tiara, golden brooches, and golden pins. There were minute double-headed battle-axes in gold less than an inch across. There were 12 enormous buttons covered with gold plate, and more than 400 round pieces of gold which may have been coins, and more than 150 gold disks. There was a lively cuttlefish in gold. There were 10 golden plates which may have served as sword handles. There were copper cauldrons, and bronze swords like rapiers, very narrow. There was a cow's head of silver with flaring horns of gold which must have been, like so many other things found in the tomb, a sacred emblem of the tribe. Amid this vast heap of gold the most surprising discovery was a large number of oyster shells, and some oysters which had never been opened.

The fourth shaft grave at Mycenae contained more treasure than he had discovered at Troy, but Schliemann was in no mood to stop. While he was still excavating this tomb, he began to dig directly north of it. Here he found his fifth and last grave, which gave every evidence of having been rifled: there was only one body in it, which quickly crumbled to powder. In the grave he found a gold diadem, a gold drinking-cup, a green vase and a few terracotta fragments.

Work on the first grave had stopped when the grave filled with mud. After weeks of bright weather the mud had dried, and he spent his last days at Mycenae carefully reexamining the first tomb. He had found it empty. By digging further he found three bodies squeezed within the inner walls. They had evidently been pushed away to make room for other bodies, but all traces of these were lost. With the bodies he found a small remnant of treasure. Two wore gold masks, and one of them still had flesh adhering to the skull. Squashed flat by the weight of debris, and without a nose, it possessed recognizable features, and Schliemann was excited beyond measure because he thought he recognized the face of Agamemnon.

It was the round face of a man about thirty-five years old, who retained all his teeth in a perfect state of preservation. He wore a large gold breastplate, and golden leaves distributed over his forehead, chest, and thighs. A flattened mask lay over the face. Schliemann raised the mask to his lips and kissed it. Then he sent off a telegram to the minister in Athens:

> In last tomb three bodies one without ornament have telegraphed Nauplia for painter to preserve features dead man with round face resembling picture of Agamemnon I formed long ago.

From all over the plain of Argos people came to view the body of an ancient hero whose face was so miraculously preserved. A painter was summoned from Nauplia to sketch it, and for two days Schliemann watched over it in a fever of anxiety, afraid lest the face would crumble into powder before it could be embalmed. Then a druggist from Argos arrived on the scene. He poured a solution over it, which rendered it hard, and shortly afterward the body was taken in triumph to Athens.

The treasure found in the first tomb could not compare with the great heaps of massive gold found in the fourth; only a small scattering had been left there by the grave-robbers. But there were gold cups and breastplates and bronze swords with golden handles—altogether Schliemann counted eighty swords, most of them wafer-thin. There were twelve gold plaques, some of them representing stags being pursued by lions. There was a battle-ax and a gold sword tassel, and long ribbons of gold were found laced over the body of one of the heroes. But the most glorious discovery was a mask even more beautiful than those he had discovered previously.

This last mask, almost the last thing Schliemann discovered at Mycenae, possesses a perfection lacking in the others. They spoke of death powerfully and were of the earth, earthy; this one speaks with a pure and serene majesty, and with no less power. Once again we are confronted not with a portrait but with an image or *ikon* of death: no human face peers up at us. Where the other masks show the heroes at the moment of dissolution, this mask shows the hero at the moment after he has become a god. There is no trace of earth's fevers, only of benignity. The large eyes are closed, the eyelids clearly marked, and the thin lips are pursed in a mysterious smile. There is a hint of a beard, and the eyebrows are heavily incised and curl upward in imitation of the flaring mustaches; but the total effect of eyebrows and mustaches and smile is to give a curious depth to the face, as though it were seen immensely magnified at the end of a long corridor, beckoning. It is a face to be compared with the great mosaics of Christ at Daphne, Cefalù, and Palermo, and belongs among the most superb achievements of ancient art.

The diadems of Troy, the crowns of Mycenae, and all the heaps of massive gold treasure speak of a people still rude and barbarous. The Warrior Vase tells us how they went to war. The gold trinkets found in the tombs tell us how they decorated themselves on exalted occasions. But only this mask tells us of the deep reverence they paid to their gods.

Now the work was done, and as Schliemann gazed around the *agora* which resembled a crumbled honeycomb after so many shafts had been dug into it, he expected to find no more treasures. He had found five royal graves and thought he had looked on the faces of Agamemnon, Clytemnestra, and the others who had taken part in that heroic tragedy. One day toward the end of November he sent off a telegram to the King of the Hellenes:

With extreme joy I announce to Your Majesty that I have discovered the tombs which tradition, echoed by Pausanias, has designated as the sepulchres of Agamemnon, Cassandra, Eurymedon and all their companions who were killed while partaking of a meal with Clytemnestra and her lover Aegisthus. They were surrounded with a double circle of stone slabs, which would not have been erected unless they were great personages. In the tombs I found immense treasures of the most ancient objects of pure gold.

These treasures alone will fill a great museum, the most wonderful in the world, and for centuries to come thousands of foreigners will flock to Greece to see them. I work only for the pure love of science, and accordingly I have no claim on these treasures. I give them intact and with a lively enthusiasm to Greece. God grant that these treasures may become the cornerstone of an immense national wealth.

He was disappointed with the reply written by the King's secretary. It was a very brief reply. He was thanked for his important discoveries, his zeal, and his love for science. The King added the pious hope that further excavations would be crowned with a similar success.

For the first time Schliemann returned from his excavations empty-handed. Everything he discovered in Mycenae became the property of the Greek government. The hated Stamatakes, so long a thorn in his side, was already making announcements about the discoveries. In horror Schliemann dispatched a telegram to the government: "Forbid publication by Stamatakes. Not the Government, but I, have the right."

Once more he was pitting himself against governments. The town of Nauplia intervened in the dispute with the demand that all the treasure should be housed there—it would be good for the town, and was not Nauplia the logical proprietor? Schliemann raged in his tent. He wrote off telegrams to all the learned societies and contemplated the huge collection of photographs he had assembled during the excavations and wrote up his notes and diaries. As usual the Germans were inclined to laugh at his claims, the French showed little interest, and only the English shared his enthusiasm.

He spent the winter in Athens. One day in January he sent one of the assistants he had employed at Mycenae to make a detailed drawing of the *agora* for his records. This assistant, Vasilios Drosinos, was a young engineer who had worked with him in the tomb-chambers. Recognizing near a partly excavated house south of the *agora* some roughly carved stones which resembled the stones in the tomb-chamber, Drosinos discussed the matter with Stamatakes, who had returned to Mycenae that day. A workman with a pickax was brought to the spot. With the first or second blow of the ax a gold cup came to light, and in less than half an hour there was a small treasure consisting of four gold cups, all of them with delicate dogs' head handles, one plain undecorated cup, a number of rings fashioned out of gold wire, and two gold signets. One of these signets showed some animal heads and ears of corn, all jumbled together, and no one has ever been able to understand what it was intended to convey. The other signet was a masterpiece.

We know it now as the Signet of the Mother Goddess, and like the gold mask found in the first tomb it hints at an unexpected depth of religious feeling among the Mycenaeans. A ceremony is being performed, the simplest of all ceremonies—an offering to the goddess. There are no temples, no altars, no veils, no rituals. In silence they make their offerings, and the artist seems to have caught the actors in the ceremony at a moment which is at once very casual and filled with significance.

The goddess sits beneath the sacred tree with flowers in

her hair and more flowers in her hands, receiving a tribute of flowers from two women of noble aspect, who may be priestesses. One of the handmaidens of the goddess stands before her, introducing these worshipers, while another handmaiden is climbing a small cairn of stones, plucking the sacred fruit from the tree and offering it to her divine mistress. All wear the flounced richly embroidered double-skirts which were characteristic of Mycenaean culture during the heroic age. Like the Mother Goddess they are all bare-breasted, and wear flowers and ornaments in their hair.

Between the first of the worshipers and the goddess stand two double axes, the smaller superimposed upon the other; these axes perhaps represent earthly and spiritual power. And beyond this strange emblem of power there floats a presiding genius who is helmeted and holds a spear and hides behind a shield shaped like a figure "8"—the first representation of an armed goddess known to us. Above this scene the sun shines in full splendor beside the crescent moon: it is at once noonday and the depth of night.

But what is most remarkable about the signet is the quiet composure and serenity of these people partaking in the offering. Such a signet could not have been carved except at a time of great self-assurance. The signet is extremely small, hardly more than an inch across, but the artist has poured into it the accumulated knowledge of centuries of religious meditation. The power of the heavens flows down in rings of light, and power wells up from the goddess as she reposes in the sacred grove. In the attitudes of the priest-esses there is no humility; they come to her as though by right, gravely, making their offerings out of affection for the goddess, towering over her, with none of the servitude which can be seen in the Egyptian paintings showing the offerings to the gods. A very human dignity informs them. Bathed in the light of the sun and moon, they stand and move according to their own volition.

We cannot hope to understand the full meaning of the signet. We do not know, for example, what meaning can be attached to the six strange objects which decorate the side facing the tree. They may be golden masks, skulls, helmets, sacred flowers, or they may simply be decorations to balance the tree with its heavy fruit. No one knows what kind of tree is being represented. Schliemann, study-ing the signet from photographs he obtained with difficulty from Stamatakes, pronounced that they were pineapples or perhaps breadfruit, such as he had seen in Central Amer-ica. He thought the women wore vizors, and was puzzled by their masculine features; and he noted that the curved parallel bands of their skirts mirrored the crescent shapes which are to be seen everywhere in the signet. For some reason he thought that the waving lines beneath the sun and moon represented the sea, though it is more likely that they represent rings of heavenly light or the Milky Way.

In the *Iliad* Homer describes how Hephaestus made for Achilles a great shield with five panels, the first representing "the earth, the sky and the sea, the indefatigable sun, the moon at the full and all the constellations," and when Schliemann first saw the signet with Sophia at his side, he exclaimed: "It must have been seen by Homer when he described all the wonders which Hephaestus wrought on the shield of Achilles." It was one of his greater griefs that he had not discovered the signet, but he took comfort in the thought that it might have lain undiscovered if he had not sent his surveyor to Mycenae.

The work at Mycenae was over. Schliemann never returned there, feeling that his work was done. He wrote a book about his finds in eight weeks, and then set about translating it into French and English; and then he wrote to Gladstone, begging for the honor of an introduction to the work from the Grand Old Man of English politics. Gladstone, an excellent Homeric scholar, was reluctant to undertake such a task, fearing that his commendation would be misinterpreted. During the summer Schliemann visited London, bringing with him the treasure of Troy, which was exhibited in the South Kensington Museum. Gladstone was not quite convinced that this was the treasure of Troy, but he was impressed by Schliemann's learning and finally wrote a rambling introduction which covers nearly forty pages.

Gladstone was particularly struck by the Signet of the Mother Goddess and debated with himself whether the six strange objects on the side were stars or lions' heads, and suggested that the waving band below the sun and moon represented mother-earth, "with its uneven surface of land and its rippling sea." He was inclined to believe that the body found in the first grave belonged to Agamemnon. The fact that the features had been preserved suggested that the body had been embalmed, and this would only apply to a very eminent personage. The *Iliad* relates that Agamemnon was always accompanied by two priestly heralds, and the heralds were no doubt the two other bodies found in the tomb.

Schliemann gloried in the attentions he received in London. He dined with Gladstone, and sent off a flood of telegrams to Sophia, who was ill in Athens. He could never tolerate her absence for long, and at last when the members of the Royal Archeological Society asked her to address them she came post-haste from Athens and stood beside her husband on the platform, telling the story of how for twenty-five days she had knelt among the tombs, carefully scraping off thin layers of clay from the bodies of the ancient kings and queens of Mycenae. She spoke very simply in English, and received an ovation. Schliemann smiled approvingly. He had written her speech, and was delighted because she recited it without faltering, and still more delighted because she was carrying his son, born later that year. Long ago he had chosen the name he would give to his son—Agamemnon.

Fame exacts its penalties, and not the least of them is the temptation to rest on one's laurels. For eighteen months Schliemann basked in his growing fame, and it was not until the summer of 1878 that he put a spade into the earth again.

Still looking for treasure, he thought he might find it in Ithaca in the great palace of Odysseus. He spent two weeks in July excavating among the immense walls at the top of Mount Aetios, but though he found the ruins of 190 houses, he found little else of value, and abandoned the excavations.

Troy summoned him—Troy where he had encountered so many defeats from the Turkish government, and so much success. Once again he was employing all his resources to obtain a *firman*. This time he was not alone, for Gladstone was sympathetic to renewed excavations at Troy and the full weight of his influence was felt in Constantinople, where Austen Layard, the discoverer of Nineveh, had become British Ambassador. The Turks granted a *firman*, but took care to send a special commissioner and ten policemen to Hissarlik to superintend the excavations.

It was Schliemann's sixth journey to Hissarlik. He began work in September, and for nearly two months nothing of value was discovered. But his luck was holding. On October 21, 1878, in the presence of some officers from a British warship, he discovered, northeast of the Palace of Priam, not far from the place where he had found the first Trojan treasure, a small hoard consisting of 20 gold earrings, a number of gold spiral rings, 2 heavy bracelets of electrum, 11 silver earrings, and 158 silver rings and a large number of gold beads. A few days later he found a still smaller treasure consisting of gold bars and pellets of gold, a gold bracelet and a silver dagger. Work stopped on November 26. This time Schliemann was allowed to keep only a third of the treasure he found; the rest went to the Imperial Museum in Constantinople.

His luck, which had been holding so well, lasted into the following spring, when digging was resumed with the assistance of Emile Burnouf and Rudolf Virchow. Schliemann arrived in Troy in February. His plan was to uncover the town wall of Troy and to make a complete map of Homeric Troy. In April he discovered two small pockets of treasure consisting of gold disks, chains, earrings, and bracelets. He never found any more treasure again. Homer had mentioned that there were three towns rich in gold—Troy, Mycenae, and Orchomenos, once a great city in Boeotia. The following year Schliemann hoped to crown his achievements with the gold treasure of Orchomenos, but though he excavated the beehive tombs and mapped the walls of the ancient city, the results were disappointing.

The years of luck were over. For the last ten years of his life he was to be a wanderer on the face of the earth, always hoping to come upon traces of gold, searching for it relentlessly, as though driven by some inner force, and never finding it. The old magic had gone. He had the eagerness of a child and the passion of an adolescent, but his skin was leathery and he was growing old. He must find roots somewhere, and so at last, having made his peace with Athens, he decided to build a house worthy of himself in the heart of the city.

Characteristically, he designed the house himself on the model of the palaces he had uncovered in Troy and Mycenae. He called it *Iliou Melathron*, or "the palace of Troy." It stands on the Boulevard de l'Université at the foot of Mount Lycabettus, overlooking the royal stables. It is a huge house, cold and chilling, with marble steps and mosaic floors on which are depicted the gold cups and vases he discovered at Troy. Along the walls run friezes with classical landscapes and paintings of the Greek heroes with appropriate Homeric quotations.

On the lower floors he displayed his treasure. Upstairs was his private study, with the notice on the door: "All who do not study geometry, remain outside." The study was crammed with books. Here were some of the more precious objects he had gathered. On the walls were fading views of New York and Indianapolis, two cities which he especially admired. For whole days he would sit there in a heavily upholstered armchair studying the Greek classics, while the smaller chair beside him was piled high with the stock exchange lists which came every morning from Paris, London, and Berlin. Telegraph forms were always at hand. He was still a businessman, and some hours every day had to be spent on superintending his financial dealings which extended over the whole world.

In his house he behaved as tyrannically as any Homeric prince. His word was law. All messages were sent to him in classical Greek, and Greek was the language employed exclusively at table. He renamed all his servants. The porter was Bellerophon, the footman Telamon, Andromache's governess was Danaë, Agamemnon's nurse was Polyxena, and the old gardener was called Calchas, after the soothsayer whose curses open the *Iliad*. Because the ancient Greeks employed little furniture, he did the same; and there were only a few chairs and sofas tucked away in the corners of the bare, draughty rooms. He refused to have curtains, because it was unthinkable that Achilles would ever stay in a curtained house. The ruins of Pompeii had always had a peculiar fascination for him, and so in this great house patterned on the palaces of ancient Greece, he built a ballroom patterned on the villas of ancient Pompeii, with a delicate blue and white frieze of putti encircling the wall. The putti were modeled on people he had known and encountered in his travels. Among them was a portrait of Schliemann in horn-rimmed spectacles.

On the flat roof of the house, facing the four corners of the sky, were twenty-four marble gods. Zeus, Aphrodite, Apollo, Athena, and all the other gods stood there, protecting and encouraging him during the declining years of his life.

The Heroes

▱▱▱▱▱▱▱▱▱▱▱▱

During the last thirty-four years of his life, Schliemann read the *Iliad* avidly. It was his bible, the book he consulted at all hours of the day, the fountainhead of nearly all the thoughts that ever occurred to him, and no single part of it was to be preferred to any other. In his library were all the available editions, many in folio and bound in heavy morocco, but there were also cheap paper-bound Tauchnitz editions which he carried on his travels and annotated heavily. Once when a correspondent wrote that he found the *Iliad* full of difficulties, Schliemann replied that on the contrary he found it as clear and pellucid as the Castalian springs, there were simply no difficulties, and anyone in his right mind could read it as he reads a modern novel. For

Schliemann both the *Iliad* and the *Odyssey* were holy writ, blessed by the gods, written with a nobility and elegance almost beyond the range of human accomplishment. In these books, if a man sat down to read them attentively, he would find all the fruitfulness and joy, and all the tragedy of man displayed. Here was the perfect story told by the perfect poet, and beyond this it was unnecessary to go.

More than once Schliemann protested that it was impossible to make any choice between the parts of the *Iliad*. On one occasion, however, he broke his own rule. He said the most splendid passage of all is in the third book: the account of Helen arising from her embroidery—she had been weaving a kind of tapestry showing the Trojans and Achaeans at one anothers' throats—and making her way to the Scaean Gate, where on one of the gate-towers overlooking the plain Priam and the elders of the city have congregated "like cicadas perched on trees chirping merrily."

News has come that there will be no more war. Instead Menelaus and Paris, her husband and her abductor, will fight a duel, and her fate will be determined by the issue of the duel. Veiled in white, accompanied by her handmaidens, she approaches the tower. The elders lower their voices as they see her coming, astonished by her beauty, and happy that a solution to the long conflict is in sight. Priam beckons her to his side, points to the enemy, and asks: "Who is that man, taller by a head than the rest, with a majestic air about him?"

She answers that it is Agamemnon, her husband's elder brother. Then Priam points to a smaller deep-chested man, who has left his armor lying on the ground, and she answers: "That is Odysseus." There is a third man, eminently tall and handsome, and she says: "That is Ajax." Then she recognizes Idomeneus, the King of Crete, the gentlest of Agamemnon's captains, but she cannot see either

Castor or Polydeuces, her two brothers, one a famous horse-tamer, the other a renowned boxer. She gazes after them, and in her silence there is all the desolation of grief, for she knows nothing of what has happened to them but suspects the worst; and Homer comments:

> The fruitful earth had laid them already on her lap,
> Far away in Lacedaemon, the land they loved.

There are seven or eight other passages in Homer where grief enters just as nakedly. Grief—grief over the lot of man—is the major theme of the story. At the very beginning Homer proclaims that his subject is the wrath of Achilles, the havoc he will create, leading to the deaths of so many good men. An explosive death-dealing force is let loose, and we watch with bated breath as he destroys everything in his path, quarrels with everyone around him, and never rests until he has not only destroyed his appointed enemy but outraged the corpse of Hector and mangled it beyond recognition, so that at last when he surrenders the body to King Priam, there is nothing human or godlike left in the appearance of the young hero—Hector is no more than a squashed fly.

Achilles is the hero, but he is a hero in love with death; and those who listened to the story were a people in love with life. They marveled at the destructiveness of the gods, who had made the earth so beautiful and filled it with so much tragic irony. The flashing armor, the bold glances, the supple bodies of men, the dancing and the gold—all end in tears. In a sense, the *Iliad* is no more than a long litany on the tragic deaths of young heroes.

All through the *Iliad* there rings the cry of suffering. Why must these things happen? Why are the Greeks determined to destroy? What pleasure do they derive from it? From the beginning we know that Hector must be dragged by the heels around the walls of Troy, and that Achilles will triumph, and that Helen in her white and shining robes will pass wraith-like through the story, always beautiful and unattainable, a ghost who lives in horror of her own beauty. For a ghost men waged this war, and for a ghost they perish. Men must die, women must weep, blood must be spilled, and it is all in vain. A grim irrational fate broods over everything.

That life was vain and therefore senseless was something Homer knew only too well. Homer knew fighting. He did not fight in the Trojan wars, but he knew the excitement of small skirmishes and what bodies looked like when they lay on the ground. He knew poverty and starvation, for otherwise he would not have taken such enjoyment in describing banquets and the embroidered raiments of heroic men. Tradition says he was blind, and this accords with his constant reference to the brightness of things; and that he was an islander from one of the islands of the Ægean, and this accords with his curious detachment, for his sympathies are neither with the Greeks nor with the Trojans, but only with the individual human beings who are caught up in the senseless war.

Three figures stand out in massive grandeur: the turbulent Achilles, the cunning Odysseus who assumes many of the characteristics of Achilles in the last terrible chapters of the *Odyssey*, and the doomed Hector, who remains the private hero of the epic, as Achilles is the public hero. Nearly all the tender and intimate passages concern Hector. Almost he is Hamlet. He is the man caught in the web, waiting impatiently for his own doom, dissembling, hoping for a way of escape, falling into dreams and out of them, remembering his childhood, more aware than anyone else of the evanescence of life and the terrible responsibilities he carries. He is speaking to his wife on the eve of a disastrous battle:

The day will come, my soul knows it is coming,
When our holy Troy will go down into ruins,
Troy and the brave King and the King's people with him.
And I am not moved so much by the grief of the Trojans—
Grief will come—Hecuba's grief, and the grief of my father,
The grief of so many good men, lying
In the bloody dust under the feet of our enemies.
I think of my death, and then your grief hurts me:
And I am grieved at the thought of you being carried away
      weeping
By the bronze-coated enemy into certain slavery.
They will set you to work over somebody's loom in Argos
Or carrying a pitcher in a remote village somewhere,
And always against your will, because you're a captive.
Seeing you weeping, they will say:
"Look, the wife of Hector, the great captain
Of the horsemen of Troy, in the days when they fought for
      their city."
Hearing them, your grief will become greater,
For having no man like me to free you from slavery.
O let me be dead and let the earth be heaped over me
Before I hear you weeping or how you were enslaved.

So he spoke, the shining one, and stretched his arms to his
      son,
But the boy cried out to his nurse with the beautiful girdle—
Frightened by the glint of steel and the horsehair crest of
      the helmet.
Suddenly both the father and mother were laughing,
And the shining Hector put his helmet away,
Set it shimmering on the ground, and threw out his hands
To his beloved son, kissing him and rocking him in his arms.

No one could have written such scenes of intolerable poignancy without being overwhelmed with affection for the character he had created. There is a sense in which the *Iliad* is Hector's *apologia*. He speaks throughout, and it is his voice, now shouting defiance, now trembling with anger, now calm and composed, which speaks most distinctly. "These things happened," he says. "This doom was brought on us. We fought back, and we extracted from every passing moment the little joy that was left to us." It is a curiously modern answer, and as we read Homer, we find ourselves continually confronting a curiously modern world.

We know Achilles only too well. He represents the violently anarchic monster in the human soul. He kills for the pure joy of killing, contemptuous of danger, certain only of the blessedness of destruction. To say he is ruthless and vengeful is to underestimate his terrible sobriety. He kills aimlessly, as huntsmen kill. He is without any sense of guilt, and cares nothing for the old or the very young. When he falls upon the child Lycaon, shouting: "Death to all!" and makes fun of the child who is pleading for his life, he is just as amused as when he fights with Hector, knowing that the gods will protect his own life. When Odysseus says to Eumaeus in the *Odyssey:* "My delight was in ships, fighting, javelins and arrows—things that make men shudder to think about," we hear once again the authentic voice of Achilles. The nihilist asks for no pardon. He despises the world, and is content to surrender all his privileges for the pleasure of destroying the world. Achilles did not take part in the Trojan war to rescue Helen: he went because he wanted to kill and because he wanted to see all Troy reduced to ashes and flame.

As we know Achilles, so we know Odysseus, "the cunning artificer," the man who cares very little for the gods, but relies on his own rude strength. He is the Good Soldier

Schweik elevated to general's rank, an excellent soldier, and the rankest amateur as a sailor, for how otherwise would he have taken so long to make the comparatively short journey from the Dardanelles to Ithaca?

Best of all do we know Hector. He is the disenchanted one, for whom no magic wand is ever waved, Hamlet and the Prince d'Aquitaine, the last of his race. Hector wears the face of our own time. He defies augury. He will do everything humanly possible to escape his fate, but he knows that it is inescapable. He will behave at all times with exquisite nobility, but he knows that honor will never win any wars. As Homer says, he has the look of nightfall on his face. "None but the gods could meet and hold him as he sprang through the gate." So in the end he is stabbed in the throat, stripped of his armor, and dragged through the dust, because the gods have aided his enemy and forsaken him, and all this was known to him from the very beginning.

In every age men have read Homer, but never has he been read so widely or attentively as in the present age; and for good reason. He holds the mirror up to nature. The world he describes is the world of today, for little has changed in the thirty centuries since the burning of Troy. The fires burn; the besieged make their desperate sorties; everywhere the cries of the doomed can be heard. We are all Trojans; and Homer, the blind wanderer among ancient islands, describes our present plight with excessive brightness. It is not that he was a prophet: it is simply that no one else has ever described the human condition with such starkness and majesty.

When Schliemann went in search of Troy, he was searching for the fountainhead of Western civilization. He, too, possessed the modern temper. Restless, feverish, moving among shadows, he possessed many of the vices of the Victorians, but he also possessed to a quite extraordinary degree the determination to break through the trappings of the cluttered civilization which surrounded him. Because he had no roots, he must search for roots even in the most ancient past, in places where there are no signposts and men must walk warily.

He had a typically modern irreverence toward scholars who are content to weave their theories without observing the evidence. He must find the evidence and bring it to light and prove incontestably that Homer existed and wrote about battles still warm in the memories of men. When he went beyond this and attempted to prove that he had looked upon the face of Agamemnon dead and hung Helen's diadem on his wife's forehead, he was greeted with derisive laughter, but it is at least possible that his claim was justified. His greatest merit was that he clothed the more shadowy statements of Homer in flesh and gave them more substance than they ever possessed before. He discovered no writing except a few scratched fragments in Troy, but all his discoveries were in the nature of a Homeric poem suddenly unearthed and laid before an unbelieving world. He found the fountainhead, and beyond this there was no need to go.

To this day we do not know what happened at Troy, and why the battle was fought. We do not know whether Homer ever visited the Troad, but the story of the fall of Troy comes to us with so much authentic detail that it is no longer possible to doubt the essential outline. Homer reshaped his heroes, magnifying and distorting them for his own purposes, as a poet will. His own sympathies were deeply involved in his portrait of Hector. He believed that the war was fought over the abduction of Helen by Paris, and the modern scholars who assert that it must have been fought for the control of the Dardanelles forget that wars often start senselessly for causes remote from economics.

Herodotus provides an ironic commentary to the Homeric story. Egyptian priests told him that the war was completely senseless, for neither Helen nor Paris were in Troy when the Greeks attacked—they had escaped to Memphis, the capital of Egypt, where they were arrested by orders of Pharaoh. Paris was interrogated and asked to explain the presence of the beautiful Helen by his side. His explanation failed to satisfy Pharaoh and he was therefore banished from the country. Shortly afterward Menelaus, Helen's lawful husband, came to Memphis, claimed her, and returned with her to Greece.

Here is Herodotus' account of the mysterious origin of the war:

> I asked the priests whether there was any truth in the Greek story of what happened at Troy, and in reply they gave me some information which (they said) came directly from the lips of Menelaus. According to the priests the Greeks sent a great force in support of Menelaus' cause when they learned of the abduction of Helen. As soon as they landed and established themselves on Trojan soil, they sent ambassadors—Menelaus was one of them—to the city. When they were received within the walls, they demanded the restoration of Helen together with the treasure which Paris had stolen, and they asked too for an indemnity. The Trojans answered that neither Helen nor the treasure were in their possession: she had fled to Egypt, where she was being detained by the Egyptian King. It was the greatest injustice that they should be punished for something over which they had no control.
>
> The Trojans always held fast to this answer, and they were always prepared to swear on oath that this is exactly what happened.
>
> The Greeks however regarded this as a perfectly frivolous answer. They laid siege to the city, and continued to fight

until it fell; but no trace of Helen was found, and in defeat the Trojans told the same story they had told at the beginning. When the Greeks at last realized that the story was true, they sent Menelaus to Proteus (the Pharaoh) in Egypt. He sailed along the river to Memphis, and after he had given a true account of what happened, he was most hospitably entertained and Helen was restored to him with all his other possessions. Helen was none the worse for her adventures.

Though Menelaus received generous treatment at the hands of the Egyptians, he himself proved no friend of Egypt. When about to leave the country, he was delayed by contrary winds for many weeks. To change the course of the winds, he seized two young Egyptian children and sacrificed them to the gods. When this terrible crime became known, the friendship of the Egyptians was turned to hatred. Menelaus was pursued, but succeeded in escaping with his ships to Libya. What happened to him afterwards none of the Egyptians could say.

Such was Herodotus' account of a Trojan war fought over shadows, and it is not altogether unsupported by some strange references in the Homeric poems to a journey by Paris to Sidon in Phoenicia and another by Menelaus to Egypt. With all his admiration for Homer, Herodotus found it difficult to believe that Priam was mad enough to sacrifice Troy and all the Trojans simply in order that Paris might possess Helen. "I do not believe," he wrote, "that even if Priam himself had been married to her, he would have failed to surrender her to bring this succession of calamities to an end." No one, not even Herodotus, knew what had happened. Only one thing is certain: it was a war so senseless that it beggars the imagination, and at the same time it was no more senseless than any other war.

But while we can never be certain about the causes of the Trojan War, we know a great deal about the men who fought in it. No Trojan graveyards have been found;

and the graves of Mycenae belong to a time before the war was fought. But we know those soldiers well: Homer and the evidence of the excavations speak with the same voice. There was little change between the time of the unknown kings found at Mycenae and the time of the Trojan War: the appearances of people, their social customs, their way of fighting and tilling the soil and worshiping their gods. We know what they wore and how they decorated themselves, and what they ate. If we saw them walking towards us across a field, we would recognize them instantly.

They wore their hair long, and bound it with gold and silver threads. In summer the men wore sleeved cloaks reaching to the knees; in winter they wore great capes, and these capes also served as bed-coverings. They delighted in ornamental belts, earrings, necklaces, jeweled diadems, and ribbons; they wore gloves and furs. Priestesses and rich women were attired in long embroidered skirts with panels of various colors, and sometimes the skirts were divided, as we see them on the Signet of the Great Mother or in the remnants of a frieze found in Tiryns. Warriors wore helmets made of rings of boars' tusks, like the helmet Meriones lent to Odysseus, and the curved tusks found in Mycenaean graves correspond perfectly to the description given by Homer. Everything we know about their skill in ornament suggests an extreme sophistication.

They had chairs and tables, but no plates; food was eaten off the table, which was afterward washed with sponges. They ate meat: mutton, goat's flesh, pork, and more rarely beef. These animals were domesticated. Fowl were kept in their farmyards, and geese wandered in and out of their houses. Game included deer, wild boar, wild goats, rabbits, and wolves. They ate fish, and especially delighted in oysters. They grew wheat, barley, millet, beans, peas, and lentils, and cultivated vines and olive trees. They sweetened their wine with honey, and enjoyed the fruit of their orchards; in the garden of Alcinoüs there were pears, apples, figs, and pomegranates. Children ate meat, marrow, relishes, fat, and wine, but there seems to have been no milk. They regarded cheese as a common dish enjoyed by even the poorest. There were no cats—the cat appeared in Greece about the sixth century B.C.—but they had hunting dogs and watchdogs.

It was a simple and primitive society, organized around the sacred persons of their kings. There was almost no industrial organization, and no coinage. Each community was fiercely proud and hostile to all other communities, yet capable at times of forming leagues of friendship and peace with them. As Walter Leaf observed long ago, "their organizations were not yet strong enough to hold in subjection the grown bodies of men." Of all people living today they resembled most the Balinese, those proud and vivid people whose lives are spent in unremitting toil, in harmony with the gods and the seasons, under the rule of cultivated and despotic rajahs.

The Trojans worshiped the gods and the spirits of the dead, but their worship was joyous. They knew no fasting or atonement, no sense of guilt, no doom descending from a crime committed long ago in a garden. They were young and fresh, living in an elemental sunlit world, the sap still new in their veins; and divinity was all around them. It did not perturb them overmuch that the gods possessed a rank and order of their own: Apollo, the lord of the silver bow, was "the mightiest of the gods," but so was Zeus. For them the gods were almost mortal, and men almost divine; and the greatest triumph of man was to enter the realm of the gods. A mortal Diomedes might wound the goddess Aphrodite. Gods walked in the market place, and they too were vulnerable, shuddering before "the dark realm of death."

Most of all they loved brightness and feared the dark. For them divinity was almost within men's grasp, a thing as light as air, as palpable as flesh, resembling the glimmering flames of campfires at night, the gleam of bronze, the shining of olive trees, the faces of people. Achilles recognizes the goddess Athena by "her mighty flaming glance." The signs of divinity were the double ax, the wheeling swastika, the little clay figurines of the Mother Goddess and those strange *carrousels*, usually of blue stone, which seem to have symbolized the womb and the mysterious beginnings of things. Every little stream possessed its attendant nymphs, and every thunder clap was a word from a hidden god. Rivers, seafoam, mountains, trees, all living things partook of divinity, but all divinity failed at the gate of death. The gods were humbled by death; men feared it with an unappeasable fear; all the heavens shuddered at it. Death was an error marked upon the face of the world: from death they recoiled with bated breath and shuddering horror. Nothing is so remarkable in Homer as the special quality of their fear of death—that fear which is also a kind of pride. Hating and fearing death, they were still capable of regarding it with laughter and derision and flashing eyes.

According to Homer the Trojans and Achaeans burned their dead; like the Balinese they danced around the funeral pyres. Patroclus was placed on a pyre, and there were consumed with him not only sheep and oxen, horses and dogs, but also twelve young Trojans. But this was a very special ceremony, ordered by the ferocious Achilles in honor of his dead friend, and it is unlikely that it was often repeated. Achilles abused the corpse of Hector for twelve days until Apollo restrained him, and this too must have happened very exceptionally. All the evidence we have suggests that the Homeric Greeks regarded the dead with grave reverence.

Scholars have remarked that the Homeric descriptions of funeral pyres have nothing in common with the grave chambers found at Mycenae. They have said repeatedly that Mycenaean burial customs point to a civilization far earlier than the Trojan War; and it is true that the shaft-graves heaped with gold antedate the Trojan War by many centuries. But gold is flame. Homer says that the spirits of the dead can only be admitted to the realm of the dead after burning. Yet it is perfectly possible to conceive that a gold mask was itself a kind of flame. The kings of Mycenae wear gold masks; Patroclus wears a raiment of flame; and to the Greeks these may have been no more than variants of the same custom.

Like nearly all the great epics, like the *Æneid, Beowulf, The Song of Roland* and *Paradise Lost,* the *Iliad* is the story of a defeat endured heroically in an evil time. Good men perish, the evil profit, but the verdict of the gods is not based upon the good or evil deeds men perform; and the gods are indifferent to men's fate. To the gods what is ultimate and significant is man's raw courage, the majesty he wraps around himself as he treads the path of danger, defying the gods to do their worst. The highest virtue of man is his audacity, which makes him most god-like; then his tenderness, which makes him most human. So Odysseus says in the *Iliad:* "Praise me not much, neither blame me, but let us go forward; for the night is far spent and the dawn is near."

Between those two worlds of the utmost audacity and the most eloquent tenderness Homer moves with enviable ease, reflecting a world where men were still innocent, and a pure fire burned in their veins, before they became intimidated by guilt and terror and the endless repetition of tragedy. They stand foursquare to the winds, simple and sensuous, before history began. Writing in old age and two hundred years after the events he described, he may have painted them brighter and more enchanting than they were, mingling the stories handed down over the years with memories of his own youth.

He had an old man's serenity, an old man's love for the ardors of youth. With his own eyes he had seen such a murder as he described in the last books of the *Odyssey*, the bodies of the suitors lying on the floor and the maidservants hanged in the courtyard. He had seen a young chieftain killed and dragged still bleeding behind a chariot around the walls of a ruined city. He had heard the old men hushing their voices "like the chattering of swallows" when a beautiful woman passed by. He had been wounded, and loved a woman as beautiful as Helen, and sat in the tents of kings when the captured women were portioned out among the victors. He had seen all this, but it all happened a long time ago; and so he wandered from town to town, telling these stories and playing on his lyre, and the same stories were told by his disciples; and in time they were written down.

Generations passed; the stories changed a little, but the unquenchable voice never died. It was so powerful and eloquent a voice that the shapes and colors of an entire civilization were carried with it, and nothing like this has ever happened since. The civilization Homer portrayed was so rich, so beautiful, so filled with sensuous majesty that men came to believe it wore the aspect of a dream. Then Schliemann came along and staggered the world by showing that it was a waking dream: it had all happened in the sunlight of the Ionian seas.

The Last Years

As the years passed Schliemann showed little sign of change. He had been inflexible in youth, and in old age he was just as inflexible, just as demanding. He still spoke in a gruff clipped voice and carried himself like a man afraid of unbending. All his life he had maintained a vast correspondence, writing his letters and books while standing at a high desk; and he had never employed a secretary. Even though he was wealthy and famous and possessed a palace worthy of him, he still saw no reason for employing a secretary and continued to write his letters in longhand, jumping from one language to another according to his mood.

His wealth increased. He kept a close watch on the stock market and the houses he owned in Paris, Berlin, and Ath-

ens; he confessed that if a house stood empty, it cost him
two sleepless nights. Occasionally there were small signs of
change. In the past he enjoyed dressing shabbily; now he
began to pay a little more attention to his clothes, his body
linen, and his hats. He had one oddity: there was always a
red silk handkerchief hanging from his coat pocket, perhaps in memory of the red shawl in which Sophia had
gathered the Trojan treasure. In company he was quiet,
rarely communicative, and he disliked discussions about his
excavations, but he was affable to the lower classes. Ambition still drove him, and he still lusted after gold. In all this
he was recognizably the same man who had been washed
ashore on the island of Texel with a burning ambition to
make good in the world.

He was always in a hurry, always restless. He had an
acute perception of the passing of time, and hated wasting
any of it. He marked out the work of the day—so many
hours for correspondence, so many hours for reading, so
many hours for studying the stock market. In summer he
would rise sharply at three o'clock in the morning and then
ride to the Bay of Phaleron for a bath, taking his wife with
him. He still thought that sea-bathing cured all the ills of
the flesh, and he was constantly celebrating the medicinal
properties of salt water. As he grew older, he became even
more spartan in his habits. He was sixty-four when he had
a cyst cut out of his lip without an anesthetic. A few months
earlier, when he fell from his horse and splinters from his
spectacles were driven into his cheeks, he did not trouble
to send for a doctor, but patiently waited for the splinters to come out of their own accord.

He did not know that his constant bathing in the sea was
slowly killing him. In November, 1877, about the time
that Gladstone was writing the famous preface to *Mycenae*, he complained for the first time of deafness and illness.

Sea water entering his ears caused inflammations and burning headaches. For the remaining thirteen years of his life he suffered intermittently from earaches and headaches, and sometimes he looked like a man frozen with horror at the thought of all the pain he had to bear.

Troy, which had given him his greatest claim to fame, still summoned him. In *Ilios*, which he published in 1879, he presented a complete account of his excavations at Hissarlik, adding a lengthy autobiographical fragment, correcting some of his earlier theories, and bringing the account of his discoveries up to date.

But there were problems which still troubled him. Was Hissarlik Troy? Was it possible that the vast city described by Homer was represented by this small mound? He calculated that this city on a mound could have held only five thousand inhabitants with an army of five hundred soldiers. Then where were the sixty-two vast and palatial rooms described by Homer? The citadel at Troy was even smaller than the citadel at Mycenae, where for a while he believed he had disinterred Agamemnon, Clytemnestra, and all the court of the golden Atridae.

The more he thought of Hissarlik, the more he was plagued by doubts. Perhaps, after all, Troy was only a figment of Homer's imagination. He wrote to his publisher Brockhaus: "The only remaining question is whether Troy really existed or was a product of the poet's imagination. If it existed, then Hissarlik must and will be universally accepted as the true site of Troy." But this was begging the question, and he knew it. To the end of his life he was to continue his excavations at Troy in the hope that some fragment of ancient writing or another hoard of treasure would somehow prove beyond doubt that Hissarlik was Homer's Troy. Like a ghost haunting the scenes of his youthful exploits, he returned again and again to the honeycombed mound which had fascinated him ever since he first set eyes on it on a summer day in 1868.

Up to this time all his knowledge of the Troad consisted of Hissarlik, Bunarbashi, the valley of the Scamander and the small villages on its banks. Now he decided to go further afield, to see whether the surrounding countryside would throw light on the problem. In May, 1881, he made a long journey by horseback across the Troad. It was a curiously uneventful journey and he learned little, but he did succeed in climbing Mount Ida, from where the gods once looked down on the battles below. Homer said Mount Ida was "the mother of wild beasts," but Schliemann saw no living creature on it except the cuckoo, which is common all over the Troad. On one spur of the mountain he found the solitary tomb of an unknown herdsman, and on another spur he came upon a slab of marble which he believed to be the remains of the throne of Zeus.

The throne was filled with blue hyacinths and violets. Hissarlik lay far below. It was about the size of a coatbutton, and he wondered how Zeus could distinguish the movements of the armies so far away. Characteristically, Schliemann announced that it was quite certain that Homer had also stood on the summit of Mount Ida. It was as though he dared never stand where Homer had never trod.

That year he did a little desultory digging at Hissarlik, but the problem which chiefly occupied his attention was the disposal of his Trojan treasure. At various times he had thought of offering it to Greece, Italy, France, and England. There was a brief period when he considered selling the jewels to Russia, and for some weeks he maintained a confused correspondence with an agent in Russia, who was promised a fair commission if the treasures were bought by the Hermitage Museum. In fact Schliemann had no very great desire to sell the treasure, which was beyond price—what price can one pay for the Sistine Chapel? It was in the character of the man to hesitate continually, while he waited upon events. At the end of 1878 he wrote to a Berlin merchant, saying he would never leave it to Berlin, a city which had never shown any appreciation of his work. He did not know that less than six months later a sprig of flowering blackthorn would profoundly affect the disposal of the treasure. In the end it would come to Berlin, because a friend plucked the blackthorn and presented it to him.

In all of Schliemann's life he made exactly two friends. One was Wilhelm Dörpfeld, a young archeologist sent out by the Prussian government to work on the excavations at Olympia. The other was Rudolf Virchow, the famous pathologist. Virchow was everything that Schlieman was not. He was calm, methodical, tactful, relentlessly logical, indifferent to money, and even more indifferent to fame. He was one of those people who are able to scatter their energies in a hundred different directions and still maintain a sense of quiet orderliness in their existence. Schliemann envied him, cherished his friendship, continually pestered him with medical questions, and asked his advice on such different matters as the proper clothes to wear at a reception and the proper formula for baby food.

On one occasion after a visit to Hanai-Tepe near Troy, Schliemann heard that Virchow was considering the publication of a report on his finds. Schliemann telegraphed immediately: "Publish nothing about Hanai-Tepe, else friendship and love for Germany both perish!"

In the spring of 1879, during a pause in digging at Hissarlik, Schliemann suggested an excursion along the banks of the Scamander. Virchow was delighted to have the opportunity of accompanying Schliemann on a brief tour along the valley. They came to the foothills of Mount Ida. Schliemann was unusually silent, immersed in his own thoughts; and when Virchow asked him what was the matter, he answered gruffly that he was concerned about so many things that it would be unreasonable to demand a full accounting of them.

A little while later, when they were resting in the shade of a blackthorn tree, Virchow asked him again what was tormenting him. Schliemann mentioned that he was preoccupied with the thought of what would happen to the treasure after his death. Suddenly Virchow plucked a sprig of flowering blackthorn, handed it to Schliemann and said quietly: "A nosegay from Ankershagen!"

Virchow could never afterwards understand why he said these words. They came unbidden. He observed the sudden change in his friend's features: it was as though a great weight had fallen from him.

"Yes, a nosegay from Ankershagen," Schliemann said, and then without exchanging any more words they both knew that the decision had been made.

Some hours later, when they were returning from the excursion, Virchow said casually: "Of course they should go to the German nation. They will be cared for, and you will be honored for giving them. It is all very simple. With your permission, I shall speak to Prince Bismarck about it."

Schliemann nodded. The answer to the question which had plagued him for seven years was suddenly revealed. Now at long last, on a spring day, gazing at the sprig of blackthorn, which reminded him of the great masses of flowers in the garden at Ankershagen, he made his decision.

When he thought about the matter coldly, he always remembered that the two countries where he had been most at home and where he was treated with the greatest

kindness were England and the United States; but his whole
life revolved around the possession of the treasure, and to
give the treasure away meant the offering up of his whole
life in a sacrifice, and where else could he turn but to his
native land? The treasure was to be a crown laid upon
the village of Ankershagen, even though it would be
housed in Berlin in a great museum bearing his name.

All through the summer and autumn Virchow worked
quietly and efficiently at the task. He was afraid Schliemann
would change his mind, and he knew he had to arrange
everything quickly, neatly, in a fashion which would soothe
Schliemann's feelings, always liable to be hurt by imagined
slights. In a long series of letters he explained that a gift
of such magnitude must be carefully prepared. The full
effect of such an outstanding gift, one which would re-
dound eternally to the credit of Schliemann, would only
be felt if the negotiations were carried on at the highest
levels. He pleaded for time. He interviewed everybody—
once he was kept waiting for two hours in Prince Bismarck's anteroom, and thought the time well-spent, for the
German Chancellor was on fire with the idea of having the
treasure on permanent exhibition in Berlin and was prepared to go to extreme lengths to honor the discoverer of
the treasure. "What honor does Dr. Schliemann want?"
Prince Bismarck asked; and on this subject Virchow was
prepared to be evasive, merely remarking that Schliemann
was a man who thirsted for recognition and sought eagerly
for every kind of tribute, provided that it came from the
most exalted circles.

As usual Schliemann temporized. He had always fought
against governments, and now he was determined to exact the best possible terms from the German government.
He complained that by offering the treasure to Germany
he had alienated himself from Great Britain, America,

France, and Italy. Henceforth he would be compelled to live only in Greece and Germany. Privately, to Virchow, he suggested his terms. They were: a special letter of commendation from the Kaiser, the order of *Pour le mérite*, the highest private order the Kaiser could bestow, the honorary citizenship of Berlin, membership in the Prussian Academy of Sciences, and the museum containing the treasure must bear his name in perpetuity. He hinted that he would not be displeased with a title, but did not insist upon it. He did not receive the *Pour le mérite*, but Virchow almost singlehandedly succeeded in arranging that all the other demands were met. Only Sophia was alarmed by the progress of the negotiations. She insisted that the treasure belonged to Greece, but she was no match for her husband when he was determined upon a course of conduct, and her fury was appeased when she saw her own name in the letter of commendation written in the Kaiser's own hand.

At last, in December 1880, the treasure, which had been on exhibition in London, was crated and sent to Berlin. Six months later Schliemann attended the royal reception in Berlin, where the treasure was solemnly handed over "to the German nation in perpetual possession and inalienable custody." It was housed in a wing of the Völkerkundemuseum, and Schliemann's name was written in bright golden letters above the doors. At the reception Crown Prince Wilhelm, later Kaiser Wilhelm II, escorted Sophia to the banquet. It was July 7, 1881. Sophia was twenty-eight, and her husband was six months short of his sixtieth birthday.

The treasure remained in Berlin until the end of the Second World War. When the war broke out, it was hidden in a secret bunker excavated deep below the Berlin Zoo. In the spring of 1945 Russian troops discovered it and sent it back through the lines. Today only the Russians know where it is.

On that July day in Berlin Schliemann reached the pinnacle of his fame. The Kaiser, the Kaiserin, the Princes and Princesses of the Court paid tribute to him, but in his view this was the least of the honors he received. The greatest was the honorary citizenship of Berlin, which had been bestowed on only two people before: Prince Bismarck and Count Helmuth von Moltke, the two men chiefly responsible for the resurgence of Germany. The boy who had glued his face to the window of an obscure parsonage, shuddering with joy as he viewed the legendary world outside, saw the world of legend come to life. Had he not summoned into his presence the most ancient kings, and a living king as well? Looking back on his life, filled with so many heroic deeds and so much accomplishment, he was content.

Still, there was much to be done. Troy was never far from his thoughts, and he hoped before he died to discover the tombs of the Trojan kings and to make a detailed map of all the cities built on the mound of Troy, where he had found his greatest happiness.

At last, after careful preparations, on March 1, 1882, he paid his ninth visit to Hissarlik and resumed digging. Fourteen years had passed since his first visit. He was once again in good humor, with no headaches or earaches. When he first visited the place he had only the most primitive implements and was almost without supplies. This time he came royally provided. Messrs. Schröder of London sent him as a gift large supplies of Chicago corned beef, peaches, English cheese, and ox-tongue. There were also 240 bottles of pale ale, and Schliemann drank all of them in the course of five months, announcing that "pale ale is the best medicine ever discovered for constipation, from which I have suffered for the past thirty years."

There was the inevitable trouble with the Turks, who despatched a certain Bedder Edin Effendi from the Ministry of Public Instruction to see that Schliemann kept to the letter of his agreement with the Turkish government. He was a monster of officiousness, who examined minutely everything that passed through the hands of Schliemann or Dörpfeld, his capable assistant, and caused no end of trouble.

Dörpfeld imported surveying instruments. Bedder Edin Effendi examined the instruments and pronounced that they must have been designed for taking measurements of the small fortress at Koum Kale, five miles from Hissarlik. Dörpfeld argued, but to no avail. The matter was reported to Said Pasha, the Grand Master of Artillery at Constantinople, and orders came back that the surveying instruments must on no account be used. More trouble came when the Turk saw Dörpfeld and Schliemann taking notes. He thought they were drawing up plans of the crumbling fort; they were ordered to commit nothing to writing, otherwise they would be sent in irons to Constantinople. Schliemann shrugged his shoulders. He had a magnificent memory, and no one could prevent him from making mental notes.

On his ninth visit Schliemann lived very much as he had lived during his first. Every morning he rose before sunrise, rode to the Hellespont and took his sea-bath as the sun was coming up. On these expeditions he was always accompanied by three guards armed with flintlocks. By day he worked with 150 workmen, wearing a battered sun helmet, enormous spectacles, and a greatcoat, with a red silk handkerchief dangling from his pocket. As before his factotum, bodyguard, and chief paymaster was Zaphyros Jannakis, who also served as a storekeeper, selling bread, tobacco, and brandy to the workmen at enormous profit.

The winter had been dry, and in July the Scamander dried up completely, and all that spring there were no flowers in the plain. In June the locusts came, and Bedder Edin Effendi, growing more officious than ever, began to make still more unreasonable demands. At the end of July Schliemann decided he could bear the presence of the Turkish official no longer, and put an end to the excavations, but not before sending an urgent telegram to Prince Bismarck, demanding protection from the Turks. Nothing came of the telegram, and little was accomplished at Troy, though Dörpfeld succeeded in making an excellent map of the various cities which had once stood on the mound. No treasure was found, only a small cache of bronze and copper objects; and these were of little value.

The next year Schliemann published *Troja*, the third of his books on the excavations at Troy, bringing the story up to date. It is the least rewarding of all his books, and consists very largely of a catalogue of his unimportant finds during the excavations of 1881 and 1882. His luck was running out. Gold no longer rose out of the earth at the touch of his magic wand. For the remaining years of his life he was to wander restlessly after treasure, only to find potsherds.

Years before there had been a period when he embarked on a large number of sporadic projects in Italy and Sicily. There were always the arrowheads of Motyë to remind him that success came at rare intervals. He thought of excavating at Thera, where he was once shipwrecked, and at Cythera, where Aphrodite rose from the sea-foam, and at Pylos on the western shore of the Peloponnesus, the scene of a great battle described by Thucydides. At a lucky moment his mind turned toward the island of Crete, still under Turkish domination. There in 1878 a merchant of Candia bearing the legendary name of Minos Kalokairinos had made some excavations on a hill called Kephala Tselempe, the traditional site of the ancient city of Cnossus. Schliemann made inquiries about the finds and thought seriously of transferring his activities to Crete. If he had dug at Cnossus he might have made the great discoveries which Sir Arthur Evans made many years later. But in those days Crete seemed a less likely prospect for the archeologist than the mainland of Greece.

Perhaps there were too many places to choose from, too many ruins beckoning him. As we see him during these last years, he seems to be hesitating, for the first time unsure of himself. He decided to dig close at hand, at Marathon near Athens, where there was a small and famous mound. Tradition, supported by Pausanias, said the bodies of 192 Athenians who fell in battle against the Persians were buried there. In February, 1884, Schliemann obtained permission to excavate the mound. It was the work of only a few days. He dug a trench through it, but found no trace of the Athenian dead. He hoped to find spears, swords, helmets, breastplates, all the trappings of warriors. All he found were a few potsherds and some evidence that the mound was raised in archaic times, before the Persians set foot on Greece.

There remained Tiryns, the great citadel on the plain of Argos, which he had visited during his first tour through Greece, and excavated for a few brief weeks before the long summer and autumn which saw the discovery of the golden masks of Mycenae.

Tiryns was old when Mycenae was young. Hercules was born there. Zeus visited the city in the shape of a shower of gold and had a child by Danaë, imprisoned there in a brazen tower. Of this union was born Perseus, the legendary hero of the Argives, who cut off the head of Medusa. Even the ancient Greeks regarded Tiryns with awe, and Pausanias cried: "Why should we trouble to go to see the Pyramids when we have this?"

On March 14, 1884, a few weeks after the unsuccessful excavations at Marathon, Schliemann arrived in Nauplia to superintend the work. He was accompanied by Wilhelm Dörpfeld, on whom a large share of the work would fall. This time, too, there were vast quantities of supplies sent by Messrs. Schröder from London: Chicago corned beef, peaches, the best English pale ale. He employed 70 workmen, and used 40 English wheelbarrows, 20 large iron crowbars, 50 pickaxes, 25 large axes, and a windlass. Never before had he planned an expedition so scientifically. Schliemann and Dörpfeld divided their responsibilities between them. Schliemann would indicate where he wanted walls torn down and digging to begin, while Dörpfeld would act as surveyor, consulting engineer, mapmaker, and principal contractor. In effect Schliemann was in charge of pottery and treasure, and Dörpfeld in charge of the buildings.

They lived at Nauplia. There every morning, according to his custom, Schliemann rose before sunrise and was carried out to sea in a rowboat just as the sun was coming up. Far from land he would jump overboard, swim for ten minutes, climb back on the boat by pulling himself up over the rudder, and shortly afterwards he would be making the twenty-five minute journey to Tiryns on horseback. At eight o'clock there would be the first pause, when all the workmen gathered in the shade of the great stone galleries and had breakfast. At sunset the work ended, and Schliemann would ride back with Dörpfeld to Nauplia.

They worked until June. During the very first summer the workmen laid bare the whole floor plan of a Homeric palace. The great fortress stood on a limestone crag projecting over a swampy plain. The galleries, vaulted with huge blocks, had served for generations as sheepfolds, and in some places the stone had been rubbed smooth by the sheep. Pausanias had seen these cyclopean walls and proclaimed that a mule team would have been unable to remove even the smallest of the stones; and though, in Tiryns as in Mycenae, Schliemann was disposed to believe every word written by Pausanias, it pleased him to discover that there were many small stones which could be lifted easily by the workmen.

He went to Tiryns again the next summer, and discovered a brilliant fresco showing a boy leaping over the back of a tawny bull, portions of a geometric frieze, and innumerable *carrousels* of blue stones. He found obsidian knives and arrowheads, but the only gold which came to light was in the form of a gold ax half an inch wide.

Schliemann's book *Tiryns*, published in 1886, was almost as disappointing as his last book on Troy. He contented himself with describing the objects found in the debris, leaving to Dörpfeld the task of discussing the great palaces they unearthed. Many of the terra-cotta vases were exquisitely fashioned, in a style which showed great advances on the vases discovered at Troy and Mycenae; but it was the huge bull with the curving horns which astonished the world. Such bulls were to be found later in Cnossus, and it is possible that the bull at Tiryns was painted by a Minoan artist. But Minoan influence on the mainland of Greece was still largely unsuspected. Schliemann believed that the citadels at Mycenae and Tiryns were built and inhabited by Phoenicians, who flooded Greece and the islands of the Ægean and Ionian Seas at a remote prehistoric age, until they were expelled by the Dorian invaders about 1100 B.C.

Among the theories which Schliemann clung to throughout his life was the gradual decay of heroism. It seemed to him that heroism was concentrated in a quite extraordinary degree in the great heroes of archaic Greece, and never since then had it flowered with the same intensity. Great men had walked the earth at Troy and Mycenae; and from that day to this the world had suffered at the hands of lesser men. There were however occasional exceptions to the rule. Schliemann was inclined to believe that Czar Alexander II, murdered by Nihilists in St. Petersburg in March 1881, belonged to the ranks of the authentic heroes. A still more shining example was General Gordon whose fortunes in the Sudan he followed with avid interest.

Schliemann and Gordon illuminate one another. They had much in common: daring, unyielding faith in themselves, a strange intimacy with the hidden things of the earth. Trusting in Homer and Pausanias, Schliemann uncovered the buried cities of Troy, Mycenae, and Tiryns. Trusting in the inspired words of the Bible, Gordon wandered over the Holy Land and believed he had discovered the exact sites of Golgotha, Gibeon, and the Garden of Eden. Both were solitaries, who confined their reading only to those works which seemed to be directly inspired. They were both haunted by dreams, ill at ease in their own civilization, seeing themselves as figures in an ancient and irrecoverable past. When Gordon wanted to examine the future, he opened the Bible at random and saw the future written clearly before his eyes. For the same reason Schliemann was constantly consulting his Homer. They were men who would have understood each other.

From Athens Schliemann looked out across the Mediterranean to Khartoum, where the real hero of the age—the man closest to Hector in his time—was being surrounded by the wild and pitiless army of the Mahdi. Relief supplies had been cut off. Food was low, and ammunition was running out. Gordon was urged to sandbag the palace windows, and refused. Instead he ordered a lantern with twenty-four candles to be placed in one of the windows, and declared: "When God was portioning out fear, it came to my turn, and there was no fear left to give me. Go, tell all the people of Khartoum that Gordon fears nothing."

On the night of February 3, 1885, the Mahdi and his dervishes approached the palace. By sunrise they were pouring through the town. Gordon was waiting for them on the palace steps. Sword in hand, he fought magnificently, flew at the enemy, and died amid a heap of corpses at the foot of the steps. When his head was cut off, wrapped in a cloth, and presented to the Mahdi, orders were given for it to be hung from a tree and for days the hawks wheeled around the bloody head.

For Schliemann it was a nightmare. Of all living men he admired Gordon most. Everyone, even Queen Victoria, believed Gordon met his death as the result of the inexplicable folly of Gladstone, who failed to send reinforcements in time. Schliemann knew Gladstone well. Had not Gladstone written the long preface to *Mycenae*, and invited him to dinner at 10 Downing Street? Trembling with indignation Schliemann removed the signed photograph of Gladstone which stood in his study. He debated what to do with it: whether to hurl it on the stone floor or tear it to pieces. He decided to be more cautious, and with typical Mecklenburger cunning punished Gladstone by installing the photograph in the lavatory.

More and more during those last years he grew convinced that the most rewarding discoveries would be made in Crete. Thera, Cythera, and Pylos would have to wait. His enthusiasm for Crete was shared by Dörpfeld. Accordingly, in 1886, they visited Cnossus together and examined the site. There were long interviews with the owner, a Turk whose business sense was at least the equal of Schliemann's. They debated endlessly over cups of Turkish coffee, and came to no conclusion. The Turk was asking $16,000 for the field, an excessive price. Schliemann was infuriated. He had already obtained from the Turkish governor of the island a *firman* permitting him to excavate provided he obtained the consent of the owner; and this consent was being withheld. He was still hopeful that he would be able to wear down the opposition when he returned to Athens.

He thought of returning to Troy, made long-range plans for the excavations in Crete, debated with himself whether to inspect his houses in Paris or to make another tour of Ithaca, and did nothing. As he grew older and wearier, he disappeared more into himself, reading Homer all day and half the night, as though Homer had become a drug, the only thing that could keep him sane. He still wrote interminable letters, sometimes beginning the letter in one language and continuing in another and concluding in still a third; but the handwriting was becoming cramped, and increasingly he wrote in the tones of one of the Trojan heroes hurling abuse at the Achaeans below. Those tremendous invocations which once poured from the mouths of Homeric heroes look curiously out of place when written by a small graying man who resembled a timid professor.

Yet there was nothing timid in Schliemann as age caught up with him. He raged interminably at those lesser men, the charlatans who refused to credit him with great discoveries, or worse still, paid him only a grudging tribute. There was, for example, a certain Captain Böttischer who wrote a monograph explaining that Hissarlik was a huge fire necropolis, probably Persian in origin. Schliemann expended reams of paper in an attempt to demolish the farcical theory. It was his custom to roar like a wounded lion at the slightest slight. The Grand Duke of Mecklenburg had never acknowledged a dedication. Schliemann sent a tele-gram—he had a passion for telegrams, and half of them were like explosives, and the other half resembled pages torn out of reports of meetings of boards of directors. The Grand Duke permitted himself the luxury of striking a gold medal in Schliemann's honor, and then there was peace again.

For months on end he put archeology aside. Instead of Schliemann the world-renowned archeologist, there was Schliemann the businessman, traveling all over the world to see that his property and investments were safe. He had large estates in Cuba, and so he made a hurried trip to Havana. He had property in Madrid and Berlin, and rushed off to inspect them and to address conferences in defense of his theories of the origin of Troy. He enjoyed money for the power it gave him to travel anywhere on earth at a moment's notice.

Physically he was changing. With his taut, weather-beaten skin, enormous forehead like an onion, and sad, wispy mustache, he was coming to resemble a mummy. Earaches drove him nearly mad, and sometimes his lips twitched. He made little jerking movements with his hands, stuttered in all the languages he knew, and now more and more it became necessary for him to keep to a strict regi-men. He was up early, took a bath in the sea, enjoyed a breakfast of three eggs and a cup of weak tea, read the newspapers and the stock exchange reports and attended to his correspondence. Then it was time to read three hundred lines of Homer, Sophocles, or Euripides—he rarely read Plato and seems never to have bothered with Aristotle. Then lunch and a brief walk and more study, and usually in the evening there were visitors. At ten he was in bed, but he suffered from insomnia and sometimes read through the night.

As he grew older, he paid particular attention to his dreams, always analyzing them carefully; and he was profoundly worried if Sophia dreamed of crows, beanstalks, or visitors from abroad. Homer spoke with the authentic voice of ancient gods, and so did dreams, and so did gold. In those years when he seemed to be slowly slipping away from the world, there were few other pleasures.

As the flesh withered, and the earache grew worse, and the cold winds of Europe made him shiver, he decided to spend his remaining winters in the south. Egypt attracted him. He had read widely in the reports of the French and English archeologists who had been excavating in Egypt for three generations. None of them possessed his genius, none of them had discovered great treasures of gold, and he suspected that they knew very little about the science of excavation. He permitted himself the thought that he might amuse himself with a little digging in Egypt.

As 1886 was coming to an end, he decided to spend three months in a leisurely progress down the Nile, alone except for a secretary and a heap of books in Greek and Arabic. It was an expensive undertaking. He hired a magnificent roomy *dahabiyeh*, luxuriously furnished with all the conveniences known to that time, at a cost of about $4,000. Sometimes as he sailed up the Nile past Theban ruins and Ptolemaic temples, he would order a halt and come ashore and wander through a village market place. He liked talking in Arabic to the villagers, and he liked to offer them simple salves for their sores. To one Egyptian girl suffering from paralysis and a swelling in the shoulder, he ordered a twice daily bath in the Nile and the application of linseed and hot herbs to the shoulder, with what result no one knows. He detested the Mohammedan sailors on the boat, who were dirty and disloyal and continually falling on their knees to pray in the direction of Mecca. He liked the

Nubians with their dark gleaming sculptured faces, the only people he had ever met who looked like heroes.

He intended to sail as far as Wadi Halfa, that small frontier post which marked the southern boundary of the Khedive's dominion. He dug occasionally, thought a good deal about Cleopatra, took soundings of the depth of the Nile, and studied cloud formations, calculating the next day's weather by the direction of the higher clouds. He recorded the temperature every day, as he always did, and copied occasional inscriptions, and paced up and down the deck, restless but strangely quiet, happiest of all when he was reading Homer and all the annoyances of Egypt were temporarily forgotten.

It annoyed him that the British military authorities in Cairo had shown no special interest in his presence, and he was inclined to sympathize with the native Egyptians against their conquerors. When he reached Assouan, he sent his secretary on shore to announce his arrival to the native officials. They had not heard of him, and were in no mood to offer him any special honors. The secretary returned empty-handed. Astonished that his fame had not penetrated the offices of the Egyptian bureaucrats in Assouan, Schliemann fretted and fumed, and swore he would not come ashore unless a welcoming party came to greet him.

That winter Assouan was crowded with tourists, who brought their lunch off the Nile steamers and went grubbing in the sand for beads. Thousands of amateur archeologists haunted the place, but there were also a number of young dedicated archeologists. Among them was E. A. Wallis Budge, then comparatively unknown, making his first mission to Egypt on behalf of the British Museum. He was a thickset, keen, uncomplicated man, and his chief task at the time was to acquire for the Museum some early Mohammedan dome-tombs inscribed with Kufic inscriptions, for Assouan had been a place of pilgrimage in the early years following the Hegira.

As soon as he heard that Schliemann had been slighted, he decided to do what he could to make amends. He rounded up two of his friends and got a boatman to row them over to the *dahabiyeh*. A butler greeted them and led them to a large saloon in the stern of the ship. Coffee was served, cigarettes were lit, and soon Schliemann was being invited by the three Englishmen to inspect the newly excavated Mohammedan tombs. And then an extraordinary thing happened. Schliemann drew himself up very stiffly, and showed that he had not the least desire to see their work.

"It is very kind of you to be so amiable," he said. "I should like to place my archeological science at your disposal and explain to you the tombs, but I have not the time as I am going to Wadi Halfa!"

There was a moment's silence, and then without another word Schliemann reached for the paper-bound copy of the *Iliad* in the Greek text, which he had been reading until disturbed by the Englishmen. He had simply laid the book face downward on a cushion while talking to them, preparing to take it up again at the first opportunity. The Englishmen were appalled, and Major Plunkett, who had accompanied Wallis Budge, asked permission "in a sweetly soft voice" to withdraw. Permission was granted, and they returned to Assouan with the curious feeling that they had set eyes on the world's most famous archeologist and everything they saw disturbed them.*

Such conduct was unusual, and perhaps due to the recurrent headaches which made the last years of his life so

* E. A. Wallis Budge, *By Nile and Tigris*. London, John Murray, 1920, p. 109.

miserable. We have another glimpse of Schliemann from another English archeologist the following year. Once again Schliemann was sailing down the Nile, this time accompanied by Rudolf Virchow. He was in better spirits. The earache no longer troubled him. He tramped for hours through the columns of Karnak and inspected the vast labyrinth which Flinders Petrie had mapped out the previous year.

Petrie was a young archeologist, and Schliemann was impressed by his painstaking excavations on the site of the labyrinth, once the greatest building in the world, with its twelve immense courts and three thousand rooms, half of them underground. As Petrie describes him, Schliemann was "short, round-headed, round-faced, round-hatted, great round-goggle-eyed, spectacled, cheeriest of beings; dogmatic, but always ready for facts." Virchow was less agreeable—"a calm, sweet-faced man with a beautiful grey beard, who nevertheless tried to make mischief for my work." * This is the last thumbnail sketch we have of Schliemann; and the story of the remaining years of his life must be pieced out from his letters and from the funeral orations pronounced at his death.

There were only three more years left to him; years of frustration and disappointment, with no great accomplishments to satisfy his desire for fame. In 1888 he worked for a short while on the island of Cythera, where Aphrodite first appeared among men, and uncovered her temple in the Byzantine chapel of Hagios Cosmas. He sent off a long telegram to the London *Times* announcing that he had made a discovery of the first magnitude, only comparable to his discoveries at Hissarlik and Mycenae, but he must have known that he was aiming too high. In the same year

* Sir Flinders Petrie, *Seventy Years of Archeology*. London, Sampson Low, Marston. 1931, p. 83.

he made excavations at Pylos and on the island of Sphac-
teria, where he laid bare the old fortifications which according to Thucydides were discovered and used by the
Spartans in 425 B.C. No doubt these were important finds,
but they could not compare with his two greatest exploits.
He wanted another triumph, and dreamed of uncovering
the royal city of Cnossus. "I would like to end my life's
labors with one great work—the prehistoric palace of the
Kings of Cnossus," he wrote on January 1, 1889, but he
seems to have guessed that this triumph would be refused
to him.

Ever since March, 1883, when he first applied for the
right to excavate at Cnossus, he had met with repeated
refusals from the owners of the land. He had visited Crete
and sent his agents there, to no avail. Now in the spring of
1889 he decided to make one last effort to buy the land. He
went with Dörpfeld and was prepared to pay a high price.
The man who claimed to own Kephala Tselempe wanted
100,000 francs, the price to include the 2,500 olive trees
that grew there. Schliemann countered with an offer of
40,000 francs. Finally it was agreed that he could purchase
the land for 50,000 francs. At the last moment before sign-
ing the contract Schliemann decided to count the olive
trees. There were only 888. He flew into a temper, and announced that he could not sign a contract with a man who
lied about the number of trees he possessed.

Dörpfeld, who was not prepared to allow the negotiations to be sabotaged so easily, thought there was still hope.
He made inquiries and discovered that Hadjidakis, the man
who claimed to own the hill, actually owned only one-
third. Negotiations were renewed with the owner of the
remaining two-thirds, and these were concluded successfully. Another contract was drawn up, and Schliemann
promised that one-third of the treasure would be given to

the owners. All that was necessary was to get Hadjidakis' signature to the contract. The Turk refused. There were bitter recriminations, and at last Schliemann saw that nothing would be gained by further negotiations. He wrote to Virchow: "It was a terrible journey, with nothing gained."*

As old age came to him, he went back to his first love. That year he held the First International Congress on the Trojan Antiquities, inviting scholars from all over the world to view his finds, accompanying them through the ruins, telling them stories about those long-distant days before the mound was carved up in trenches and great galleries. He still spoke excitedly about further explorations, particularly in Crete, but he was aging rapidly. A photograph taken that year shows him with a strange pleading expression. He looks helpless and miserable, and there is something about him which suggests a bank clerk who is being retired from the office where he worked industriously all his life, a face empty of hope, and without strength. Photographs rarely flattered him. But there was strength in him still, and he still climbed among the ruins like a young chamois.

He was at Troy again the next year, holding his Second International Congress. Scholars came, and he addressed them gracefully, no longer thundering against their obtuseness, their mediocrity, and their malice. One day he decided to make an excursion to Mount Ida, so that he could look once more on Troy, but the journey was abandoned when they came in the evening to a village in the foothills, and he complained of deafness and an excruciating pain in his ear.

---

* Schliemann never described the negotiations at length. I have based this account on the version given by Sir Arthur Evans, who eventually bought the property. Evans went to some pains to discover exactly what happened, and tells the story in his diary for March 22, 1894, printed in Joan Evans, *Time and Chance: The Story of Arthur Evans*. London, Longmans Green & Co., 1943, p. 313.

Virchow examined the ear, found a large swelling in the aural passage, and suggested an immediate return to Troy.

According to Virchow, there was one last attempt to scale Mount Ida. When the Congress came to an end, Schliemann decided to make a seven-day excursion in the valley. They rode on horseback. When they reached the foot of Mount Ida, Schliemann decided he could not let the opportunity pass. Once more he must sit on the throne of Zeus and gaze down on the beloved plain. They were near the top when a storm broke. It was such a storm as Schliemann had rarely encountered, with a magnificent display of thunder and lightning illuminating the four corners of the heavens. To escape the storm they took shelter under some rocks, but the rain was driven horizontally, and they were soaked to the skin. Then the storm cleared, and in the rain-washed light Schliemann looked down for the last time at the plain of Troy, the Hellespont, the islands of the Ægean, Samothrace, Lemnos, and Tenedos, and the long coastline reaching to Smyrna. Then like Moses, having seen the vision, he came down from the mountain.

The Congress was over, but the work went on, with Dörpfeld largely in control. As usual Dörpfeld was insisting that everything had to be photographed, labeled, ticketed, minutely examined, before it was thrown on the rubbish heap, and sometimes Schliemann would complain testily about the waste of time. But there were occasional rewards, like the fragments of gray Mycenaean pottery with characteristic stirrup-cup designs which were found during these last days. More fortress walls came to light, and soon they found a building formed of great boulders piled one on top of the other, and it was like Tiryns again. Once more Schliemann began to hope that the whole plan of Homeric Troy would be revealed to him before he died. To Virchow and Dörpfeld he spoke lightheartedly of how all of Homeric Troy would be laid bare by the following spring. Meanwhile the hot winds roared across the plain, and some of the workmen were struck with fever, and Schliemann continued to superintend the excavations, a small wizened man wearing a sun helmet who smiled easily and sadly.

Suddenly toward the end of July he decided to abandon the excavations until the next year. On August 1, 1890 he returned to Athens: the great stone house, the children growing up, the table piled high with notes on the year's work, and the ever-healing presence of Sophia to lighten his burdens. He did not know then that he would never see Troy again.

In Athens he was still restless, still pursuing dreams. He wrote to Virchow that he planned to visit the islands of Atlantis and to make a voyage to Mexico—perhaps somewhere there he would find the traces of Odysseus. He was sure he could find Atlantis in the Canary Islands, and had not Homer himself proclaimed that these islands enjoyed perpetual spring? Then, of course, the book on the recent excavations in Troy must be finished, and there would be another scientific congress and they would spend all spring and summer at Troy.

He no longer suffered from earache; the swelling had died down; perhaps there would be no need for an operation. Virchow advised postponing the operation as long as possible, and Schliemann was duly grateful for the advice. When Sophia went off to Vienna for a visit, he wandered round the house like a ghost, remembering one day toward the end of September that they had never celebrated their wedding anniversary together in Athens. So he wrote to her a long letter in classical Greek, chiding her for her absence:

I am proud of this day, and so I am inviting your relatives, and I pray the gods will permit us to celebrate together next year, for we have lived together in health and happiness for twenty-one years. When I look back over those many years, I see that the fates have offered us much that is sweet and much that is bitter. I can never celebrate our marriage enough, for you have always been my beloved wife and at the same time my comrade, my guide in difficulties, and a friendly and faithful companion in arms, and always an exceptional mother. So I rejoice continually in your virtues, and by Zeus! I will marry you again in the next world!

About this time he decided to go to a clinic in Halle which had been recommended by Virchow. Sophia hurried back to Athens to help him pack. He seems to have had some premonition of his approaching death, for he was unusually solemn and quiet. He discussed his will with the directors of the bank. Once, when he was folding his clothes and putting them in a trunk, he was heard saying: "I wonder who will wear these clothes." The mood passed, but sometimes in the letters he wrote at this time we are aware of a strange apathy, a sense of brooding disquiet. Sophia wanted to accompany him on the journey, but he said he would be gone for only six weeks and there were the children to be looked after. At the last moment, when he was leaving for the train, Sophia held him back by the watch-chain. She seemed to know she would never see him again.

He arrived in Halle early in November. It was a cold winter, the snow falling outside the windows of the clinic. The doctors examined his ears and pronounced that an operation on both ears was advisable. The next day they operated on him while he lay stretched out on a board covered with white oilcloth, which resembled, as he told a friend some days later, "one of those tables used for the dissection of the dead." The operation lasted one and three-quarter hours.

According to the doctors the operation was completely successful. Schliemann had some doubts. He felt miserable. He was not allowed to receive visitors. His head bandaged, surrounded by books, he kept up his vast correspondence. He wrote to Dörpfeld, begging forgiveness for all the sins he had committed and asking, if any shadow of discord ever rose between them, that they would declare themselves frankly face to face. On receiving a letter from his wife, he wrote: "To the wisest of all women, I read with wet eyes what you have written."

Though the doctors had declared that the operation was successful, the pain returned, more terrible than ever. It seemed that the periosteum was injured and inflammation was spreading through the inner ear. Against the advice of the doctors he decided to leave the hospital. He was given two little boxes containing the bones extracted from his ears, and then he went off to Leipzig to visit his publishers, and to Berlin to visit Virchow, who found him in good humor, though quite deaf. Schliemann reminded Virchow of his promise to come to the Canary Islands in the early spring, and then took the train for Paris.

He reached Paris on December 15, one of the coldest days of winter. He found six letters waiting for him from the faithful Sophia, who was almost beside herself with worry. He calculated that he would reach Athens by Christmas and still have time to visit the Museum at Naples, where the recent excavations at Pompeii were on display. To his wife he admitted it was his fault that the pain had returned—he had simply forgotten to put cotton wadding in his ears in the draughty railway carriage when he was immersed in reading the *Arabian Nights* in the original

Arabic. He wrote his last letter to Virchow: "Long live Pallas Athene! At least I can hear again with the right ear, and the left will get better."

Pallas Athene and all the other Greek gods had protected him throughout his life, but now at last they withdrew into the clouds of Olympus. For the last time they permitted him to see treasure: but only for a brief moment, on a winter afternoon, suffering from high fever, in agony, with a doctor by his side.

He was already dying when he reached Naples. The pain was excruciating, and the two-day journey from Paris had weakened him. When the pains grew worse, he summoned first one doctor, then another. A ship was waiting for him, but he was too ill to make the sea journey and telegraphed to Athens, asking Sophia to delay the Christmas celebrations, and then went to visit another doctor, who recognized him and spoke gravely about archeology and suggested a drive to Pompeii.

Bundled up in his greatcoat, Schliemann sat back in the carriage during the long journey around the bay in the shadow of Vesuvius. He saw Pompeii. The colonnades, the roads rutted by ancient Roman carts, the *tabernae* where the wine-sellers stood two thousand years before—they were all as he expected them to be. Then he returned to his hotel room, sent off more telegrams, announced that he would soon be making his way to Athens, and fought against the raging pain in his ears.

On Christmas Day he was crossing the Piazza della Santa Carità, perhaps on his way to the post office, when he suddenly collapsed on the cobblestones, conscious, his eyes wide open. A crowd gathered. People asked him questions, but he could only nod his head: he had lost the power of speech.

The police carried him to a hospital, but since he appeared to be perfectly well, only dazed and strangely mute, he was refused admittance. It was decided to take him to the police station. There he was searched for papers and money, but they found none. They did find the address of his doctor, who was summoned and immediately recognized his patient. The police were perplexed. Judging by his clothes, he was a poor man. Then why was the doctor so solicitous?

"No, he is a rich man," the doctor said. "I have seen him holding a wallet filled with gold coins!"

Then the doctor reached under the shirt and pulled out a heavy wallet full of gold.

Schliemann was carried back to his hotel, still conscious and still in command of all his faculties except speech. At the hotel the ear was opened, but the malady had already attacked the brain, and there was little that could be done. He passed a quiet night. The next day it was discovered that the whole of his right side was paralyzed, and there was some talk of trepanning. Eight specialists were called in, and while they were in another room discussing what steps they would take, he died quietly in bed, conscious to the last.

Telegrams were sent off to Athens and Berlin, and soon Dörpfeld and Sophia's elder brother were on their way to Naples to escort the body back to Athens. On Sunday, January 4, 1891, nine days after his death, the coffin lay in the great hall of his palace in Athens, where the twenty-four marble gods towered against the sky. King George and the Crown Prince Constantine came to pay their respects and to lay wreaths beside the coffin, and messages of sympathy came from all over the world.

He had long ago chosen the place where he would be buried. He would be buried among the Greeks he loved in their own cemetery south of the Ilissus, in a tomb fit for a hero. From there his unquiet spirit could look out upon the Acropolis and the blue waters of the Saronic Gulf and the distant hills of Argolis. Beyond those hills the Kings of Mycenae and Tiryns had been buried. At the very end he was close to the heroes he worshiped, and the most adorable of the goddesses, clear-eyed Athena, gazed down at him from the ruined Parthenon on the cliffs.

With his death his new life began. The man who had conjured gold out of the earth had been a legend while he lived, but he was still more of a legend when he was dead. His rages, his arrogance, his embarrassing eccentricities were forgotten. They remembered his faith in Homer and the vastness of his determination to reveal the mysteries buried in the earth. His vices became virtues—his ruthless egoism no more than natural pride, his exaggerations the pardonable excesses of a man impatient for discovery. Men forgot that he retained to the end of his life the habits which had made him a successful bank clerk. Matthew Arnold said that Homer was eminently rapid, eminently plain and direct, and eminently noble, and Schliemann was the contrary of all these—a slow, cautious, complex, devious man, often pompous and ill-tempered, with no natural nobility in him.

Yet the legend which depicted him as a man of indomitable spirit, standing upon the battlements of Troy and waging implacable war on his enemies, was sufficiently truthful to be credible. When his coffin was laid on trestles in the hall of his palace, a bust of Homer was placed at its head; there was something wonderfully appropriate in the gesture, even though in all his life Schliemann never discovered any object dating from Homeric times.

So in the end he became one of the great forerunners, the man who opened the way, the first of archeologists because he was the enemy of classical archeology, the pure romantic who threw the windows wide open and let the air in. Faith and dreams led him on his journey, and he was not so very far from the Homeric heroes whom he had adored ever since he was a child. There was more greatness in him than he knew; and it was not the greatness he thought he had achieved. Homer paints the gods as all-seeing, strangely remote from the earth, given to displays of ironical affection. A sense of irony was the one god-like quality he lacked.

A few days after Schliemann's death Gladstone, who was then eighty-one, wrote in a failing hand a letter of consolation to Sophia. He described how deeply he had felt the force of Schliemann's particular genius, and in a single paragraph he described the nature of Schliemann's triumph. He wrote:

> His enthusiasm called back into being the ancient spirit of chivalry in a thoroughly pure and bloodless form. He had to encounter in the early stages of his work both frowns and indifference, yet the one and the other alike had to give way, as the force and value of his discoveries became clear, like mists upon the sun. The history of his boyhood and youth were not less remarkable than that of his later life. Indeed they cannot be separated, for one aim and purpose moved them from first to last. Either his generosity without his energy, or his energy without his generosity might well have gained celebrity; in their union they were no less than wonderful.

The spirit of chivalry in a thoroughly pure and bloodless form . . . Schliemann would have disagreed. He would have said he had given blood and flesh to the ancient heroes, for had he not resurrected them from the grave? Like a magician he had waved his wand over the buried cities and brought them to life. We know those ancient people now because he employed all his energy in coming to grips with them. Once there were heroes who walked the earth, vast and magnificent and mysterious, and now they were still vast and magnificent, but less mysterious. Gaunt Achilles, cunning Odysseus, Hector of the dancing helmet-crest— he had served them well and never for a moment lost faith in them.

The Enduring Flame

As he sought shelter in the haunted house of his imagination, an old man mad for gold, Schliemann sometimes gave the impression of being a man for whom only the Homeric heroes were real and all the rest of the world was anathema. During the last five years of his life, he wrote and spoke in ancient Greek and seemed strangely uninterested in anything that was not touched by Homer's magic wand. He told a friend: "Only Homer interests me: I am increasingly indifferent to everything else." It was not only that Homer spoke to him with the force of the tablets of the law. For him Homer was a sign and a watchword, a way of life, a history of the earth, and the prophecy of a more vivid life in the future. Schliemann was not mad, but close to madness. His mania was to believe that a very bright and wonderfully pure civilization had once existed, and that it was worth while to enter that civilization even at the risk of lunacy.

Schliemann's mania was one he shared with many others. Keats, too, had gazed upon a Greek vase and in a moment of illumination observed the ancient sacrifices being performed before his eyes. Goethe and Schiller proclaimed their loyalty to a civilization which had long ago vanished from the earth. The young poet Friedrich Hölderlin rejoiced in the Greek gods and celebrated them as though there still existed temples for their worship, himself a priest, an acolyte, a wanderer among the Greek islands, which he never saw except in the flaming light of his imagination.

In his greatest poem he made the imaginary journey across Greece to share the Last Supper with the disciples and then to take refuge on the island of Patmos with St. John. For Hölderlin, Christ was the greatest of gods, and all the Greek heroes were his sons:

> Calm is His sign
> In the thundering heavens. And One stands beneath
> His whole life long. For Christ lives still.
> For they, the heroes, His sons, and Holy Scripture
> Have all come from Him; and the lightning declares
> The deeds of the world till now,
> A conflict unceasing. But He is there.
> His works are known to Him from everlasting.

In the end, striving in the same breath after Christ and the gods of Greece, Hölderlin went mad, but not before he had composed poetry so rich in the music of the ancient Greeks and so passionately Christian that he became one of the greatest of Christian poets, while at the same time owing allegiance to Greece.

For Schliemann it was altogether simpler. Though he was brought up in a parsonage, he denied his Christian heritage, attended no church, and regarded the Bible as fiction. He was baffled by the New Testament: there were so many Greek words which had no equivalent in Homer. When Sophia's mother died, and he entered the death-chamber where the priests were intoning the prayers for the dead, he was heard muttering: "Oh, it is all nonsense! There is no resurrection—there is only immortality!" The entire European tradition since the death of Homer meant nothing to him. Moses crossed the deserts of Sinai; Christ died; the Roman empire rose and fell; there came the flowering of the Renaissance, and then one by one the petals dropped from their stems; and it was all meaningless to him. To the end there was only Homer: the enduring flame.

After Schliemann's death the work he had begun so fruitfully continued. From all over Europe eager archeologists came to Greece and the Near East to dig among ruins and to take part in the process of resurrecting an ancient heroic society which had almost nothing in common with the society of their own age. Discoveries in Crete and Upper Egypt threw light on the Ægean civilization. In 1889, the year before Schliemann's death, Chrestos Tsountas discovered at Vaphio in Laconia two exquisite golden cups, one showing a bull enmeshed in a net, the other showing bulls wandering among olive trees in an idyllic landscape. These, too, must have belonged to a royal treasury. The next year he discovered in a tomb-chamber at Mycenae two amphorae bearing three strange signs on one of the handles; and the search for the Mycenaean script had begun.

Troy was not forgotten. Sophia set aside a sum of money to enable the excavations to go on under the direc-

tion of Wilhelm Dörpfeld. The excavations ended in the
summer of 1893, partly because of the heat and partly because Dörpfeld had exhausted his grant. That August he
hurried to Potsdam, bearing photographs and plans of the
ruins which he showed to the Kaiser Wilhelm II. When
winter came he received the welcome news that the German Imperial Chancellor had been pleased to make a
special grant of 30,000 marks for the excavations, and work
was resumed in the spring of the following year.

Dörpfeld made a surprising discovery. By examining the
plans and retracing Schliemann's earlier work, he found
that Schliemann had completely missed Homeric Troy. At
the point where Schliemann had been digging, Homeric
Troy had been leveled to make room for the Roman
city of Novum Ilium. All that remained of Priam's Troy
was a house corner and a length of fortification wall,
which Schliemann had assumed to be Macedonian because
it was in an excellent state of preservation. He had touched
Troy, but failed to recognize it, because he worked with
such astonishing speed and because he was tempted to remove everything that was not Homeric from his path.

Dörpfeld later published an account of his excavations.
With painstaking accuracy he went over the ground which
Schliemann had uncovered, pointed to the errors which
had been made, and listed the treasure. It is a long book,
and very weighty in its Germanic way, but one of
his conclusions would have been especially pleasing to
Schliemann. After examining the traces of Homeric Troy
and the earlier settlements, he wrote: "The Princes of
Troy were in no way behind the Achaean Princes in their
striving to build great citadels and magnificent palaces:
they were a match for the rulers of Mycenae and Tiryns."

Meanwhile the French School at Athens was attempting
to begin excavations at Crete. Nothing came of these

efforts until 1898, when the Turks were expelled from the island. Then, not the French, but a rich Englishman, a former curator of the Ashmolean Museum at Oxford, succeeded in buying the land and uncovering the treasures which Schliemann had hoped to find as "the crown of my career." In a series of campaigns from 1900 to 1905, Sir Arthur Evans succeeded in winning a king's share of treasure from the ruined city of Cnossus. There was little gold, but he found magnificent frescoes and whole palaces and vast quantities of clay tablets inscribed with written signs. He unearthed a civilization which had existed in the sixth millenium B.C. and progressed continually until in some unexplained way, perhaps by fire and earthquake, the city was destroyed. When the dust had settled, it was possible to trace close affiliations between Cnossus and Mycenae.

About the time that Evans was uncovering written records from the abandoned library of Cnossus, more inscriptions dating back to the heroic age came to light in Greece. Keramopoullos discovered thirty inscribed vases in a storeroom of the "Palace of Cadmus" in Thebes. Here and there a few other inscriptions were discovered, but none could be deciphered. Evans continued his excavations without a break except during the war of 1914-1918, but he published his finds rarely and his monumental work, *The Palace of Minos*, gives only the sketchiest outline of the three scripts found in the ruins of the palace.

These scripts were of three kinds: one hieroglyphic or picture writing, another in a more sophisticated style called Minoan Linear A, and a third which was discovered in much greater quantities, called Minoan Linear B, which seemed to be derived from Linear A, as this in turn was derived from the hieroglyphics. To the end of his life Evans hoped to decipher these strange carved letters on the sunbaked bricks. He failed, and his failure was largely of his own choosing, for he hoarded his finds, rarely allowed other scholars to examine them, and regarded any attempt to decipher them as invasions on his own privacy. He had Schliemann's passion for keeping secrets.

Cnossus filled in the colors of the heroic age. The young cupbearers, the sloe-eyed girls, the delicate paintings of bulls tossing their youthful riders between their horns demonstrated the tenderness of the heroic age, as the graves of Mycenae described the lives of the warrior-kings. But when Cnossus had been unearthed—most of the work was finished by the summer of 1905—there followed a long period of frustration. It was as though the earth had given up all its secrets, and there were no more. A few unimportant finds were made. In 1926 Swedish scholars opened the unrifled tomb of a king, a queen, and a princess at Mideia near Mycenae; and learned little more than they knew before.

From 1932 to 1938 Carl Blegen of the University of Cincinnati worked at Hissarlik. He had the pure scholar's desire for accuracy, and a curious contempt for Schliemann. "It seems desirable, timely, and worth while," he wrote, "to return to Troy to undertake an exhaustive, painstaking re-examination of the whole site." He planned a work of sober research "with no compulsion to recover objects of startling or sensational character with high publicity value." His admirably detailed and documented volumes list innumerable pieces of gray pottery, and he was able to correct many of the mistakes of Schliemann and Dörpfeld, but he found no treasure. One gets the impression that he would have been a little annoyed if any treasure had fallen into his hands.

In 1938 the excavations at Hissarlik were abandoned, and Blegen turned his attention to a Mycenaean palace at

Ano Englianos in western Messenia, the probable site of Nestor's Pylos. Here he discovered some objects which appeared at first sight to be even more valuable than treasure. In a narrow room of the palace he discovered a total of 618 sunbaked clay tablets, 20 of them intact, the others in fragments. All of them were in a slightly modified form of Minoan Linear B. The tablets appeared to form inventories, perhaps of slaves, soldiers, and objects of value belonging to the palace. But since the key to the script was still unknown, they defied translation. Then the war came, and all archeological work in Greece came to a stop.

The war supplied a breathing space. Men had time to ruminate over the finds, to move cautiously and fit the pieces of the jigsaw puzzle together. In particular it gave to young Michael Ventris, who had once listened with bated breath to Sir Arthur Evans discussing his discoveries at Cnossus, a clue to the decipherment of the mysterious illegible script which fascinated Blegen and Evans and all those who were brought in contact with it. Wartime cryptography provided the needed method.

Studying Blegen's finds at Pylos, Alice Kober, an American scholar, who did not live to see the final decipherment, had noted by an examination of the signs that they appeared to represent syllables of an inflectional language. The same groups of syllables would appear, but in each case they would be followed by a different final sign. So in Latin *dominus* becomes *dominum* in the accusative, *domini* in the genitive, and *domino* in the ablative.

There followed in quick succession a number of important discoveries. In 1950, while excavating a house outside the citadel at Mycenae, Alan Wace and George Mylonas discovered thirty-eight more tablets in Minoan Linear B. In November of the following year John Papademetriou discovered a new grave at Mycenae containing four skeletons, swords, daggers, vases, and gold ornaments. The most important find was a mask in electrum very close in form to the most archaic mask found by Schliemann. Gradually a whole new grave circle was being uncovered at Mycenae, but no more tablets were found there.

In February 1952 the tablets discovered by Evans were at last published in a reasonably complete form by Myers in his book *Scripta Minoa II*, and with the evidence from Cnossus, Mycenae, and Pylos before him, Michael Ventris was able to go to work. Two months later the mystery was magnificently solved.

Ventris attacked the problem as an experiment in logic. He made no hypotheses about the nature of the language, though for some time he had held to the belief that it was akin to Etruscan. What he did was to assemble the signs and establish a complex pattern of their relationships, like the "grids" employed in cryptography. Toying with his grid, he did exactly what Champollion had done in attempting to decipher Egyptian hieroglyphics: he simply substituted for an often repeated syllable what seemed to be a likely sound. From the moment when he gave the value of *ko* to the first sign of one of the triplets, all the pieces in the jigsaw puzzle began to fall into place. To his astonishment he discovered that he was reading a language remarkably like ancient Greek, but strangely coarse and sometimes indistinct, as though spoken by a man with a cleft palate in a thunderstorm. It was recognizably Greek, in an ancient dialect, and though rough-edged and barbaric, would have been understood by Socrates. The Greek language was proved to be one of the oldest in existence: and words spoken at Cnossus in 1400 B.C. are still employed in the streets of Athens today.

While Michael Ventris was drafting his article on his discovery, Blegen found three hundred new tablets at

Pylos. Among them there was one so striking and simple that he decided to publish it at once. It was quite evidently an inventory of one of the royal storerooms. On a single slab of baked clay, on nine registers, there was carved a series of syllables, nearly all of them followed by a picture of a vase with one, two, three, or four handles. The syllables evidently described the vases. Ventris substituted for the syllables the sounds he had previously deduced. Accordingly, before the picture of a four-handled vase, he read out the syllables *di-pas me-zo-he que-to-ro-wes.* In Homeric Greek *depas* is a "vase," *meizon* means "greater," *tessares* is "four." Ventris translated: "One larger cup with four handles." So he went on until he had deciphered all the remaining passages on the tablet, which read:

Three wine-jars
Two tripods brought by Aigeus the Cretan
One tripod defective in one leg
One tripod brought by the Cretan charred around the legs
Two larger cups with three handles
One smaller cup with three handles
One smaller cup with no handle
One smaller cup with three handles
One larger cup with four handles

Unfortunately, most of these documents consist of similar inventories. There are lists of slaves, sewing women, bath-pourers, soldiers. One document found at Pylos describes preparations for coastal defense and contains a long list of the military units and their commanders, among them a certain Orestes. Familiar names appear. We find Achilles and Hector on land records, and Æneas appears on a Mycenaean tablet as a man who was given a ration of oil. We find a reference to "a regiment of Tros," which may be Troy. On one tablet from Crete we can decipher the words: "To all the gods—a pot of honey," and "To the lady of our Labyrinth—a pot of honey." There are references to swords "with gold rivets around the hilt" and chariots "inlaid with ivory, fully rigged, fitted with reins, ivory head-stalls, and horn bits." No poems, no royal edicts, no letters have been found, though more clay tablets are continually turning up. Yet bit by bit archeologists are filling in the gaps of the Homeric story.

Significantly, Michael Ventris and John Chadwick dedicated their monumental *Documents in Mycenaean Greek* to the memory of Schliemann. The book, which reads like a detective story, was published in 1956, and in the same year Ventris was killed in an automobile accident at the age of thirty-four.

In the roll-call of those who have brought the Homeric age to life there are many names. Tsountas, Wace, Blegen, Mylonas, Papademetriou, Stamatakes, Ventris—there are many others; but all of them recognized the primacy of Schliemann. He stands above them all like a giant, because he was the boldest and saw farthest and never betrayed his faith in Homer.

> The long toll of the brave
> Is not lost in darkness:
> Neither hath counting the cost
> Fretted away the zeal of their hopes.
> Over the fruitful earth
> And athwart the seas
> Hath passed the light of noble deeds
> Unquenchable forever——

Select Bibliography

ARNOLD, MATTHEW. On Translating Homer. London: John
 Murray, 1905.
BOSSERT, HELMUTH THEODOR. *Kunst und Handwerk in Griech-
 enland, Kreta und in der Agais.* Berlin: E. Wasmuth, 1937.
BUDGE, E. A. WALLIS. By Nile and Tigris. London: John
 Murray, 1920.
EVANS, JOAN. Time and Chance: the Story of Arthur Evans.
 London: Longmans, Green & Co., 1943.
GLOTZ, GUSTAVE. The Ægean Civilization. New York: Al-
 fred A. Knopf, 1925.
HALL, H. R. Ægean Archeology. London: Philip Lee Warner,
 1915.
KARO, GEORG. *Die Schachtgräber von Mykenae.* Munich:
 F. Brockmann, 1930-33.

KELLER, ALBERT GALLOWAY. Homeric Society. London: Longmans, Green & Co., 1906.

KINROSS, LORD. Europa Minor. New York: William Morrow, 1956.

LANCASTER, OSBERT. Classical Landscape with Figures. Boston: Houghton Mifflin Co., 1949.

LANG, ANDREW. Homer and his Age. London: Longmans, Green & Co., 1906.

LEAF, WALTER. Homer and History. London: Macmillan & Co., 1915.

LLOYD, SETON. Early Anatolia. Harmondsworth: Penguin Books, 1956.

LUDWIG, EMIL. Schliemann: the Story of a Goldseeker. Boston: Little, Brown & Co., 1931.

MEYER, ERNST. Rudolf Virchow. Wiesbaden: Limes Verlag, 1956.

MEYER, ERNST (ed.) *Briefe von Heinrich Schliemann.* Berlin: Walter de Gruyter, 1936.

———— *Briefwechsel: Heinrich Schliemann.* Berlin: Verlag Gebr. Mann, 1953.

MYLONAS, GEORGE E. Ancient Mycenae: the Capital City of Agamemnon. London: Routledge & Kegan Paul, 1957.

NILSSON, MARTIN P. The Mycenaean Origin of Greek Mythology. Cambridge: Cambridge University Press, 1932.

OTTO, WALTER. The Homeric Gods. New York: Pantheon, 1954.

PETRIE, SIR FLINDERS. Seventy Years of Archeology. London: Sampson Low, Marston, 1931.

SCHLIEMANN, HEINRICH. Ilios: the City and Country of the Trojans. New York: Harper & Bros., 1880.

———— *Ithaka, der Peloponnes und Troja.* Leipzig: Gieske & Derrient, 1869.

———— Mycenae: a Narrative of Researches and Discoveries. New York: Scribner, Armstrong & Co., 1878.

———— *Orchomenos: Bericht über meine Ausgrabungen.* Leipzig: F. A. Brockhaus, 1881.

———— *Reise in der Troas im Mai 1881*. Leipzig: F. A. Brockhaus, 1881.

———— Tiryns: the Prehistoric Palace of the King of Tiryns. New York: Charles Scribner's Sons, 1885.

———— Troja: Results of the Latest Researches. New York: Harper & Bros., 1884.

———— Troy and Its Remains. London: John Murray, 1875.

SCHUCHHARDT, KARL. Schliemann's Excavations. London: Macmillan & Co., 1891.

VENTRIS, M. and CHADWICK, J. Documents in Mycenaean Greek. Cambridge: Cambridge University Press, 1956.

WACE, ALAN J. B. Mycenae: an Archeological and Historical Guide. Princeton: Princeton University Press, 1949.

WEBER, SHIRLEY H. (ed.) Schliemann's First Visit to America 1850-1851. Cambridge: Harvard University Press, 1942.